DISTRIBUTED MULTIMEDIA RETRIEVAL STRATEGIES FOR LARGE SCALE NETWORKED SYSTEMS

MULTIMEDIA SYSTEMS AND APPLICATIONS SERIES

Consulting Editor

Borko Furht
Florida Atlantic University

Recently Published Titles:

MULTIMEDIA ENCRYPTION AND WATERMARKING by *Borko Furht, Edin Muharemagic, Daniel Socek:* ISBN: 0-387-24425-5

SIGNAL PROCESSING FOR TELECOMMUNICATIONS AND MULTIMEDIA edited by T.A Wysocki,. B. Honary, B.J. Wysocki; ISBN 0-387-22847-0

ADVANCED WIRED AND WIRELESS NETWORKS by T.A.Wysocki,, A. Dadej, B.J. Wysocki; ISBN 0-387-22781-4

CONTENT-BASED VIDEO RETRIEVAL: *A Database Perspective* by Milan Petkovic and Willem Jonker; ISBN: 1-4020-7617-7

MASTERING E-BUSINESS INFRASTRUCTURE, edited by Veljko Milutinović, Frédéric Patricelli; ISBN: 1-4020-7413-1

SHAPE ANALYSIS AND RETRIEVAL OF MULTIMEDIA OBJECTS by Maytham H. Safar and Cyrus Shahabi; ISBN: 1-4020-7252-X

MULTIMEDIA MINING: *A Highway to Intelligent Multimedia Documents* edited by Chabane Djeraba; ISBN: 1-4020-7247-3

CONTENT-BASED IMAGE AND VIDEO RETRIEVAL by Oge Marques and Borko Furht; ISBN: 1-4020-7004-7

ELECTRONIC BUSINESS AND EDUCATION: *Recent Advances in Internet Infrastructures,* edited by Wendy Chin, Frédéric Patricelli, Veljko Milutinović; ISBN: 0-7923-7508-4

INFRASTRUCTURE FOR ELECTRONIC BUSINESS ON THE INTERNET by Veljko Milutinović; ISBN: 0-7923-7384-7

DELIVERING MPEG-4 BASED AUDIO-VISUAL SERVICES by Hari Kalva; ISBN: 0-7923-7255-7

CODING AND MODULATION FOR DIGITAL TELEVISION by Gordon Drury, Garegin Markarian, Keith Pickavance; ISBN: 0-7923-7969-1

CELLULAR AUTOMATA TRANSFORMS: *Theory and Applications in Multimedia Compression, Encryption, and Modeling* by Olu Lafe; ISBN: 0-7923-7857-1

COMPUTED SYNCHRONIZATION FOR MULTIMEDIA APPLICATIONS by Charles B. Owen and Fillia Makedon; ISBN: 0-7923-8565-9

STILL IMAGE COMPRESSION ON PARALLEL COMPUTER ARCHITECTURES by Savitri Bevinakoppa; ISBN: 0-7923-8322-2

Visit the series on our website: www.springeronline.com

DISTRIBUTED MULTIMEDIA RETRIEVAL STRATEGIES FOR LARGE SCALE NETWORKED SYSTEMS

by

Bharadwaj Veeravalli
National University of Singapore
Singapore

Gerassimos Barlas
American University of Sharjah
UAE

 Springer

Bharadwaj Veeravalli
Department of Electrical and
  Computer Engineering
National University of Singapore
Singapore 117576

Gerassimos Barlas
Computer Science Department
School of Engineering
American University of Sharjah
Sharjah, UAE

Library of Congress Control Number: 2005934523

DISTRIBUTED MULTIMEDIA RETRIEVAL STRATEGIES FOR LARGE SCALE
NETWORKED SYSTEMS
by Bharadwaj Veeravalli and Gerassimos Barlas

ISBN-13: 978-0-387-28873-4
ISBN-10: 0-387-28873-2
e-ISBN-13: 978-0-387-29675-3
e-ISBN-10: 0-387-29675-1

Printed on acid-free paper.

Printed in the United States of America.

9 8 7 6 5 4 3 2 1   SPIN 11498742, 11573913

springeronline.com

Dedicated to*:*

My Parent's(late),
My Wife Lavanya,
My Daughters Tanya &
Harshitha,
All my Teachers who got me
here!

–Bharadwaj Veeravalli

My wife Katerina
My parents, Dimitrios and
Maria

–Gerassimos Barlas

Contents

List of Figures

List of Tables

Preface

Deriving entertainment and availing a variety of multimedia services via home-computers/laptops or mobile devices, have become commonplace for Internet users in this modern era. Growing high-speed networking technology coupled with the development of ultra-speed multimedia high-end machines facilitates the notion of rendering such media services at attractive costs. Network based multimedia services attempt to render best effort services at cheaper prices. For instance, a video rental store allows users to rent video cassettes, CDs/DVDs at a fixed price. In contrast, a networked multimedia service (NMS) allows a user to surf through a range of collections and obtain the desired content, without having to satisfy timing, or physical location restrictions. Furthermore, a user need not even be confined to a specific location, but could be roaming with a mobile device. Modern Video/Movie-on-Demand (V/MoD) services even allow complete interactivity by supporting functionality that includes variable-speed playback, fast-forward/backward, etc.

In the published literature there are several papers that present comprehensive studies of such NMS systems that are based on a wide spectrum of performance goals and topics. There are several text-books that expose fundamental multimedia technology at undergraduate to graduate level and even serve as guides to practitioners. However, the emphasis in this book is purely on the research perspective of a focused topic in the domain of multimedia. The emphasis in this book is in exposing a specific state-of-the-art NMS technology that is of recent vintage. The service infrastructure we are concerned in this book is for VOD and/or MoD. Although such services have been in place for some time with a varying degree of success, the manner in which these are deployed leaves many things to be desired in terms of supporting large client populations with adaptability, quality of service and low cost. With increasing user demands for multimedia on-demand services, rendering cost effective and reliable services becomes an imperative requirement.

The design of high-fidelity network-based VOD/MoD service infrastructure must carefully consider issues in optimizing various parameters, ranging from the data storage level to customer satisfaction, in terms of providing high quality, reliability and interactivity. To provide an idea of the challenge ahead, since 1997 the Internet traffic has doubled every 6 months, while in the past 5 years hard disk storage has doubled every year. In particular, the number of large size (typically >3GB) multimedia documents keeps increasing on the Internet and experts conjecture that by the year 2005/2006, more than 50% of the information available over the Internet will constitute of large multimedia documents. It is also conjectured that the percentage of requests to such large-volume multimedia document increases in a greater that linear fashion with time. NMSs are attractive from an economic perspective. For instance, in the case of VOD services, depending on the popularity of the movie, the cost per user can be reduced when clever placement of movies on the network is carried out. Thus, the design of a VOD system employs several technologies, ranging from disk arrays, to clever scheduling policies that maximize the use of networked resources.

Contemporary technology, more-or-less uses sophisticated high-end machines to render such NMS. These are typically maintained by the service providers, taking care of services at various physical network domains. Thus, users in a particular domain can avail service when subscribed to a local service provider. However, when a requested movie or a digital media document is not available with a local service provider, it may be fetched from other domains, when such a contract exists between parties when they are from different service providers. In contrast, a recent technology that is introduced in this book, exploits a distributed approach in rendering NMS to the clients by making use of time-and-bandwidth multiplexed strategies and data partitioning strategies. These strategies are shown to be very effective in minimizing large annoying waiting times for the users and simultaneously maximizing the number of customers that a service provider can attract. This technology, during its incipient stages, has stemmed from a mere theoretical interest and has subsequently been conceived as a practically viable scheme in addressing several issues that are akin to NMS elegantly. The key idea is to employ more than one server in rendering NMS to the clients. This technology can be referred to as a *Multiple Server Retrieval* (MSR) strategy, in general. A variety of issues that are germane to this domain, such as the minimization of access times/waiting times, buffer management, networking issues, fault-tolerance, etc are studied and thoroughly presented. A prototype that has been realized as a (working) proof-of-concept is also presented.

In this book, we expose most of the major research issues and challenges in this MSR media retrieval technology. As a word of caution, this technology specifically suits retrieving long duration media documents, such as complete movies and Gbytes of both time continuous and discrete media data, over delay sensitive and unreliable network channels. Thus, this technology constitutes an alternative solution to existing problems, opening in the process avenues on how to make use of current Internet-like networks to render such NMSs.

The organization, presentation, and contents of the book are pitched at a research monograph level. The contents are carefully sorted in tune with the specific focus of the book and they are being derived from a number of published papers and articles from the recent literature. As this technology is still in its infancy, the available material is pooled from research efforts of the past 4 to 5 years and peripheral related material from the past 12 years. The mathematical background that is expected to go through the material is modest. Fundamental knowledge of Linear Algebra, Calculus, and Probability theory is expected as these are used throughout the contents, in a variety of occasions, to make the treatment more rigorous and complete. Proofs of all the theoretical claims in the form of Lemmas and Theorems are provided in an emphatic, comprehensive, and step-by-step fashion to render clarity. Several numerical examples in addition to rigorous simulation studies and implementations were provided to clarify all the results. Each chapter has been carefully written to have a continuous flow of contents in a systematic fashion and carries design recommendations for implementation specialists and system level designers. In every chapter, we provide a summary of source material in the form of bibliographic notes.

When it comes to the question of who are the potential users of this monograph, we see a wide spectrum of audience with diversified interests in this multimedia domain. This monograph can be used as a reference text for an advanced undergraduate level course in *Multimedia Networking* courses and in courses that use NMS topics. For graduate study, this book serves as a directly useful reference in introducing the state-of-the-art technology for students wishing to pursue research in this area. Certain chapters (specifically Chapters 3, 5, 6, and 7) can be a part of advanced graduate level courses. For teachers, additional material and notes are provided in bibliographic notes section at the end of each chapter for quick reference to other allied materials in this domain. This monograph can be used by researchers working directly in this and other related domains such as multimedia networking (at the applications and the network layers), multimedia computing & scheduling, distributed system design, digital document storage and retrieval, to quote a few. Researchers working in the area of Storage Area Networks (SANs) may find this material useful in terms of deriving ideas and algorithms for an alternate implementation, while handling large scale data storage and retrieval. Research organizations and corporate sectors can use this technology to enhance their existing solutions with the use of an appropriately designed MSR wherever required, as distributed infrastructures and their mastery is what this monograph is all about. For entrepreneurs, certainly this monograph is challenging and entertaining as it exposes several new ideas that can be tuned to fit the current day market and technology trends. For instance, service providers can immensely benefit from this technology in terms of maximizing the number of customers who can subscribe to their NMS, as it has the potential to be a cost-effective and welcomed scheme for customers. Clearly, this technology renders a win-win situation!

In Chapter 1, we first explore a number of different technologies that are related to multimedia retrieval in general. We examine their characteristics from the viewpoint of how they relate to MSR, how they could benefit from MSR or vice-versa, or how they could be superceded by it.

In Chapter 2, we present an introduction to the MSR technology, and the underlying problem setting. We proceed to the design and analysis of a single and multiple installment servicing policy to minimize the access time. This chapter serves as a first, gentle exposure to the ideas underlying MSR design.

In Chapter 3, we extend the study of Chapter 2, to handle multiple clients and discuss a channel partitioning approach. We present a rigorous analytical study to quantify the performance gains which are validated by extensive realistic simulation models.

While Chapters 2 & 3 analyze in detail the design and performance of MSR technology, in Chapter 4, we introduce a modification to the overall approach taken by MSR, that reflects on how video playback can be performed in real-life. Here the client is allowed to initiate the playback soon after a critical portion is downloaded, as opposed to awaiting the completion of the download of an entire portion before kick-starting the playback.

In Chapter 5, we address the issue of packet loss and generic network unreliability that is one of the main issues hampering the deployment of VoD services. We show that small modifications to our mathematical framework suffice to make it capable of producing a robust schedule that is impervious to certain network problems. The trick is to allow the relaxation of the constraints it is based on.

In Chapter 6, we investigate ways for adapting to network variability, in the process extending the robustness of the schedules we can produce. In particular, we compare two competing approaches, one based on a multi-installment strategy and one based on the repetitive application of a single installment strategy. Rigorous discrete event simulations show that the latter can truly offer a robust, adaptable approach to handling network variability.

In Chapter 7 we present fault-tolerance analysis studies pertaining to server crashes and show how availability can be maximized. We specifically present analysis on how to retrieve media data that is lost either due to server crashes or channel failures. Here, we present deterministic and probabilistic approaches in deriving some significant analytical results. The results of this chapter are particularly useful in choosing a set of servers from a given pool depending on reliability/availability criteria.

The results of chapters 5, 6 and 7 indeed demonstrate the fact that MSR is a viable and useful technology to adopt for deploying multimedia services over public networks.

In Chapter 8, we present the design and implementation of a working MSR system based on the Jini platform. We provide a detailed account of the design and implementation of all system components, including the Client, the Server and other essential parts of the service infrastructure.

In Chapter 9, we present our view on the future and scope of MSR and discuss some other dimensions associated with the realization of MSR technologies.

Acknowledgments

We wish to extend our heartfelt thanks to those who have directly and indirectly helped in this book project. We thank the editorial efforts rendered by the Kluwer Academic team and special thanks go to Mr. John Martindale and Ms. Robert Saley in bringing out this book in good shape. We acknowledge all timely transactions over countless emails with John and Saley over the last one year time frame. We would also like to thank Ms. Susan Largerstrom-Fife and Ms. Sharon Palleschi in rendering continuous support from the manuscript preparation stage till its production. We would like to extend our appreciation to Dr. Wujuan Lin of Data Storage Institute of Singapore (DSI), Singapore, for his suggestions on formatting, proof-reading of certain chapters, and suggestions on Chapter 1 contents on SANs. Parts of the work presented in this book have been reviewed earlier by Professor Viktor K.Prasanna, Department of Electrical & Systems Engineering, USC, LA, USA. We would like to thank Professor Prasanna for his effort. Bharadwaj Veeravalli would like to thank Mrs. Xiaorong Li, Mr. Jingxi Jia, and Qiao Yunhai, for their help in formatting and fixing certain figures in Chapters 2, 4, 7, and 8.

On the personal front, Bharadwaj Veeravalli would like to thank his wonderful wife, Lavanya for her patience, understanding, and encouragement rendered throughout the book writing process. He would like to thank his daughters Tanya & Harshitha. He would like to render special thanks to Harshitha for keeping him awake during long night hours, in a way, helping to complete this paramount task on time!! He would like to thank his brother Sivakumar and his family for all the encouragement provided during this time. He would like to render special thanks to his parents-in-law for their unflagging support during this period (2004/2005) without which this task would not have been undertaken. Their help in taking care of the new born and assuming most of the house-hold work helped to squeeze in long writing hours!! He would like to render special thanks to (his Gurus!) Professor Debasish Ghose and Professor

Venkatraman Mani, Department of Aerospace Engineering, Indian Institute of Science, Bangalore, India, who had always a word of encouragement on any research endeavor ventured by him. He would also like to pass a special thanks to his good friend and colleague Professor Tom Robertazzi, Department of EE, SUNY, Stony Brook, NY, USA, who always had a great deal of interest in all his works. Finally, he would like to say a BIG THANK YOU to all his friends in NUS with the Department of ECE, NUS, for providing a conducive and joyful ambience. Special thanks to *The Tea Club* members who had discussions, almost everyday, on all topics ranging from International affairs to everyday life in Singapore! Thanks Guys!

On a personal note, Gerassimos Barlas would like to thank his parents Dimitrios and Maria for their sacrifices, love and support that helped him go so far. Special thanks go to his dearest wife Katerina for her love, patience, dedication and sacrifice.

Chapter 1

DISTRIBUTED TECHNOLOGIES FOR MULTIMEDIA RETRIEVAL OVER NETWORKS

1.1. Video on Demand: The Challenge and Contemporary Solutions

Video or Movie on Demand (VoD/MoD) has been touted for a long time as the next best thing to be delivered over the public Internet. The problem is that the size of the data involved and the strict timing constraints that must be maintained are overwhelming challenges that have limited VoD to proprietary networks or niche markets.

The quality of offered services in the VoD domain is usually measured by:

- Access Time : how much time the client has to wait between making the request and the beginning of the actual playback (also referred to as initiation latency [39])

- Movie Quality: the number or interruptions, artifacts or distortions present in the playback due to network errors, packet losses, etc.

Although there is no universally acceptable quality (or distortion) metric [111], it is natural for a client to expect the highest possible quality, or at least the quality promised by the Service Provider.

If one considers only the elimination of playback artifacts, storing the movie before actual playback is an option. However, the delay involved and associated problems in Digital Rights Management (DRM) make this option a very unpopular one. Hence, the persistence of the research community in perfecting streaming in its various shapes and forms. Streaming, which is the popular term used to refer to concurrent playback and download, is not without problems as anyone who has actually tried it will attest.

A few examples can shed light to the problems involved:

- An MPEG-2 coded, DVD quality, feature-length movie has a typical bit rate of 7.5Mbps. If we assume that the movie is 100 minutes long and the playback must commence at the most 5 minutes after the client requests the particular media, then the above characteristics and requirements translate to the need to communicate a 5.24 GB document at a rate of 872 Kbytes/sec!

- Although the above example is extreme, moving to an advanced codec (e.g. MPEG-4) coupled with a modest SIF resolution (352x240 pixels), would enable the use of bit rates in the range of 300 kbps. If we again assume that the movie is 100 minutes long and the playback must commence 5 minutes after the client makes the request, then the client machine needs to receive a total of 214.58 MB at a rate of 34.88 Kbytes/sec which is still not a trivial task while at the same time the quality offered is a far cry even from TV-broadcast quality.

Past experience has shown that just "buffering" the data, i.e. storing a portion of the data before playback can start, is only part of the solution in VoD service deployment. The unpredictability of the communication media and the bulk of the data involved, require either special conditioning by the underlying network (e.g. multicasting) or dedicated architectures to be deployed (e.g. simulcasting). Contemporary solutions to these problems try to avoid the creation of bottlenecks or hot-spots in the network, by employing multiple "entities" in various stages of the data delivery process. The manifestations of this approach are:

- Scalable video : a video stream can be split into multiple streams, each carrying a piece of the information needed to reconstitute the original. Typically, a base and detail streams are created, where the detail stream can provide better temporal and/or spatial resolution but it is not required for decoding the base stream.

- Multicasting : in the case of a real-time video feed that is of interest to a wide audience, multicasting can provide the "goods" to multiple recipients with a minimum of network overhead.

- Simulcasting : was conceived as a unicast-based alternative to multicasting that uses the clients as repeaters and requires no special network support in the fashion that multicasting does. Several schemes have been proposed for building and maintaining the tree of participating nodes. It is also known as overlay or peer-to-peer (P2P) multicast.

- Multiple distributed servers: the content is delivered in disjoint parts by multiple servers, thus allowing for dynamic adaptation to network conditions and server loads.

In tandem with the above methods and depending on the possibility of data loss and its impact on the provided service quality, error correction and error concealment techniques can be utilized. In the sections that follow, each of the above techniques is presented and discussed in greater length.

The focus of this book is on the *multi-server* approach and what it has to offer towards realizing VoD over the public Internet. The distributed multi-server approach provides scalability and fault tolerance at the network connection level, as parallel video servers offer both at the storage level [66].

1.2. General Multimedia Storage and Retrieval Architectures

Under a network based service infrastructure, we will now study the following:

- Issues and challenges in the design of multimedia storage servers[1]

- Different types of media delivery architectures and certain important criteria for jitter free presentation

- Basics principles in the design of admission control algorithms

Specifically, we will study some possible storage server architectures, the nature of data/objects being stored, and derive admissibility criteria for a jitter-free high quality service.

1.2.1 Multimedia servers: A resource management perspective

Future advances in multimedia technology will make it feasible for distributed systems to support a range of multimedia services on networks. Already there are a host of applications running on the network, however, somewhat restricted in their service abilities. Most of the systems are dedicated to cater a single service to a subscribed community. However, technology still needs to be improved in order to make a single server support a range of applications. As a networked multimedia server is expected to serve a large pool of clients, it is possible to view this server as a resource. In the following, we shall see how a single multimedia server manages the storage of media documents and present an admission control procedure that cleverly adapts to a large client pool.

1.2.1.1 Storage requirements

Multiple data streams: A multimedia object may consist of three types of components: audio, video, and text. By and large, these three components

---

[1]These are referred to as VoD/MoD servers or just plain multimedia servers in the literature.

are separate when captured or composed and they could be handled as three different streams. Of course, conventional movies are exceptional to this case. Similarly, during the retrieval and delivery, these three streams are routed to three different output devices. Storing these media may entail additional processing for combining them during storage (multiplexing), and for separating them during retrieval at the time of delivery (demultiplexing). On the other hand, if the three media are stored separately, what needs to be stored is the *temporal* relationships between the media types so as to ensure proper synchronization between them during retrieval.

Continuous recording and retrieval of data streams: Recording and playback of motion video and audio are time continuous operations. The file system must organize the multimedia data on the disks so as to guarantee that their storage and retrieval proceed at their respective real-time rates.

Large size files: In general, the audio and video require very large storage spaces. If the file system is to act as a basis for supporting media services such as document editing, mail, distribution of news, VoD, entertainment, etc., it must provide mechanisms for manipulating and sharing stored data. For these mechanisms to be efficient on large data, disk access must be stream-lined. The design of a file system that addresses the above issues is what a multimedia storage server is all about. We will first see some most commonly used terminology and notations used in this domain.

1.2.1.2   Some most commonly used terminology and notations

Following is a list of commonly encountered terms in video coding:

- **Frame**: A basic unit of video.

- **Sample**: A basic unit of audio.

- **Strand**: is an immutable, sequence of continuously recorded audio samples or video frames. The immutability of strands is a necessary condition to simplify the process of garbage collection.

- **Block**: is the basic unit of disk storage. There are two types of blocks: (i) *Homogeneous* and (ii) *Heterogeneous*. In the case of (i), all the data belong to only one type of media and in (ii), the data contains multiple media.

- **Rope**: A collection of multiple strands (of same and different media) tied together by synchronization information.

Table 1.1 summarizes a list of notations that will be used in subsequent paragraphs for deriving continuity constraints. Thus, with the above notations, we can write the expression for

Table 1.1. List of notations used in continuity constraints derivation

Symbol	Explanation	Unit
R_{ar}	Audio recording rate	samples/sec
R_{vr}	Video recording rate	frames/sec
R_{dr}	Rate of data transfer from the disk	bits/sec
R_{vd}	rate of video display	bits/sec
η_{vs}	Granularity of video storage	frames/block
η_{as}	Granularity of audio storage	samples/block
S_{vf}	Size of the video frame	bits/frame
S_{as}	Size of audio sample	bits/sample
l_{ds}	Scattering parameter	sec

(i) The duration of the playback of a video block as, η_{vs}/R_{vr},

(ii) The total delay to read a video block from a disk as, $l_{ds} + (\eta_{vs}S_{vf})/R_{dr}$

(iii) The time to display a video block as, $(\eta_{vs}S_{vf})/R_{vd}$. Note that this time is for decompression and Digital-to-Analog conversion.

1.2.1.3   Continuity requirements

For continuous retrieval of media data, it is essential that the media information are available at the display device at or before the time of playback. We refer to this as the *continuity requirement* or *continuity constraint*. If this constraint is violated, then the displaying device will starve for the data and the presentation continuity will be lost. We now analyze three kinds of service architectures - sequential, pipelined, and concurrent architectures for continuity requirements.

Sequential Architectures: These architectures serialize the read and display (similarly capture and store) operations. Each block is transferred from the disk to a buffer in the video device, and then displayed before initiating the transfer of the next block. the continuity requirement is met in this case *if* the sum of time to read a block from disk and the time to display it does not exceed the duration of its playback. That is,

$$\left(l_{ds} + \frac{\eta_{vs}S_{vf}}{R_{dr}}\right) + \frac{\eta_{vs}S_{vf}}{R_{vd}} \leq \frac{\eta_{vs}}{R_{vr}} \tag{1.1}$$

Pipelined Architectures: These perform read and display operations in parallel. If there are a minimum of two buffers on the video device, one holding the block being displayed, the continuity requirement is met *if* the time to read a block does not exceed the duration of its playback. That is,

$$\left(l_{ds} + \frac{\eta_{vs} S_{vf}}{R_{dr}} \right) \leq \frac{\eta_{vs}}{R_{vr}} \tag{1.2}$$

Concurrent Architectures: These architectures perform multiple disk read operations in parallel. Let p be the degree of concurrency, i.e., the number of concurrent disk accesses. if there are p buffers in the video device to hold the p blocks being transferred simultaneously, continuity of playback will be maintained *if* the time to read a block does not exceed the duration for playback of $(p-1)$ blocks. Hence,

$$\left(l_{ds} + \frac{\eta_{vs} S_{vf}}{R_{dr}} \right) \leq (p-1) \frac{\eta_{vs}}{R_{vr}} \tag{1.3}$$

Thus, the performance of the multimedia server system largely depends on the type of architecture chosen. We will consider the scenario of a single server single client system (client-server paradigm) in which the server is referred to as a VoD server.

1.2.2   Client-Server VoD system

Consider a VoD system consisting of a single server and a single client. A request arrives at the server for a movie of length L Kbytes. Let the movie playback rate expected by the client to be R_p Kbytes/sec and the data retrieval rate offered by the server, referred to as *server bandwidth*, to be bw Kbytes/sec. Usually, in such systems, the server services this request in n rounds(*round-robin schedule*) by continuously fetching the blocks of video data. In order to guarantee a *continuous presentation* at the client site, the retrieval time of the current block must be less than the playback of the previous block. Let x_i be the size of the block retrieved in the i-th round. We will determine the individual sizes required to maintain the continuity relationship as follows.

Clearly, the solution to the above design problem lies in choosing the appropriate sizes meant for each round. Failure to deliver these will cause a "gap" in the presentation. The following inequality must hold in each round:

$$x_i/bw \leq x_{i-1}/R_p, \ i = 2, ..., n \tag{1.4}$$

The above recursive equation generates $(n-1)$ equations involving n variables. However, with

$$\sum_{j=1}^{n} x_j = L \tag{1.5}$$

we have n linear inequalities. Solving these equations with *equality constraints* yield the appropriate block sizes that have to be fetched in order to have a continuous presentation. Thus, we obtain,

$$x_i = \frac{L\sigma^{i-1}}{\sum_{k=0}^{n-1} \sigma^k}, \quad i = 2, ..., n, \tag{1.6}$$

where $\sigma = bw/R_p$. x_1 is automatically decided when you solve these equations. One can quickly verify (1.6) to determine the value of x_1.

1.2.3 Designing an admission control algorithm: Single Server multiple clients system

In the previous section, we have seen a simple client-server system. As long as the continuity requirements are satisfied, the system *guarantees* a jitter free presentation. However, if the server is to serve multiple requests on a distributed network, it has to guarantee the continuity for each request. Also, it is impossible to accommodate a very large (theoretically infinite) number of customers, as the server has a limited bandwidth to split among the requests. Thus, for a network based multimedia service to be attractive to the customers, the server must

(i) guarantee a continuous presentation,

(ii) maximize the number of customers it can serve so that it can reduce the overall cost of the system

While guaranteeing a continuous presentation is restricted by the inherent delays and the rates of the playback and the read operations, maximizing the number of customers can be achieved by designing efficient strategies. Thus, our objective is to design a strategy that maximizes the number of customers that a server can serve and that guarantees the continuity relationships for each request it has admitted.

As mentioned earlier, a file server has to process requests from several clients simultaneously. Given a maximum rate of disk transfer, the file system can only accept a limited number of requests without violating the continuity requirements of any of the requests. The problem of administering a single resource's bandwidth is referred to as *resource allocation* problem in the literature.

Consider a scenario in which a multimedia server is servicing n requests. In order to service multiple requests simultaneously, the server proceeds in *rounds*. In each round, it multiplexes among the media block transfers of the n requests. Let k_i, for $i \in [1, n]$, be the number of consecutive blocks retrieved for the i-th request before switching to the next request. Let $\eta_{vs}^1, \eta_{vs}^2, ..., \eta_{vs}^n$, and $R_{vr}^1, ..., R_{vr}^n$ be the granularities and the recording rates of the strands corresponding to the n requests. When the server switches from one request to another, it may encounter an overhead of up to the maximum disk seek time to move from a block in the first strand to a block in the second strand. The total time spent in servicing i-th request in each round can be divided into two parts:

1. θ_i^1: the overhead of switching from the previous request to the i-th request, and then transferring the first block of the i-th request. That is,

$$\theta_i^1 = l_{seek}^{max} + \eta_{vs}^i S_{vf}^i / R_{dr} \qquad (1.7)$$

2. θ_i^2: The time to transfer remaining $(k_i - 1)$ blocks of this request in this round. That is,

$$\theta_i^2 = \sum_{j=1}^{k_i-1} l_{ds}^{i,j} + \eta_{vs}^i S_{vf}^i / R_{dr} \qquad (1.8)$$

Thus, the total time spent servicing the i-th request in a round is,

$$\theta_i = \theta_i^1 + \theta_i^2 \qquad (1.9)$$

The total time spent servicing **one round** of all the n requests is,

$$
\begin{aligned}
\theta &= \sum_{i=1}^n \theta_i \\
&= n l_{seek}^{max} + \sum_{i=1}^n \left(\eta_{vs}^i S_{vf}^i / R_{dr} \right) \\
&+ \sum_{i=1}^n \sum_{j=1}^{k_i-1} \left(l_{ds}^{i,j} + \eta_{vs}^i S_{vf}^i / R_{dr} \right)
\end{aligned} \qquad (1.10)
$$

The continuity requirement for each of the requests can be satisfied *if and only if* the service time per round does not exceed the minimum of the playback duration of all the requests. That is,

$$
n l_{seek}^{max} + \sum_{i=1}^n \left(\eta_{vs}^i S_{vf}^i / R_{dr} \right) \;+\; \sum_{i=1}^n \sum_{j=1}^{k_i-1} \left(l_{ds}^{i,j} + \eta_{vs}^i S_{vf}^i / R_{dr} \right)
$$
$$
\leq \; min(k_i \eta_{vs}^i / R_{vr}^i), \; i \in [1, n] \qquad (1.11)
$$

Thus, the multimedia server can service all the n requests simultaneously *if and only if* k_i, for all i in each round can be determined. Determining these k_i in this most generalized formulation is extremely complex. Thus, we make some simplifying assumptions trying in the process to provide as much a realistic scenario as possible.

Let $k_i = k$, for all i. We assume that,

$$\sum_{i=1}^{n} \left(\eta_{vs}^i S_{vf}^i / R_{dr} \right) \approx n \left(\eta_{vs}^{avg} S_{vf}^{avg} / R_{dr} \right) \tag{1.12}$$

and,

$$\sum_{i=1}^{n} \sum_{j=1}^{k_i-1} \left(l_{ds}^{i,j} + \eta_{vs}^i S_{vf}^i / R_{dr} \right) \approx n(k-1) \left(\left(l_{ds}^{avg} + \eta_{vs}^{avg} S_{vf}^{avg} / R_{dr} \right) \right) \tag{1.13}$$

where, individual values of the granularity, size of the video frames and the scattering parameter, are replaced by their respective average values in the summation. With these approximations, we have

$$n\alpha + n(k-1)\beta < k\gamma \tag{1.14}$$

where $\alpha = l_{ds}^{max} + \eta_{vs}^{avg} S_{vf}^{avg} / R_{dr}$

$\beta = l_{ds}^{avg} + \eta_{vs}^{avg} S_{vf}^{avg} / R_{dr}$

$\gamma = min \left(\eta_{vs}^i / R_{vr}^i \right), i \in [1, n]$

From this relationship, we can determine the value of $k > 0$ as,

$$k \geq \frac{n(\alpha - \beta)}{\gamma - n\beta}, \text{if} \gamma > n\beta \tag{1.15}$$

Thus, the **maximum** number of requests that can be serviced by the multimedia server is given by,

$$n_{max} = \lceil (\gamma/\beta - 1) \rceil \tag{1.16}$$

There are some interesting implications on the above derived admissibility criteria. If the system is adequately loaded and another request arrives then if the current population is less than the one given by (1.16) we can admit this request provided the remaining bandwidth is sufficient to avoid creating any jitter. Thus, an admission algorithm should consider not only the above equation but the available bandwidth also. Also, during service rounds, when clients leave the system, the system can fetch larger chunks of media portions for the existing clients if there are no further requests and that the buffers at the client side are adequate to accommodate these portions. Issues pertaining to buffer management at the client side are dealt extensively in Chapters 3 and 4, respectively.

The above analysis stands as a considerable motivation for us to go for data and channel partitioning approaches using multiple server technology, which is the primary focus of this book. Thus, if one employs several servers the service infrastructure becomes obviously attractive owing to the large pool of customer requests that can be admitted. Of course, related issues in the implementation must be taken care of duly to make the scheme practically viable. These are discussed in the subsequent chapters.

As the population of clients served by media servers increases, storage technology and management must maintain efficiency and scalability. If the content retrieval is not fast enough, the service becomes unattractive, commercially non-viable. While there is a host of literature available for disk scheduling policies [2] maturing of VoD technology requires leveraging of all available assets to provide the best available service. In Chapter 2 we shall present a very powerful technique that organizes and retrieves the data in a clever way so as to support a large pool of clients. This way of retrieval delivers high concurrency and matches servers and networks bandwidth to yield a higher throughput. The discussion in Chapter 2 is not a complete one, however the purpose is to introduce the technology and viewpoint associated with *Multiple Server Retrieval* (MSR) strategies.

1.2.4   The *Fellini* Multimedia storage server: Brief case study

The Fellini multimedia storage server is a classical architecture designed in mid-90's at AT&T Bell Laboratories. Fellini can be also considered as a typical implementation of a Single Server Retrieval Strategy (SSRS). Fellini subsumes most of the imperative components such as storage aspects, admission control, and process control in its design. The architecture completely supports storage and retrieval of time-continuous and non-continuous(discrete) media. The retrieval process multiplexes several clients concurrently and has an efficient admission control mechanism. The admission control typically follows our derivation presented in the previous section. The algorithms for retrieving media data from disks guarantee high throughput by reducing disk seek latencies. Fellini has an excellent buffer management process that manages cache data and implements replacement algorithms. The buffer management operates in a pre-fetching mode by pre-allocating the buffers for disk pages that will be written by updating the client or disk pages that will be read by clients. The process of buffer pre-allocation is crucial to the buffer management mechanism and it governs the overall efficiency of the scheme.

---

[2]Many operating systems and multimedia technology books discuss extensively disk scheduling algorithms.

The overall Fellini process architecture can be described at two levels: at the process and at the system level. A server process is made to run on a dedicated machine while clients can run at remote machines. There exist a buffer cache, which is a shared memory, bridging the gap between the server(fetching the data from disks) and the clients. For data storage in the Fellini system, a peer client process receives the data over the network from a remote client and writes it to the buffer cache. This data eventually gets transferred to the disk by the server process. When data are to be read from Fellini, a peer client reads the data from the buffer cache and sends it to the remote client. Of course, a client process can also run on the same machine on which the server process runs, however in this case, there is no need for a peer client to assist the transactions.

Fellini has three additional components: the *Admission controller*(AC), the *Cache manager*(CM), and the *Storage manager*(SM). The resources in the system are allocated by the AC module such that rate guarantees for all the accepted clients are always met. This does not preempt the possibilities of a non-real-time client requesting a service. A balance is sought between allocating resources between the clients and admissibility test is carried out at this module to avoid any starvation of resources. The role of CM is to optimize the availability of the pages in the buffer cache. The SM module coordinates the file and space management processes. It also stores the file layout information on the disk and manages the free space on the disk efficiently. In real-life situations the potential applications of Fellini are several: video-conferencing, co-operative file editing, etc, are just a few of the possible ones.

1.3.   RAID Array Technology: A Useful Insight

Past decades have been characterized by rapid improvements in processor speed (doubled every 18 months), network speed (doubled every nine months) and magnetic storage capacity (doubled every twelve months). Alas, secondary storage interfaces haven't been able to follow this trend, setting the stage for a performance bottleneck.

A research group in UC-Berkeley introduced RAID (**R**edundant **A**rray of **In**expensive **D**isks) in 1988 as an answer to this problem, by utilizing multiple physical storage units to build a single logical device. The disks in a RAID array operate independently offering the potential for substantially higher transfer speeds. However, the Mean Time Between Failures (MTBF) of an array is equal to the MTBF of a single device divided by the number of devices. The increased risk of data-loss is addressed by having RAID configurations, a.k.a. levels that support data-redundancy and error recovery.

Central to RAID is the concept of **striping** where the physical storage space is split into disjoint areas of equal size called **stripes**. The logical storage space is

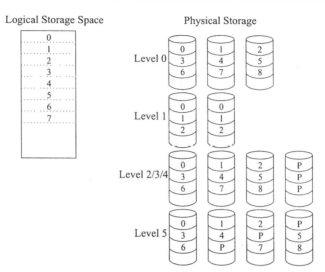

Figure 1.1. Illustration of the 6 original RAID levels. Levels 2, 3 and 4 differ mainly in the size of the stripe used (bit, byte and sector accordingly). Levels 2, 3 and 4 have dedicated parity (P) or error correcting code devices. Level 5 distributes the parity sectors over all participating devices.

mapped to the stripes in a fashion that suits the particular RAID level. The size of the stripes is also subject to the RAID level requirements. The six original RAID levels are (also shown in Fig. 1.1):

- Level 0: data are mapped across multiple drives in a round-robin fashion. No redundancy is provided.

- Level 1: commonly referred to mirroring as two drives are used, each an identical copy of the other.

- Level 2: stripes are bit-sized, with some devices dedicated for storing Error Correcting Codes (ECC). Outclassed by levels 3 and 4.

- Level 3: byte-sized stripes are used, along with parity stored on a dedicated drive.

- Level 4: sector-sized stripes are used. A parity drive is also used in a fashion similar to level 3. Offers good read performance but writes require access to the parity drive.

- Level 5: similar to level 4 but the parity is distributed among all the drives.

Several manufacturers have introduced variations to the above levels by combining two of them (dual level or nested level arrays). For example, RAID 50 utilizes several RAID 5 arrays as elements in a level 0 array. Any drive failure will go unnoticed because of the redundancy offered by RAID 5 while RAID 0 offers increased transfer speeds.

The principle behind employing multiple distributed servers to provide disjoint parts of a video stream to a client, is very similar to the underlying principle of the RAID technology. Actually, many of the attributes that the RAID technology brings to the storage domain can be offered by MSR in the VoD domain. Independent server operation means that a client can receive data from a MSR system at rates that could not be offered by a stand-alone server. Additional benefits include:

- Reduced access times: The client can begin the playback at a much earlier time without the risk of introducing interrupts.

- Fault-tolerance: In the case of a server or a link failure, data can be retrieved from other servers.

- Server load-balancing: A client can adapt its download schedule to the state of the MSR servers and the underlying network, effectively offering a distributed load-balancing mechanism

The challenges in building a MSR system in the fashion of a RAID array, stem from the inherent heterogeneity of such a system, particularly the communication speeds. So while a data break-up in the fashion of stripes is possible, almost all systems reported in the literature go for 'mirroring', i.e. keeping complete copies of media in multiple servers, similarly to RAID level 0. However, the choice of which movies to offer and their placement (for example not all servers need to carry all movies) is another question as illustrated in Fig. 1.2.

1.4.   Related Network Technologies

The network is one of the most challenging components of a VoD system, the reason being the lack of control over the corresponding media and the circumstances involved in their operation. One of the earliest attempts to offer scalability to VoD services involved *multicast* [101, 31]. Multicast achieves scalability by letting a video server/source send a packet only once to all the clients that should be receiving it, thus reducing the corresponding traffic substantially (see Figure 1.3). Multicast can be also used to serve the components of a multimedia presentation if we can make sure that their temporal relationships are preserved during playback, as it is described in [52] where a presentation system called Mcast is presented.

	Server 0	Server 1	Server 2	Server 3
(a)	Movie A	Movie A	Movie A	Movie A
	Movie B	Movie B	Movie B	Movie B
	Movie C	Movie C	Movie C	Movie C
	Movie D	Movie D	Movie D	Movie D

	Server 0	Server 1	Server 2	Server 3
(b)	Movie A	Movie A	Movie A	Movie B
	Movie C	Movie B	Movie B	Movie D
	Movie D	Movie C	Movie D	Movie E
	Movie F	Movie F	Movie E	Movie F

Figure 1.2. (a) A multiple distributed server system where all movies are copied in all servers. (b) Limiting the number of copies can provide a greater variety of offerings at the cost of reduced availability.

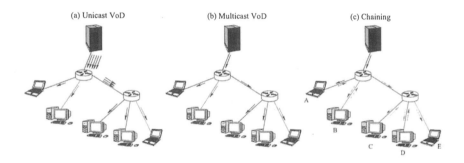

Figure 1.3. A multicast based system has two advantaged over a unicast based one: reduced server load and reduced traffic between routers. The chaining example shown in (c), uses color coding to indicate the pipeline/virtual batch of machines: $A \rightarrow B \rightarrow C \rightarrow D \rightarrow E$

Multicast however, does not come free as it requires infrastructure changes like special routers for supporting operations spanning more that a single LAN. The routers should be capable of handling the replication and forwarding of packets, plus the regular traffic for group management according to the IGMP protocol [101].

A major issue with the use of multicast is that the content must be delivered simultaneously to all clients, or at least within strict time limits. This effectively narrows the applications of interest to live news/sport feeds or collaborative/workgroup communication applications [33], unless special constraints are imposed as discussed below. The timing constraints also dictate the use of UDP instead of TCP as a transport mechanism. Since UDP is inherently unreliable, basic IP multicast is also unreliable. The number of additional protocols that have been proposed to address this issue, can be categorized as belonging to one of the following categories [33]:

- Forward Error Correction (FEC): The multicast server sends in addition to the original N message packets, k redundant packets that can facilitate reconstruction of the original message as long as less that k packets are lost.

- Negative ACK (NACK): The receivers send a negative acknowledgment to the server when they detect the a missing packet. NACK message consolidation eliminates the problem of ACK implosion at the server.

- Scalable Reliable Multicast: Every receiver keeps a log of the packets received. In case a neighboring receiver misses a packet, the retransmission can be localized, without the need to involve the server.

To overcome the problem of random client request arrival times, a number of techniques have been proposed. *Batching* [4] works by delaying all the requests for a particular content that arrive within an interval, called the batching interval, until they can be serviced simultaneously with a single data stream. Aggarwal et al. in [5] discuss a scheduling policy for batching that can minimize the average access time (a.k.a. as latency time) by sorting the waiting queues according to the ratio of their length and the square root of the relative frequency of the incoming arrivals.

Letting clients join the multicast tree in the middle of a transmission can be achieved by a technique called *patching* [23]. Patching requires that a separate stream is send to the client to compensate for the missed content that was communicated before the client joined the multicast tree. Thus, the advantages of multicast can be realized with a minimum overhead.

Minimizing the data that need to be "patched" is discussed in [86], where Qingsong et al. propose two techniques for managing the media cache at streaming proxies. This study is limited to one media file and therefore its scalability is unknown.

Batching, patching and periodic multicast have been combined in the SS-VoD system by Kong and Lee [59], which has been designed to support Variable Bit Rate (VBR) content. The peak data rates that could cause disruption of the playback, are treated by sending the excess data on a separate multicast channel concurrently with other data. SS-VoD requires however clients capable of receiving data at least at twice the rate of the video content. This requirement. which is shared by systems employing patching, severely hinders their capability of spanning more than an Intranet, unless very low quality/low bit rate content is used.

Batching strategies depend on a time interval used to decide when to schedule a new multicast channel for waiting clients. Depending on this interval a system maybe classified as near VoD (NVoD). Examples of a batching and a patching system are shown in Figure 1.4. The examples shown assume that the server schedules a multicast stream every Δ seconds, at times T_n, T_{n+1}, etc. Clients requests arrive at times t_i, t_{i+1}, etc. In Fig. 1.4(a), clients that make a request past the beginning of a multicast transmission have to wait for the next scheduled multicast channel. In contrast, in Fig. 1.4(b) a dynamic channel is allocated for allowing the clients to "catch up" by having the data missed since the beginning of the most recent transmission uploaded to them. At the same time, the clients download the data from the most recent multicast channel. To avoid exhausting the server resources, a dynamic channel is allocated only if the access time of a client would exceed a certain threshold d, hence client C_{i+1} in the example of Fig. 1.4(b) waits for channel n.

Chaining [96] is a batching technique that while predating P2P multicast protocols discussed below, introduced the concept of client assisted content delivery. All requests to a particular media are grouped together in a "virtual batch". The virtual batch is essentially a data pipeline which is formed as long as there is enough buffer space to accommodate the data communication between the peers. Chaining improves responsiveness (reduces access time) over classic batching although in extended chaining a number of clients can be delayed to maximize the availability of a virtual batch. Despite Sheu et al. claim that chaining reduces the burden on the network, practically it alleviates only server load. As can be seen in the example displayed in Fig. 1.3(c) routers will continue to manage a traffic volume which is substantially higher than what multicast generates.

Harmonic broadcasting (HB) [81] is a technique that breaks a video into n equally sized portions that are broadcasted constantly using n different channels. Each portion S_i for $1 \leq i \leq n$, is further broken into i subsegments such that the broadcasting of each subsegment lasts exactly time $d = \frac{D}{n}$ where D is the duration of the movie. Hence, if b is the movie bitrate, each segment S_i is transmitted at a rate of $\frac{b}{i}$. Thus, a client has to spend a total of $i \cdot d$ time in order to get segment S_i. Paris et al. [81] have shown that if the client waits for $\frac{(n-1)d}{n}$ time past the beginning of the first S_1 segment it can download, it can playback the movie with no interrupts as long as all the other segments are also downloaded simultaneously. This results in the need to have a total client

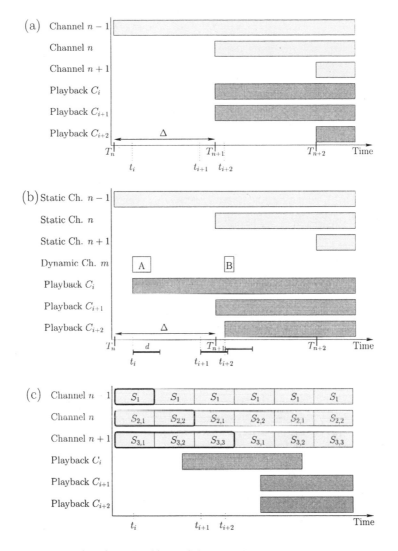

Figure 1.4. Examples of (a) a batching and (b) a patching system. In (b) patch A is used for client C_i and patch B for client C_{i+2}. The time threshold d is displayed as a horizontal bar, following each of the request arrivals. (c) shows a harmonic broadcast arrangement where the video stream is split in 3 parts and broadcasted in the same number of channels/streams. Please note that the medium communicated in Fig. (c) is of much smaller duration than the one assumed in (a) and (b). In particular, the duration of the movie is 3 times the duration of part S_1.

bandwidth equal to

$$\sum_{i=1}^{n} \frac{b}{i} = b \sum_{i=1}^{n} \frac{1}{i} = b \cdot H(n)$$

where $H(n)$ is the harmonic number of n. Several improvements to the basic harmonic broadcasting have been proposed [81, 82], aiming to reduce the access time of the client for the given bandwidth spend. However, the main problem associated with the use of the harmonic broadcast class of techniques remains the need for excessive client bandwidth. Even for $n = 3$ as shown in Figure 1.4(c), this bandwidth is roughly 1.84 times the movie bitrate, for an access time that for classical HB can be as high as $\frac{5}{9}$ of the movie's duration.

The access time can be reduced by using the *polyharmonic broadcasting protocol* (PHB) [82], which has the client start the download immediately following its request, instead of waiting for the beginning of the next S_1. In PHB the access time is fixed at $\frac{D}{k}$ where $k = \frac{n}{m}$ and $m \geq 1$ determines the number of subsegments each S_i is split into: $m + i - 1$. Each subsegment is broadcasted over d time, hence each channel requires bandwidth equal to $\frac{b}{m+i-1}$ for a grand total of $b \cdot (H(n + m - 1) - H(m - 1))$. The PHB scheme still translates to an access time of $25\%D$ for a consumed client bandwidth equal to 1.714 times that of the movie's bitrate for $m = 4$ and $n = 16$. Achieving a $5\%D$ access time would require $n = 80$ streams for $m = 4$ at the expense of $3.168 \cdot b$ bandwidth.

The family of *pyramid broadcasting* (PB) techniques [72] works in a similar fashion to harmonic broadcasting, i.e. breaking up the content in disjoint pieces and broadcasting it along different channels. Each piece is connected with its previous one by a geometric formula, e.g. $S_i = 2S_{i-1}$. The pieces are broadcasted at twice the bitrate of the movie. The main difference of PB is that the client has to download at any time only one or two of the available channels. As Paris and Long have shown [81], harmonic broadcast offers superior access time for any given consumed bandwidth.

In order to be able to accommodate heterogeneous clients, multiple streams of varying quality can be broadcasted by the servers. These streams can be, either, different versions of the same content, or, in a more elaborate and cost-saving scheme components of a scalable video stream (see Section 1.5). The former technique has been explored in association with multiple replicated servers by Hiromori et al. in [46]. Hiromori et al. propose a technique for dynamically selecting the group a client subscribes to, by keeping a record of packet arrival ratios at routers and path-to-server lengths.

The dependence of multicast on appropriate network support is a liability also for another reason. In a study performed by Rajvaidya and Almeroth [87], it is shown that spatial and temporal routing instabilities which are a major problem in the robust deployment of multicast, can be attributed to configuration inconsistencies. Hence, multicast must be not only supported universally, but also the policies and configurations used in the individual routers must adhere to specific rules to assist the elimination of routing inconsistencies.

This dependence has lead to the proposal of many techniques that offer a form of multicasting by using peer-to-peer (P2P) unicast communications [35, 103, 17] also known as *overlay multicast* or *simulcast*. It should be noted that the term "simulcast" has been also used in the literature to denote the use of multiple streams with different rates, targeting heterogeneous clients [70].

In [17, 16] Birrer and Bustamante compare a number of P2P multicast protocols against their P2P multicast protocol named Nemo. Nemo is based on a hierarchical organization of the peers into clusters. Each cluster has an elected leader and co-leader that affords fault-tolerance in the case of a node failure and enhances the scalability of the scheme by offering alternate routes. NACKs are used for error recovery.

El-Gindy et al. [30] proposed a variation of multicast called "scheduled multicast", that involves using intermediate network nodes as buffers to hold the content that could be requested. This technique can be only used if the requests made for the same content are closely timed. In a different case, the memory requirements could easily overwhelm the nodes that buffer the content.

A similar approach to simulcast and its variations is being used by the Bit-Torrent project (http://bitconjurer .org/BitTorrent) and the Kontiki Delivery Management System (http://www.kontiki.com). BitTorrent uses the clients as content publishers, striving at the same time to satisfy fairness constraints. Files are split into $\frac{1}{4}$MB pieces that are transferred between the peers. Other P2P file sharing approaches include the ever-popular KaZaa (http://www.kazaa.com), eDonkey (http://www.edonkey.com) and WinMX (http://www.winmx.com) systems. The major difference of these systems with the VoD P2P technologies is the objective: while the latter try to minimize latency or access time, the former try to maximize content availability in the face of even the originating server's failure.

In summary, all the techniques employing multicasting in one form or the other, suffer from the need to have all the participating nodes receive data at a rate matching or far exceeding the video rate. Given that even the best video codecs require on average around 900kbps for good quality content [45], the deployment of multicast/broadcast techniques over the public Internet presents severe problems.

1.5.   Scalable Video

Scalable or *layered* video is a technology that has been originally introduced to increase the resilience of video coders in video transmission over
packet switched networks [40]. As the name suggests, layered video is de-
composed into two or more layers, each incorporating a different part of the
video stream information. In the simplest form of this technique, there are two
layers, a *base-layer* carrying a rough approximation of the video signal, plus an
enhancement-layer that carries the remaining information. The decoder needs
only the base-layer for uninterrupted playback, thus reducing the effect of los-
ing the enhancement-layer data.

Of course, the key for deploying a scalable video solution is to determine how
such a separation could be accomplished and in the process, how could the
encoder maintain efficient predictors for the component layers such as to avoid
producing a bloated stream. There are several answers to these questions, each
identified as a different kind of *scalability*.

Scalability is extensively covered in the context of MPEG-2 in [40](section 7.5)
and in the context of MPEG-4 in [84](section 8.4). MPEG-4 generalizes the
concept of scalability to cover video objects, i.e. arbitrarily shaped sequences
of bitplanes. In the following paragraphs we summarize the main types of
scalability:

- **Data partitioning** : The two resulting layers carry two totally independent
  parts of the original stream. The partitioning is performed by selecting a
  priority break point in the 8x8 DCT coefficient scan sequence, and assigning
  the two sets to different layers. The low-frequency coefficients end up in
  the base layer. The main drawback of this simple technique is that loss of
  the enhancement layer causes loss of synchronization between the coder
  and decoder (picture drift). An I-frame is required for reestablishing the
  synchronization.

- **Signal-to-Noise-Ratio (SNR) Scalability** : The base layer consists of a
  rough approximation (quantized with a large step) of the DCT coefficients.
  The enhancement layer consists of the differences required to better approximate (i.e. enhance the SNR) the input DCT coefficients. Several ways can
  be used to calculate the enhancement layer, trading between complexity and
  picture drift issues. The block diagram of an SNR-scalable coder is shown
  in Figure 1.5.

  SNR scalability has been totally revamped in the MPEG-4 standard (where
  it is called Fine Granularity Scalability), essentially allowing an adaptation
  of the enhancement layer to the network conditions.

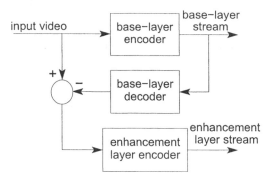

Figure 1.5. Block diagram of a SNR scalable coder.

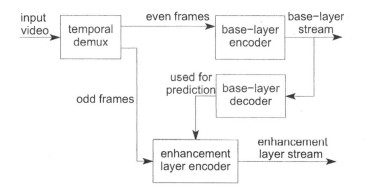

Figure 1.6. Block diagram of a temporal scalable coder.

- **Temporal Scalability** : The video stream is partitioned along the time axis, i.e. frames are split into two groups providing the corresponding layers. The difference between the base and enhancement layer lies in the predictors used for them, i.e. the enhancement layer can use the base layer frames for motion compensation. Typically, the enhancement layer consists of B-frames. The block diagram of a spatial scalable coder is shown in Figure 1.6

- **Spatial Scalability** : In this case the two layers represent different spatial resolutions of the input stream, e.g. the base layer is $\frac{1}{4}$ of the original. The enhancement layer carries the difference of the scaled-up base layer and the input stream. The block diagram of a spatial scalable coder is shown in Figure 1.7

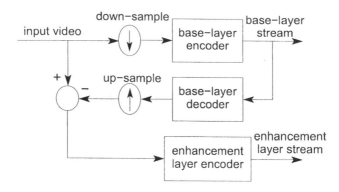

Figure 1.7. Block diagram of a spatial scalable coder.

- **Hybrid Scalability** : Hybrid scalability combines two or more of the above techniques, to produce three or more layers. When two scalabilities are used, three layers are produced: base-layer, enhancement-layer-1 and enhancement-layer-2. Such an arrangement is shown in the example of Figure 1.8, where a spatial-temporal hybrid encoder is displayed.

In conclusion, while scalable video is an answer for using communication media that do not provide QoS, it presents a number of drawbacks:

- It cannot handle situations were the available bandwidth is less that the playback rate of the base-layer.

- Typically, the sum of the resulting layers is larger that the original stream, possible accentuating network congestion.

- Encoders and decoders can be quite complicated.

In favor of scalability we should mention that it is a very powerful technique albeit complicated, for quality adaptation. An indication of the flexibility offered is that it is possible to use this technique to integrate two different encoders.

1.6.   Are SANs an Efficient Solution?

Network and server performance in terms of management and availability is costing network companies hundreds of thousands of dollars in business and productivity losses. At the same time, the amount of information to be managed and stored is prohibitively proliferating. Storage Area Network (SAN) is a relatively new concept that could offer a solution to large volume data storage and communication. SANs have no specific topologies but their defining

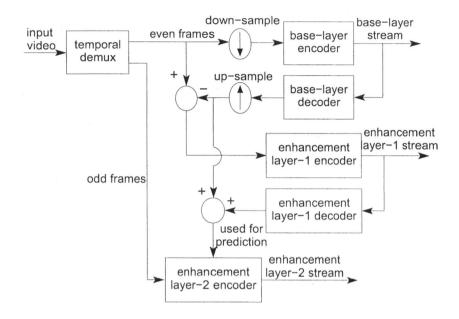

Figure 1.8. Block diagram of a hybrid scalable coder, employing a temporal followed by a spatial decomposition.

characteristic is that they are capable of rendering high-speed authenticated data access to networked machines. The nodes offering the service are mostly referred to as servers, although they are typically very different than run-of-the-mill computational or data servers. The service can be also collectively offered by a storage site which can be considered as a data repository or data-oriented service provider. While a typical server can be viewed either as an independent or as a shared resource, a storage device/site is not owned by any node. Thus storage devices are shared among all networked servers as peer resources. This thinking is not novel to SANs as it is similar to a LAN which is used to bridge clients to servers. The novelty in SANs lies in the *physical* and not just logical separation of the storage service nodes of a LAN. The benefits are platform independence, very-high speed data access, high availability, fault-tolerance and scalability. In the previous sections, we had a glimpse of storage techniques on RAID systems. While the underling networks in which RAID arrays form a part was considered generic, having them on SANs would make a difference in performance. In the following, we shall present general discussions on SANs

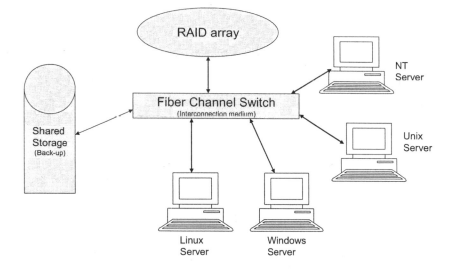

Figure 1.9. A typical SAN Architecture showing the interconnection medium with storage and networks nodes

and certain key components and present a discussion as to the use of SANs in our MSR technology context.

1.6.1   SANs: A brief discussion on salient features and components

SANs by no means can stand alone. They use a mix of technologies just as our traditional networks like LAN/WAN/MAN use today. These include, FDDI, ATM and IBM's Serial Storage Architecture, the emerging iSCSI, and the Fibre Channel over IP standards like iFCP. SAN architectures also allow for the use of a number of underlying protocols, including TCP/IP and variants of SCSI. Current technology is limited and focuses on Fibre Channel implementation perspective as the advent of SANs is somewhat very recent. A typical SAN architecture is shown in Figure 1.9. As of now, SANs are mostly recommended infrastructures for large scale corporate offices and government organizations due to cost considerations. Small scale SANs can also be deployed in smaller sectors that are trying to leverage fibre channel's device sharing capabilities. However, this possibility is highly discouraged for companies that do not have fibre channel expertise in house. Thus, the size of the network in terms of scalability is something questionable at this stage. We bring up the impact of this issue in the context of our MSR in the Chapters that follow.

As far as physical storage is concerned, SANs can incorporate any major technology including mainframe disks, tape drives, and RAID configurations, while making them available under any OS: Windows NT/XP, Unix, Linux, MacOS X and OS/390. With this shared capacity, organizations can acquire, deploy and use storage devices more cost-effectively. SANs do not discriminate the platforms in use and allow free utilization all of their storage resources without any affinity. This also means that within a SAN group of users one can backup or archive data from different servers to the same storage system; allow stored information to be accessed by all servers; create and store a mirror image of data as it is created; and share data between different environments. Thus, we see clearly the use of SANs in off-loading the storage traffic from mainstream network traffic to yield a significant performance improvement. This is one of the positive aspects which our MSR should facilitate.

With respect to supportive networking technologies, with a SAN, there is no need for a physically separate network because the SAN can function as a virtual subnet operating on a shared network infrastructure, provided that different priorities or classes of service are established. Fibre Channel and ATM allow for these different classes of service. Early implementations of SANs have been local or campus-based. But as new WAN technologies such as ATM mature, and especially as class-of-service capabilities improve, the SAN can be extended over a much wider area. Despite a prevailing hype about the coming of unlimited bandwidth, WAN services remain costly today. However, as WAN technologies improve their quality of service, they will provide the robustness needed for each application, including networked I/O, even over public WANs. SANs would play a crucial role then in accommodating profound volume of storage related traffic for several classes of service.

Finally on storage aspects, hooking a storage device or a site is easy over SANs, as a SAN is primarily a network and has no affinity to any device. All that is required is to assign the storage unit a LUN (logical unit number) and connect it to the SAN. Once storage is added to a SAN, an IT manager can use this newly added storage to increase the size of a given storage volume. This makes the newly added storage available to all users and applications without having to reprogram every workstation or application. This is a key feature that makes SANs useful to large enterprises that are experiencing rapid growth. Similar to the RAID technology discussed in Section 1.3, partitioning is also a key feature that is allowed by SANs. The partitioning here refers to parts of SANs functioning as smaller groups, clusters, specific to certain applications. For example, a RAID system first pools multiple physical hard drives into a single large virtual volume. This large virtual volume can then be partitioned into smaller volumes.

Each of the partitioned volumes on a RAID subsystem can be the same size as a single hard disk, but the volumes benefit from the redundancies and performance advantages inherent in RAID technology. Partitioning lets operating system file systems use disk space more efficiently. It gives system administrators flexibility when planning security and assigning users their storage access. SANs can be partitioned just like a RAID system, only the partitioning takes place over the entire storage network rather than individual storage subsystems. So, if a SAN is composed of multiple RAID systems of various speeds, plus tape and optical archives, each partition of the SAN may include portions of these different storage resources. This is something a MSR strategy may use when client population grows beyond certain thresholds. Furthermore, each partition in a SAN can be controlled by its own server or server cluster. Of course the network and system administrators have the freedom of assigning storage resources to different partitions in any combination. Each department in an organization might be allocated its own partition, and can determine its own file migration, redundancy, and backup requirements. Applications demanding large volume space for their intermediate computational steps will find the idea of using small scale partitioned storage networks very useful.

1.6.2   SANs& MSR Technology: a handshake?

We have seen some specific components and technologies underlying the SANs in the above section. Below we shall discuss their use and impact in the context of MSR technology, the subject matter of this book.

Although SANs hold great promise for scalability and efficiency in handling of huge volumes of data, their prospects of a successful deployment as primary components of a VoD architecture are dim, at least based on the specifications and cost of contemporary Fibre-channel based implementations. This is mainly due to their overwhelming cost, especially when viewed as part of a networked multimedia (public) service infrastructure. Also, given that VoD services generate traffic that can be easily anticipated and predicted for the duration of a client's session, their needs can be more easily and economically catered for by strategically placing existing multimedia databases and repositories at vantage locations to minimize large client access times.

Since MSR strategies operate at the application level there is still room for a future fusion between the two technologies. SANs will make a difference to multimedia applications when operated on smaller domains. With MSR, if service providers decide to operate in smaller domains with proxy-based control, the integration of SANs would speed up content retrieval, especially with a multitude of storage devices and vast storage space available for local users. With SANs, MSR can make a difference in rendering highly customized services

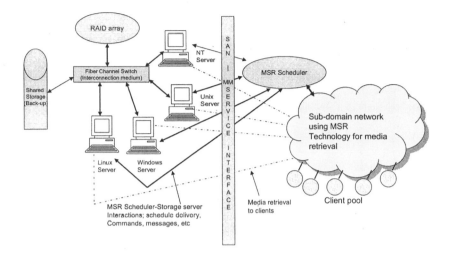

Figure 1.10. Diagram showing the integration of MSR technology with SANs on a small scale multimedia service domain

to users, as the domains are now considered smaller with fairly larger storage space.

One could envisage a typical SAN-MSR architecture as the one shown in Figure 1.10. MSR built-in with SANs will wisely discriminate user data traffic and media traffic and it is expected to maximize the number of users or user requests that can be supported from such a smaller domain. This does not preclude the possibility of services to users outside the domain. Employment of smaller domains will boil down to improved service levels while accommodating a larger number of user's requests. Thus with distributed control being exercised in the implementation of MSR technology, support of SANs will be indefatigable and unavoidable, especially due to ever surmounting user demands.

One of the welcoming aspects of SANs under MSR technology is the gain that is achieved by splitting the storage/retrieval traffic from main network-user traffic. Since in every local domain a huge amount of space could be available, media data migration that is transparent to the users can be carried out between domain controllers/schedulers, without much effort or lengthy negotiations. This is particularly useful when, say, movie profiles are used to control the storage space. This means that as long as the popularity of a movie is fairly large, a site continues to retain the corresponding data files. However, when popularity degrades, which means lesser demand traffic, then it is wiser to move it to remote sites or slower/cheaper storage sites/devices. Usually in conventional and existing implementations, negotiations need to be performed and least-recently-used type algorithms work to provide space for a newly incoming movie. With SANs in place, this seldom becomes a primary issue of concern and movie can be migrated to a remote site. Possibly, an infrequent broadcast of the capacities available within the domains is what needs to be implemented. In addition, mirroring/replicating of media data for casual and sporadic demands can be easily accommodated.

A huge benefit for MSR-based systems from the deployment of SANs in local domains, would materialize because of the existence of large pervasive storage space. Inter-net traffic that currently bogs down large-scale VoD systems could be largely replaced by intranet traffic between the clients and their local SAN.

1.7. Concluding Remarks

In this chapter we have introduced some of the key concepts that underlie the design philosophy of the MSR strategies. Also, we have discussed contemporary solutions used in the VoD domain, along with their associated advantages and shortcomings. We have studied and elaborated on the constraints imposed on the workings of single-server VoD systems, that are usually employed by service providers. The Fellini server, a typical architecture representing mid-1990s works is also presented. We have also discussed a number of enabling technologies that relate to the storage and the network subsystems respectively. RAID arrays provide availability and speed improvements, while multicasting, simulcasting and other network protocols can conserve network resources and allow for improved scalability. Network scalability and quality adaptation is also the motivation behind the scalable video technology presented in Section 1.5. With the focus of the book being the design of MSR technologies, we devoted a significant part of this chapter on Storage Area Networks, as an MSR system could profusely use SANs technology. The discussion that follows our introduction of SANs and associated technology, raises many possibilities for interoperability between SANs and MSR systems. In Chapter 2 we discuss the theoretical design, analysis and performance evaluation of two MSR strategies. Chapter 8 demonstrates one real-life MSR implementation showing the feasibility of the technology.

Chapter 2

MULTIPLE SERVERS RETRIEVAL STRATEGY : DATA PARTITIONING APPROACH

2.1. Introduction to Multiple Server Technology

In Section 1.2.3, we have seen how to retrieve a long duration media document form a single-server system. The recommended portions considered the link bandwidth between the client and the server as well as the playback rate of the media at the client end. This is a typical service style of a networked client server system. We have also seen how a single server serves more than one client and uses an admission controller to maximize the number of clients it can serve in Section 1.2.3. However, in this analysis, we have not taken into account the non-zero network delays. In contrast, the formulation of Section 1.2.3 focused on the impact of disk systems and also showed how storage specifications affect the admission control and service quality. However, several real-time applications demand the response of the media servers to be as quick as possible in order to make the underlying mission successful, hence network delays cannot be ignored. In this chapter, we will introduce a novel retrieval strategy that particularly suits long duration media such as feature-length movies (typically longer than 60 and usually around 90 minutes in duration) for Video-on-Demand (VoD) or Movie-on-Demand (MoD) applications[1]. Below we will see the need for such a multiple server technology for modern day high-bandwidth applications.

With the increasing popularity of multimedia services on network based environments, there is a continuous thrust in achieving an optimized design for multimedia servers and network service providers. The main attraction of these services is that viewing and presentation control is handed over to the user, in

---

[1] Hereafter we will use VoD and MoD interchangeably in this book.

contrast with conventional video broadcast services as cable TV. A particular movie can not only be made available to a user at his/her convenience (as with video cassettes), but the user can also have complete control on all aspects of the different media involved (audio, video), as for example the physical layout of the screen. Also, with an increase in demand for a particular movie, depending on the popularity profile, viewing cost per user can also be reduced considerably when clever placement of movies at strategic locations on the network is carried out. The effort for the development of such systems and services would be futile without the availability of high performance computers and high speed fiber optic networks that offer the capability of supporting such demands.

The above mentioned application and other (futuristic) applications like MoD, collaborative video editing and synthesis of multimedia objects and other network based distributed applications, will be attractive only when the available network bandwidth and other necessary resources are cleverly utilized. While using state-of-the-art technology to realize such applications is always a solution, the established -network mostly- and slowly changing infrastructure leaves no alternative but to carefully plan and utilize what is currently available. Owing to the continuous thrust in developing multimedia services on network based environments, the service providers situated at geographically large distances can co-operate and share their documents in order to serve their local subscribers. Once a document is available locally, in turn, each service provider can choose the appropriate admission control and scheduling algorithms to maximize their servicing capabilities. We believe that this multi-tier service architecture, provides an elegant solution for developing such multimedia services, since the data sizes that are involved are very large. Another motivation underlying this support is from monetary aspects. It will be prohibitively costly if one tries to replicate all the media documents across all the sites, to provide efficient service. Of course, replication of the documents may take care of the performance to certain extent, although monetarily such a scheme may not be desirable.

Also, applications like virtual multimedia conferencing or virtual group discussions, will be attractive and viable, only when the on-line discussions are captured and presented without any temporal delays. If however, the subject of discussion is currently not available at the local service provider, then the corresponding document would have to be downloaded from a remote site in which it is available. Since the sites are typically geographically apart and downloading would involve the transmission of large volumes of data, it would take quite an amount of time before the entire document is downloaded and the discussion at the local site initiated. This waiting time may be annoying to end users, especially if the discussion depends on making time critical decisions.

An illustrative example presented in the next section clearly describes the motivation for this research. In this chapter we precisely address the problem of minimizing this waiting time or the access time for similar and allied network based multimedia services. The key idea is to divide the media document into several disjoint portions, which are then retrieved from several servers, taking into account each client-server connection bandwidth. Since we partition the document, this approach shall be referred to as *data partitioning approach*, hereafter. Also, this data partitioning approach, to a large extent presents a unified theoretical framework that suits most of the existing network-based distributed multimedia services and also opens a new avenue for the researchers in this field. The theoretical framework is accompanied by an in-depth analysis of the behavior of the proposed strategies that leads to the design of more refined approaches in the chapters that follow. Whenever appropriate, we also make comparisons with the Single Server Retrieval Strategy (SSRS), that bring out the true potential of the suggested multiple server strategies.

2.1.1 Network architecture

We envision a network consisting of a set of service providers serving each locality (see figure 2.1)[2]. Each service provider has a directory facility, which registers the available documents at various sites. Whenever a user requests a movie, this directory service will produce a list of servers that can supply the requested multimedia document. Thus, if the requested multimedia document is not locally available, the service provider will request the other service providers to upload that document to its local site. Thereafter, whenever a request for this document arrives, the local server can use the stored document. This service provider could be the multimedia server itself, if it has adequate resources for supporting this service. In such a large network, the user requests may originate anywhere, and servicing these requests should incur the minimum possible delay. If not, such a multimedia service becomes less attractive. A survey [16] on monetary issues provides a good hope of realizing such multimedia applications on network based environments and opens avenues to pursue further research in this domain.

In the case of networks that span a large area wherein the server sites are geographically distributed, communication from one site to the other will incur a finite amount of non-zero delay. One of the attractive features of such multimedia services on networks lies in keeping up the promise of a smooth presentation without any audio-visual discontinuities. Unless clever strategies are adopted in retrieving the video blocks amidst the presence of these communication delays, this objective may not be met. We model the communication delay as a quantity that is directly proportional to the length of the video data that is

---

[2]Figure 4.1 presents a slightly more detailed version.

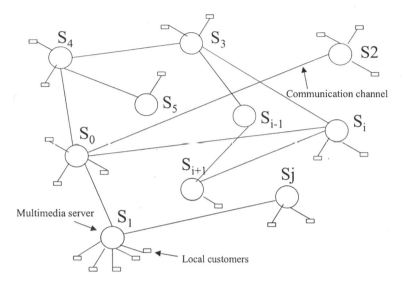

Figure 2.1. Networked Multimedia Servers Servicing Customers

carried over that established communication path (virtual or circuit switched) to the service provider. This is unlike the model proposed for pyramid broadcasting technique[3], in which the video blocks in the successive retrievals are of increasing sizes. In this multiple server technology, the available communication bandwidth and the display/playback rate of the video clip are the two major system parameters that are considered, and this chapter focuses in the design and analysis of retrieval strategies that minimize the access or the wait time of the users.

2.1.2   Distinct advantages in using Multiple Server Retrieval

We now highlight some of the key inherent advantages in using a multiple server approach. Since this strategy primarily involves more than one server for retrieving the document and rendering the VoD/MoD service, this strategy, and hence the technology associated with this service infrastructure is referred to as *Multiple Server Retrieval*(MSR) strategy, hereafter in this book. A MSR scheme inherently subsumes the following advantages. Firstly, on a network-based service rendering environment, if a single server system, however sophisticated it may be (in terms of speed and capacity) is used there is a continuous "work pressure" that is enforced on the system. For instance, when there is

---

[3] See the bibliographic notes for pyramid broadcasting.

a continuous demand for a long duration video retrieval by several clients, a significant amount of the time is spent in servicing these requests, while some small number of requests demanding short services may undergo long waiting times. By employing a MSR strategy, the work pressure can be balanced among the servers. Secondly, by using a MSR strategy, even low-bandwidth or heavily-loaded servers, that may not be usable on their own, can now be significantly contributing to a group of several servers that upload a movie. Thirdly, considering fault-tolerance aspects, which are treated in Chapter 7, even under server/link failures, the workload imbalance can be gracefully taken care of by the remaining servers, in a multiple server environment. Since multiple servers are engaged in the retrieval process, failure of one or more servers, will allow the service to continue without any interruption so long as there is at least one server operational. In fact, with a clever design of a retrieval strategy, the clients will continue to view the presentation while a certain number of servers may "die" and come back to "life" after some time. In contrast, with a conventional system, the clients will most probably need to be rescheduled at the expense of their presentation continuity. Also, as shown in rigorous simulation studies in the literature [105, 11], scalability of the physical system and heterogeneity of the system, can be easily accounted in the design, as the size of the portions retrieved from each of the servers depends on the available bandwidth and playback rate of the movie. In effect, a MSR strategy has a natural load balancing capability built-in its design. Each server participates according to its available capacity and/or its connection bandwidth to the client, collectively offering a service far superior than anything it could offer on its own. Finally, from service provider's perspective, since each server, on the whole, is engaged only for a short while in retrieving a portion of the media document, the number of clients that can be entertained simultaneously can be potentially maximized. Thus MSR offers a clear win-win situation for both the customers and the service providers.

2.2.   Problem Definition and Preliminary Remarks

In this section, we present the problem more formally, describe the network architecture that is considered, and introduce the necessary definitions, notations and terminology

The network model consists of a pool of N multimedia servers each serving their respective customers (see figure 2.1). The requests for viewing a movie of a long duration (typically of 100 to 120 minutes) arrive at these servers from its local customers. These servers are by and large, powerful workstations with sufficient amount of bandwidth capacity and memory space to serve a maximum number of users concurrently by employing efficient admission control algorithms. Upon an arrival of a request, the server seeks the requested multimedia document. We interchangeably use the terms service providers and servers as per the context. If the document is available locally, then usual retrieval and presentation techniques as described in the so far literature can be employed to serve the request. However, if the requested document is not available, then the server with its directory service facility, a kind of look-up table procedure, determines the server sites at which the requested multimedia document is present. It then obtains a set of server addresses from which the document may be retrieved. The requested multimedia document is then retrieved by employing a MSR strategy demonstrated through the following motivating example. We introduce the necessary notations and terminology in the example for the ease of understanding.

2.2.1 Motivating example

Consider a scenario in which a requested multimedia document is not available locally at a server denoted as, S. Let the requested multimedia document be present at the sites S_0, S_1, and S_2. Let the total size of the movie requested be $L = 1GB$. Further, let the channel bandwidths in terms of the time delay encountered per unit load transfer, measured in *seconds per unit load*, between each of these servers to S be denoted as $bw_i \ i = 0, 1, 2$. It may be noted that we are referring to the inverse of the channel bandwidth, however, we will continue to use the terminology *bandwidth* while referring to this quantity. Let these quantities(expressed in seconds per Mbit or in seconds per Mbyte) be $bw_0 = 1$, $bw_1 = 2$, and $bw_2 = 3$, respectively. Thus, with our definition, in this example, bw_0 is the fastest channel, bw_1 is the next fastest and so on. Hence, sending a unit load on bw_0 takes less time to reach S than from others. We assume that when the server S receives the document from another server, it starts the playback simultaneously at the user terminal. A discussion on this aspect is presented in 2.5. After locating the respective servers having the requested multimedia document (in this case servers 0 to 2), server S adopts the following strategy. From each server a portion of the entire document is retrieved and the parts are collected by S in a particular order. Upon receiving a portion from S_0, the playback is started at the user terminal. Let the inverse of the playback rate(expressed in the same units as the bw_i's), denoted as R_p be 5.3333 units (MPEG I stream). Now, the retrieval strategy is such that before the playback of this portion comes to an end, the next portion of the requested multimedia document is collected from S_1. This process is repeated for all the servers participating in the retrieval process.

This example describes one of the possible MSR strategies, namely the *single installment* retrieval strategy. Later, we will see an example for the case of the multi-installment strategy. This strategy has some inherent advantages. Firstly, it retrieves disjoint portions from different servers and thus, minimizes the retrieval time. Secondly, the strategy inherently takes care of continuity requirements, which are crucial when implementing such a strategy on network based environments. Thus, the continuity in the presentation is one of the aspects that a MSR strategy guarantees in the retrieval process apart from access time minimization. A fundamental assumption of all the analysis that follows is that the playback of a portion of the document is (or can be) initiated after this portion is completely received from the corresponding server. For the reason we also call this approach as a Play-After-Retrieval (PAR) strategy. In Chapter 4, we relax this assumption and examine the effect on performance when playback and retrieval are concurrent.

The *access time* or the *wait time* is defined as the time between the start of the downloading and the start of the playback [13]. The access time is directly proportional to the size of the portion retrieved from server S_0, i.e., starting from the time at which the downloading starts to the time at which the playback starts. An immediate naive choice would be to make this size as small as possible to minimize the access time of the entire multimedia document. However, in that case we will later show that the *presentation continuity* cannot be guaranteed by choosing the first retrieved portion arbitrarily as small as we desire. Hence, using this strategy, the problem now is to decide on the optimal sizes of the portions of the multimedia document to be retrieved from each of the servers, satisfying the presentation continuity, using the bandwidth constraints, and the playback rate constraints to minimize the access time.

In the above example, we see that the following size distribution $m_0 = 85.997$ MBytes, $m_1 = 272.3235$ MBytes, $m_2 = 665.679$ MBytes satisfies the constraints, where m_i is the size of the data retrieved from server S_i, $i = 0, 1, 2$, respectively. For this distribution, the access time (following the definition) is given by $m_0 bw_0 = 85.997$ secs.

An elegant representation of this retrieval strategy is by means of *directed flow graphs* (DFGs)[4]. Figure 2.2 shows the directed flow graph for this example. The communication nodes at the first level are assigned a weight equal to the total communication time of the portions of the multimedia document they are transferring to S. The dots on these communication nodes indicate that all these servers start their downloading simultaneously at time t units. Without loss of generality, we assume $t = 0$. If m_0 is the portion of the multimedia document communicated by S_0, then the total communication delay (which is the weight of the node 0 (see figure 2.2) is given by $m_0 bw_0$. The second level nodes are referred to as *playback* nodes. The weight of the playback node 0 is propor-

---

[4]Directed graphs are usually used to capture any precedence relationships between the nodes in the graph. The nodes of the graph may represent program modules, events or states in general.

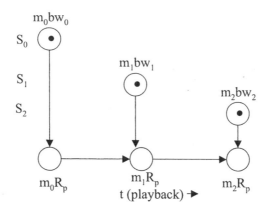

Figure 2.2. Directed Flow Graph representation for the case of 3 servers.

tional to the total time of playback of that portion of video, given by $m_0 R_p$, where R_p is the inverse of the rate of playback expressed in seconds per unit load of display. The directed arrows depict the *causal precedence* relationships between the node events. Thus, at S, the display of the portion from S_2 starts only after the display of the portion from S_1 is completed and also the portion from S_2 must be completely available.

2.2.2   Some definitions

Throughout the chapter we will use the following definitions.

1. *Retrieval schedule distribution*: This is defined as an N ordered tuple m given by

$$m = (m_0, m_1, ..., m_{N-1}) \qquad (2.1)$$

where, m_i is the portion of the multimedia document downloaded from server S_i, $i = 0, 1, 2, ..., N-1$. Further,

$$\sum_{k=0}^{N-1} m_k = L \qquad (2.2)$$

and

$$0 \leq m_i \leq L, \quad i = 0, 1, ...N - 1, \qquad (2.3)$$

The set of all such retrieval schedule distributions is denoted as Γ.

2. The *Access Time* or the *wait time* is defined as the time between the instant at which the servers start uploading their portions to the time at which the

presentation starts. This is denoted as, $AT(m)$.

Typically, this is the time to access the first portion of the downloaded data, given by $m_0 bw_0$, where bw_0 is the bandwidth of the established communication path from S_0 to S. Hereafter, we shall use the term "access time" throughout the chapter.

3. *Minimum access time* is defined as,

$$AT^* = min_{m \in \Gamma} AT(m) \tag{2.4}$$

Thus, from the above set of definitions and the strategy illustrated in the above example, the objective is to minimize the access time by determining the optimal sizes of the portions of the video to be retrieved from different servers involved in the retrieval process.

2.3. Single Installment Retrieval Policy

In this section, following the retrieval strategy mentioned in the previous section, we shall analytically determine the sizes of the various portions retrieved from all the N servers. We then derive a closed-form solution for the minimum access time. It will be shown that the continuity and the bandwidth constraints are implicitly considered, stemming naturally as a property of the optimal solution in the analysis.

Figure 2.3 shows a generalized version of the example illustrated in the previous section, with N servers. From figure 2.3, we can derive a relationship between the communication nodes i and $i + 1$ and the playback time of the portion m_i with the use of causal precedence relations and continuity constraint as,

$$m_{i+1} bw_{i+1} \leq m_i bw_i + m_i R_p, \quad i = 0, 1, ..., N - 2. \tag{2.5}$$

Let us denote $(bw_i + R_p)/bw_{i+1} = \rho_i$. Using in (2.5), we have,

$$m_{i+1} \leq m_i \rho_i, , \quad i = 0, ..., N - 2. \tag{2.6}$$

One can solve these set of recursive relations with equality conditions. Using equality relations in (2.5) and (2.6) produces the *maximum* size of all document portions other than m_0. So under the constraint of (2.2), this yields the *minimum* m_0 or equivalently the minimum access time. Thus, we have a recursive set of $(N - 1)$ equations with equality relations from (2.6). Each m_j in (2.6) can be expressed in terms m_0 as,

$$m_j = m_0 \prod_{k=0}^{j-1} \rho_k, \quad j = 1, ..., N - 1. \tag{2.7}$$

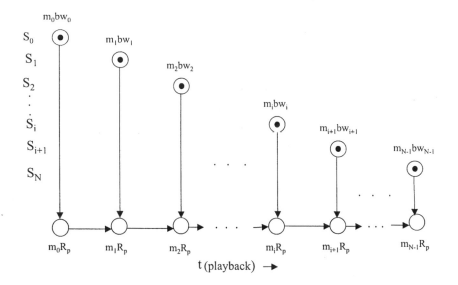

Figure 2.3. Directed Flow Graph representation using single-installment strategy for multimedia document retrieval from N servers

In general, the continuity relationship[5] states that *the playback duration of a portion of a video must be greater than or equal to the total retrieval time of the immediate successive portion of the video.* Otherwise, the continuity of the presentation will be lost and leads to a considerable performance degradation. In the above set of recursive equations, it may be noted that we have taken care of this continuity constraint by using the equality relationships rather than the inequality relationships. That is, the next playback will start immediately after the current playback comes to an end. Thus, when these set of linear recursive equations are solved with equality relationships, we obtain the minimum access time, as the solution set (m_0 to m_{N-1} through this procedure) gives the minimum value of m_0. Equation (2.7) generates $N - 1$ equations, but we have N media portions. However, along with (2.2), we have N equations which can be solved to obtain the individual disjoint portions of the requested multimedia document. Substituting each m_i from (2.7) into (2.2), we obtain,

$$m_0 = \frac{L}{\left(1 + \sum_{p=1}^{N-1} \prod_{k=0}^{p-1} \rho_k\right)} \qquad (2.8)$$

---

[5]See [89] for further reading on continuity constraints.

Substituting (2.8) in (2.7), we obtain the individual sizes of the portions as,

$$m_j = \frac{L \prod_{k=0}^{j-1} \rho_k}{\left(1 + \sum_{p=1}^{N-1} \prod_{k=0}^{p-1} \rho_k\right)} \tag{2.9}$$

for all $j = 1, ..., N - 1$. Note that the access time (see figure 2.3) is given by,

$$AT(m) = m_0 b w_0 = \frac{L \, b w_0}{\left(1 + \sum_{p=1}^{N-1} \prod_{k=0}^{p-1} \rho_k\right)} \tag{2.10}$$

where we have used (2.8) for m_0. The retrieval schedule distribution demonstrated in the motivating example in the previous section is derived through these set of formulas.

2.3.1 Homogeneous channels

We consider a network with identical channel bandwidths or a channel that is shared by several servers. In other words, we have, $bw_i = bw$, for all $i = 0, ..., N - 1$. The individual sizes of the portions retrieved from the servers S_0 till S_{N-1} are given by,

$$m_0 = \frac{L(\rho - 1)}{\rho^N - 1} \tag{2.11}$$

$$m_j = \frac{L(\rho - 1)\rho^j}{\rho^N - 1}, \quad j = 1, ..., N - 1, \tag{2.12}$$

where we have used $bw_i = bw$ for all $i = 0, 1, ..., N$ 1 in (2.8) and (2.9) to obtain these expressions. Hence, the access time is given by,

$$AT(m) = m_0 b w_0 = \frac{L \, bw \, (\rho - 1)}{\rho^N - 1} \tag{2.13}$$

We shall later present a detailed discussion on the behavior of this homogeneous system.

2.3.2 Effect of sequencing on the access time

It is worth noting at this juncture that throughout the above analysis we have assumed that retrieval follows a particular order, referred to as *fixed sequence*, S_0 to S_{N-1}. Given a set of N servers, we have $N!$ retrieval sequences possible. However, one may wonder if it could be possible to gain performance by varying the sequence in which the multimedia document is retrieved from the servers. The following lemma and theorem prove that such a behavior is not possible when a single installment strategy is employed.

Lemma 1. Let the access time of a requested multimedia document by the server S be denoted as $AT(m, \sigma(k, k + 1))$, where

$$\sigma(k, k + 1) = (S_0, ..., S_{k-1}, S_k, S_{k+1}, S_{k+2}, ..., S_{N-1}),$$

denotes the sequence in which the requested multimedia document is retrieved from the servers. Then, for a sequence

$$\sigma'(k, k + 1) = (S_0, ..., S_{k-1}, S_{k+1}, S_k, S_{k+2}, ..., S_{N-1})$$

, the access time $AT(m', \sigma'(k, k + 1))$ is equal to $AT(m, \sigma(k, k + 1))$ where, $\sigma'(k, k + 1)$ denotes a retrieval sequence in which the adjacent channels k and $k + 1$ are swapped, i.e., portion from server S_{k+1} is retrieved first and then from server S_k.

Proof. The denominator of (2.10) can be written as:

$$denom(m) = 1 + \rho_0 + \rho_0\rho_1 + \rho_0\rho_1\rho_2 + ... = 1 + \rho_0(1 + \rho_1(1 + \rho_2(...)))) \tag{2.14}$$

We can distinguish two cases depending on whether the first server S_0 is involved or not. If S_0 is not involved, when a switch is made between two successive servers, the new denominator is different from the original one in three ρterms. This difference can be written as

$$denom(m') - denom(m) =$$
$$\frac{R_p + bw_{i-1}}{bw_{i+1}}\left(1 + \frac{R_p + bw_{i+1}}{bw_i}\left(1 + \frac{R_p + bw_i}{bw_{i+2}}\right)\right)$$
$$- \frac{R_p + bw_{i-1}}{bw_i}\left(1 + \frac{R_p + bw_i}{bw_{i+1}}\left(1 + \frac{R_p + bw_{i+1}}{bw_{i+2}}\right)\right) \tag{2.15}$$

With little algebraic manipulation, the above equation returns zero.

In the second case, where the first two servers S_0 and S_1 are switched, the difference in access time is,

$$AT(m) - AT(m') = \frac{L\,bw_0}{denom(m)} - \frac{L\,bw_1}{denom(m')}$$

$$= L\frac{(bw_0 denom(m') - bw_1 denom(m))}{denom(m)\,denom(m')} \tag{2.16}$$

By using (2.14) ($denom(m)$ and $denom(m')$ differ in two ρ-terms), the numerator of the above fraction becomes equal to

$$bw_0\left(1 + \frac{R_p + bw_1}{bw_0}\left(1 + \frac{R_p + bw_0}{bw_2}\right)\right)$$

$$-bw_1 \left(1 + \frac{R_p + bw_0}{bw_1} \left(1 + \frac{R_p + bw_1}{bw_2} \right) \right) \qquad (2.17)$$

which in turn can be easily proven to be equal to zero. □

The significance of the lemma is that the order in which the portions are downloaded affects only the respective size distribution, but not the access time when adjacent servers are swapped. We prove this claim in general for the case of N servers, as follows.

Theorem 1. Given a pool of N multimedia servers capable of rendering the requested multimedia document, using the single installment strategy, the access time is independent of the retrieval sequence used.

Proof. Direct application of Lemma 1 proves the theorem. Any valid sequence of servers can be derived from a single sequence by iteratively switching the positions between adjacent servers. Lemma 1 guarantees that these operations do not affect access time. □

2.4. Multi-Installment Servicing Policy

In this section, we present a generalized servicing policy, which provides a tuning control mechanism for the access time. This tuning provides a better control on the retrieval process and allows the system to adapt to the variations in the bandwidth of the network. This policy constitutes of retrieving the multimedia data from each of the servers S_0 to S_{N-1} in more than one installment. This means that every server participates more than once in the process of uploading disjoint portions of the requested document one after other, in a particular order. Since this facilitates the accessing of the data by S at a much earlier time, the access time decreases. As in the case of the single installment policy, the continuity of the presentation must be guaranteed. The necessary and sufficient conditions for the multi-installment policy, can be derived by extending the directed graph representation of the previous section. By assuming that each server uploads a disjoint portion of the multimedia data in n installments, we can use the extended graph to derive a set of recursive equations.

2.4.1 Recursive equations and solution methodology

Figure 2.4 shows the directed graph for this policy. Note that we have extended the communication and playback processes from single installment to multi-installment using causal precedence relations (time orderliness). Let $m_{i,j}$ represents the part of the L in total multimedia data, that is downloaded from the S_i server during the j-th installment, where $j = 0, \ldots, n-1$. Thus, there is a total of Nn portions of the multimedia document that are retrieved from servers S_0 to S_{N-1} in n installments. These are $m_{0,0}, m_{1,0}, \ldots, m_{N-1,0}, m_{0,1}, \ldots,$

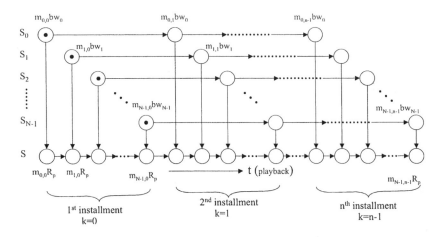

Figure 2.4. Directed Flow Graph representation using Multi-installment strategy for multimedia document retrieval from N servers

$m_{N-1,1}, \ldots, m_{0,n-1}, \ldots, m_{N-1,n-1}$. It can be easily deducted from (see figure 2.4) that the causal precedence relations and the continuity relationships impose the following inequalities:

$$m_{k,0}bw_k \leq m_{k-1,0}bw_{k-1} + m_{k-1,0}R_p, \qquad (2.18)$$

for all $k = 1, 2, ..., N - 1$. For $i = 1, 2, ..., n - 1$, we have,

$$m_{k,i}bw_k \leq \left(\sum_{p=k}^{N-1} m_{p,i-1} + \sum_{p=1}^{k-1} m_{p,i} \right) R_p \qquad (2.19)$$

for all $k = 0, 1, ..., N - 1$.

The $m_{i,j}$ parts are also connected by the normalizing equation:

$$\sum_{i=0}^{N-1} \sum_{j=0}^{n-1} m_{i,j} = L \qquad (2.20)$$

The *minimum* size of $m_{0,0}$, which determines the minimum access time, can be obtained by seeking the *maximization* of all other $m_{i,j}$. This goal can be achieved by using the equality relations in Equations (2.19) and (2.20). Deriving a closed-form solution from the above set of recursive equations is too tedious. However, since

$$m_{1,0} = m_{0,0} \cdot \frac{bw_0 + R_p}{bw_1} \qquad (2.21)$$

$$m_{k,0} = m_{0,0} \cdot \prod_{j=1}^{k} \frac{bw_{j-1} + R_p}{bw_j} \tag{2.22}$$

$$m_{k,i} = \left(\sum_{j=k}^{N-1} m_{j,i-1} + \sum_{j=0}^{k-1} m_{j,i} \right) \frac{R_p}{bw_k} \tag{2.23}$$

we can reach a solution by using the following procedure. If we assume that $m_{0,0} = 1$ we can obtain from (2.21) $m_{1,0}$, and from Eq. (2.22) and (2.23) successively all $m_{k,i}$. The original assumption is the equivalent of multiplying $m_{0,0}$ by a constant K so that it equals unity. Because of the way $m_{i,j}$ are related through Eq. (2.21), (2.22) and (2.23), this process returns all $m_{k,i}$ also multiplied by K. K can in turn be estimated from the normalizing Equation (2.20), which becomes:

$$\sum_{j=0}^{N-1} \sum_{l=0}^{n-1} m_{j,l} = K \cdot L \tag{2.24}$$

and this completes the solution. We denote the access time, using multi-installment strategy, as $AT(N, n)$, as we have now two parameters N an n to control the access time. The access time is given by,

$$AT(N, n) - m_{0,0} bw_0, \tag{2.25}$$

where $m_{0,0}$ is obtained by solving the recursive equations a mentioned above. Following example demonstrates this strategy.

Example 2. Suppose that the client at S requests a 2GB multimedia document from servers S_0, S_1, S_2 and S_3, which are linked with S with 128KByte/sec connections. If we assume a playback rate of 4Mbits/sec, typical of a MPEG II document, then a single installment, i.e. $n - 1$, results in an access time of 2841.67 seconds. However, doubling the number of installments results in an access time of 1362.0 seconds. Thus, we gain a significant decrease (of 52%) in the access time.

2.4.2 Homogeneous channels

Here too, we shall consider analysis for homogeneous channels. Thus, the above set of recursive relations ((2.18) and (2.19)) reduces to,

$$m_{k,0} bw \leq m_{k-1,0} bw + m_{k-1,0} R_p, \tag{2.26}$$

for all $k = 1, 2, ..., N - 1$. Then, for $i = 1, 2, ..., n - 1$, we have,

$$m_{k,i} bw \leq \left(\sum_{p=k}^{N} m_{p,i-1} + \sum_{p=1}^{k-1} m_{p,i} \right) R_p \tag{2.27}$$

for all $k = 0, 1, ..., N - 1$. Denoting, R_p/bw as σ, we have,

$$m_{k,0} \leq m_{k-1,0}(1 + \sigma) \tag{2.28}$$

for all $k = 1, 2, ..., N - 1$. Then, for $i = 1, 2, ..., n - 1$, we have,

$$m_{k,i} \leq \left(\sum_{p=k}^{N} m_{p,i-1} + \sum_{p=1}^{k-1} m_{p,i} \right) \sigma \tag{2.29}$$

for all $k = 0, 1, ..., N - 1$. Using the equality relationship, we write,

$$m_{k,0} = m_{k-1,0}(1 + \sigma) \tag{2.30}$$

for all $k = 1, 2, ..., N - 1$. Then, for $i = 1, 2, ..., n - 1$, we have,

$$m_{k,i} = \left(\sum_{p=k}^{N} m_{p,i-1} + \sum_{p=1}^{k-1} m_{p,i} \right) \sigma \tag{2.31}$$

for all $k = 0, 1, ..., N - 1$. Each of the $m_{k,0}$, $k = 1, ..., N - 1$ from (2.30) can be expressed as a function of $m_{0,0}$ as,

$$m_{k,0} = m_{0,0} P(\sigma, k), \tag{2.32}$$

where, $P(\sigma, k) = (1 + \sigma)^{k-1}$. It is worth noting that the polynomial $P(\sigma, k)$ contains binomial coefficients when expanded. Also, it may be observed from (2.31) that to obtain $m_{k,i}$ for any $i > 0$, we need to simply add N of its preceding terms and multiply by a σ.

We define a transformation $k = i(n - 1) + jN$, and denote the portions of the multimedia document retrieved from $S_0, ..., S_{N-1}$ in n installments as, Q_k, $k = 0, 1, ..., Nn - 1$, where k is as defined above. For instance, when $N = 4$ and $n = 2$, $m_{1,1}$ which is actually the second installment for server S_1 is denoted by Q_5, as $k = 1.(1) + 1.(4) = 5$. Thus, with this notation and transformation, and with (2.31) and (2.32), we can easily generate the following table. We have shown the table for $N = 4$ and $n = 2$ case. The entries in each row of the table are the coefficients of the respective powers of σ. Thus, the maximum number of columns will be $Nn - 1$. As an example, $m_{1,1}$ corresponds to the row Q_5, given by (2.31) as $3\sigma + 10\sigma^2 + 10\sigma^3 + 5\sigma^4 + \sigma^5$, and the entries are precisely these coefficients of the various powers of σ.

$m_{i,j}$	k	$j \to$ 0	1	2	3	4	5	6	7
0,0	0	1	0	0	0	0	0	0	0
1,0	1	1	1	0	0	0	0	0	0
2,0	2	1	2	1	0	0	0	0	0
3,0	3	1	3	3	1	0	0	0	0
0,1	4	0	4	6	4	1	0	0	0
1,1	5	0	3	10	10	5	1	0	0
2,1	6	0	2	12	20	15	6	1	0
3,1	7	0	1	12	31	35	21	7	1

Thus, generalizing this idea, we have the following boundary conditions and a recursive definition to generate a particular entry E(i,j) in the table for arbitrary N and n.

The boundary conditions, which generate entries for the first installment $n = 0$ are given by,

$$E(k,0) = 1, \forall k = 0, 1, ..., N - 1, \tag{2.33}$$
$$E(k,0) = 0, \forall k = N, ..., Nn - 1, \tag{2.34}$$
$$E(k,j) = 0, \forall j > k, \text{ and} k, j = 0, 1, ..., Nn - 1, \tag{2.35}$$
$$E(k,j) = E(k - 1, j - 1) + E(k - 1, j), \forall k = 1, 2, ..., N - 1 \tag{2.36}$$

Note that the first entry $E(0,0)$ is assumed to be equal to 1. This is just for the purpose of generating the table entries as a function of $m_{0,0}$ which is assumed to be unity. However, when actually solving the recursive equations, we can express each of the $m_{i,j}$ as a function of $m_{0,0}$. Now, for the remaining rows, $Q_N, ..., Q_{Nn-1}$, we have,

$$E(k,j) = \sum_{p=k-N}^{k-1} E(p, j - 1), \forall k = N, ..., Nn - 1, j = 1, 2, ..., Nn - 1,$$
$$\tag{2.37}$$

Thus, we have for $Q_5 = m_{1,1} = E(5,0) + E(5,1)\sigma + ... + E(5,4)\sigma^4 + E(5,5)\sigma^5$. This is nothing but the polynomial shown above. Following this notion, we can write $m_{i,j}$ as,

$$m_{i,j} = Q_k = \sum_{j=0}^{i} E(i,j)\sigma^j, \forall i = 0, 1, ..., Nn - 1, \tag{2.38}$$

We have a total of Nn unknowns with $Nn - 1$ equations. As in the previous section, we use the normalizing equation,

$$\sum_{i=0}^{Nn-1} \sum_{j=0}^{i} E(i,j)\sigma^j = L \tag{2.39}$$

to have a total of Nn equations to solve for all the unknowns. Note that each of the $m_{i,j}$ can be expressed in terms of $m_{0,0}$, by using the recursive definition of (2.38) and using (2.39), we obtain,

$$m_{0,0} = \frac{L}{\sum_{i=0}^{Nn-1} \sum_{j=0}^{i} E(i,j)\sigma^j}, \tag{2.40}$$

where, $E(i,j)$ is generated by using equations (2.34) to (2.37).

Thus, given a set of N multimedia servers having identical channel bandwidth connections, it is easier to obtain the optimal sizes of the portions of the multimedia document to be retrieved from each server by immediately using equations (2.34) to (2.40).

2.5. Discussions on MSR Strategy

The problem tackled in this chapter presents a generalized approach to the theory of minimizing the access time for network based multimedia document retrieval/distribution. Researchers in this field have addressed the problem from different perspective, however, on different application specific requirements. For instance, the results equally apply to a single server multiple client multimedia video-On demand system by replacing the bandwidths specified in this chapter by the disk bandwidths. On a network based environment, one of the crucial bottlenecks being the available bandwidth, the treatment we presented suggests an elegant solution to minimize the access time. Future network based multimedia applications demanding a trade-off between the available network bandwidth and the service from geographically well separated servers become the natural candidates of the problem addressed in this chapter. We shall now present some interesting observations made during the analysis.

We have derived the closed-form solution for the partitioning problem in a single-installment strategy. By using the recursive procedure, obtaining the optimal sizes of the media portions (solution set) retrieved from the servers, can be achieved with $O(N)$ time complexity. An attractive and interesting feature of this strategy is that the optimal solution evolves naturally as we solve the set of recursive equations (2.7) with equality constraints (capturing the continuity relationships) together with (2.2). As it is evident from the closed-form solution, the access time monotonically decreases as we tend to utilize more and more servers. Figure 2.5 shows the behavior of the access time with respect to the number of servers utilized for the case of homogeneous channels, i.e., when $bw_i = bw$, for all the channels. As expected, as the requested multimedia document is available on more servers, the access time decreases, as we tend to utilize all the probable servers. In the figure, we have shown the plots for typical MPEG-I and MPEG-II video streams with 1.5MB/s and 4MB/s playback rates, respectively. Another important contribution in this research is the proof of *access time invariance property on sequencing*. The non-triviality lies in identifying such a behavior of the access time. The result of Lemma 1, though not astonishing, clears the fact that the access time is independent of the order in which the multimedia document is retrieved from the server pool, at least as long as communication costs do not suffer from start-up latencies. If the latter apply, a different outcome is produced as discussed in Chapter 5.

Alternative to this strategy and as a future extension to the problem considered in this chapter is the following. It may be possible with the current day technology that a client may be able to download multiple streams at the same time depending on its available buffer and the bandwidth. This scheme is attractive as it is adaptable to varying system loads. However, the implementation of this scheme involves the design of efficient resource management and scheduling policies at the client site. In the case of multi-installment strategy, obtaining a closed-form as in single-installment strategy, is tedious as equations are complex to solve. However, the recursive procedure proposed in Section 2.4.1 generates the optimal sizes of the media portions from the servers in $O(Nn)$ time complexity. Also, the recursive expressions presented in Section 2.4.2 for the case of homogeneous channels are easier to implement as the entries of the table (shown for $N = 4$ and $n = 2$ case) can be automatically generated and can be reused when the number of installments or the servers varies. Another attractive feature of this methodology is that the speed parameters (channel bandwidth and the playback rates) do not influence or affect the entries of the table, and hence these entries ($E(i, j)$, $\forall i, j$ can be generated a-priori and can be stored using the best possible data structure for computation purposes.

As far as the performance of this strategy is concerned, a set of questions that might arise are the following:

• What is the relationship between the number of servers used and the number of installments?

• Can we expect that ever-increasing the number of installments will always result in gains with respect to access time?

Answers to the above questions are attempted by means of an experiment. An iterative procedure was employed in order to compute the access time under

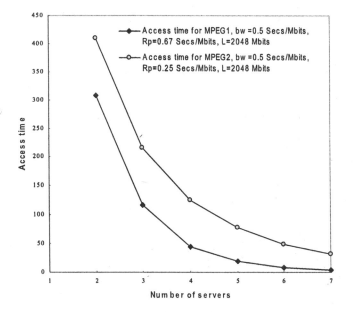

Figure 2.5. Access Time vs Number of multimedia servers using MPEG-I and MPEG-II Streams

ever-increasing number of installments. The document size was set to 2GBytes and the playback rate R_p to 2sec/MByte, typical of a MPEG II stream. The number of servers varied from 2 to 30 and their bandwidth from 1sec/MByte to 32sec/MByte. All connections were considered identical, i.e. $bw_i \equiv bw$ The iteration stopped, either when increasing the number of installments by 1 resulted in less than 5% gain in access time, or when the access time fell below 1 second. The number of installments at which the process ended is plotted in figure 2.6(a). Figure 2.6(b) shows the corresponding access times. The y-axis is labeled as $L\ bw$ in order to give a measure of the time necessary to download the multimedia document from a single server. The usage of the $L\ bw$ product is not a way for normalizing things. Actually, using different bandwidths with loads that have identical $L\ bw$ products results in different (quantitative) behaviors.

A striking observation (see figure 2.6) is that there is a barrier beyond which increasing the number of installments and/or the number of servers cannot benefit the access time. This barrier is network capacity related and it can result in very poor performance. Just before this barrier is reached, the number of installments that are suitable for near optimum performance grows rapidly and falls the same way after the barrier is exceeded. Before the barrier is reached,

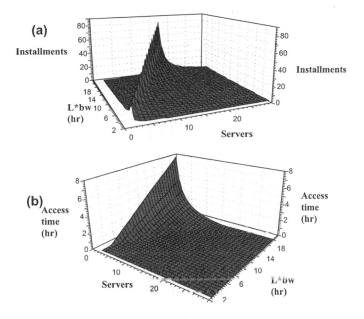

Figure 2.6. (a) Number of installments where the access time falls below 1 sec, or where an additional installment would improve the access time less than 5%, against the number of servers and connection speed. (b) The corresponding access times for the installments shown in (a).

the network connections are fast enough to guarantee that even with a small $m_{0,0}$ the portions of the document will reach the client prior to their turn for playback. Increasing the number of installments has just that effect, i.e. keeping $m_{0,0}$ small. After the barrier is exceeded, $m_{0,0}$ must be a large portion of the document in order to guarantee that the continuity constraints hold. As a result, the access time escalates while increasing the number of installments does not serve the purpose.

The relationship between the number of servers and number of installments is more clearly seen in Figures 2.7(a) and (b) which depict an experiment identical to the one described above, with the exceptions of

1 Adding more servers in the previous case, actually scales the client's connection bandwidth, which is not the usual case -for Internet at least- connections. So in this case, there is a shared connection whose bandwidth is divided among all servers.

2 The shared bandwidth ranged from 0.5 sec/MB to 4 sec/MB .

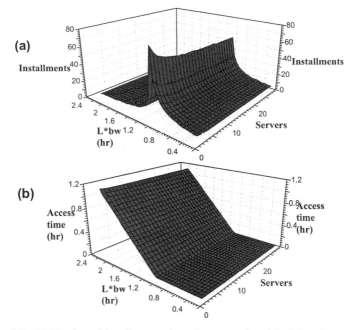

Figure 2.7. (a) Number of installments where the access time falls below 1 sec, or where an additional installment would improve the access time less than 5%, against the number of servers and connection speed. The difference from Figure 2.6(a) is that the servers share the same connection to the document requesting party. (b) The corresponding access times for the installments shown in (a).

The number of servers and installments are perpendicular ways for maximizing server utilization under the multi-installment strategy. This is clearly seen in figure 2.7(a), where as the number of servers increases, the near optimum number of installments decreases. This can work the other way around, i.e. instead of increasing the number of servers, the number of installments can be modified to achieve a target access time. Of course, there are limits to this approach especially if each connection is independent of the others (see figure 2.6). As a final remark, the multi-installment strategy has an inherent advantage in managing the available buffer at the client's site. If the buffer size available is limited, then the best possible way to optimize the performance is by the use of multi-installment strategy, as the sizes of the individual chunks retrieved are smaller than the individual sizes recommended by the single installment strategy. This in a way makes the scheme attractive, as the existing limited resources(buffer capacities) are cleverly utilized without any additional resource investment.

One may suggest that the multi-installment strategy fails to address the need to use the available multimedia servers for servicing multiple client requests. This, however, falls outside the scope of this chapter. Serving multiple clients, calls for employing other administration policies for allocating the bandwidth of each server. The strategies presented here are suited for analytical or otherwise systematical evaluation of such policies, which could very well be the subject of further research. For example, as Figures 2.6 and 2.7 indicate, MSRSs can be used to determine the minimum bandwidth that each server should allocate for a single request while keeping the access time to a minimum. In Chapter 3 we discuss on strategies that can handle multiple clients using this MSR strategy.

2.6.   Concluding Remarks

In this chapter, we have introduced the MSR technology and the key idea behind it. We presented a generalized approach to the theory of minimizing the access time of retrieving a multimedia document requested by a client. On a network based environment, we have shown the impact of non-zero communication delays on the performance. We have designed and analyzed two different retrieval strategies that minimize the access time of the multimedia document. The single and multi-installment strategies proposed, can provide a basis for improved quality services in the emerging markets of VoD or MoD. Given the limiting technological aspects of the current network -mainly- infrastructure, these strategies form not just the basis for improved services, but can be the only way to realize them. In general, these strategies are designed to suit most of the network based multimedia applications in which a large volume of data needs to be transferred between sites incurring a considerable amount of communication delays. Approximations to the strategies and the model presented in this chapter precisely address the problems in the domain of multimedia applications in which the impact of network delays and bandwidth are significant.

In the case of the single-installment strategy, we have derived closed-form solution for the individual sizes of the portions retrieved from various servers and the corresponding access time. We have extended the analysis to the case of homogeneous or shared channels. In the case of the multi-installment strategy, we have presented a recursive procedure to obtain the individual sizes of the document portions from various servers. It has been shown that the multi-installment strategy has the added advantage of fine tuning the access time, which is crucial to time and delay sensitive applications. Rigorous performance tests were conducted to study the trade-off relationship between using several servers and using multiple installments. It was observed that the gain achieved by increasing the number of installments is in effect similar to employing more servers for the job. Of course, the former approach is far more attractive as a means towards minimization of the access time. This also means that the available servers can be appropriately partitioned to attend to different service requests, while at the same time keeping the access time as low as possible. This observation is not only non-trivial, but also allows an increase of the overall servicing capability of the network and makes such network based multimedia applications viable and more attractive. In the case of the single installment strategy, we have proved an important theorem which eliminates the need for seeking a particular server sequence. Although, the access time is independent of the sequence chosen, a deployed system may elaborate on the sequence in order to 'release' some servers before others. Of course, as the number of installments increases such actions become pointless.

The analysis presented in the Section 2.5 can be a stimulus for developing more fine-tuned approaches, that take into account the ever-changing nature of the network environment parameters. Firstly, an interesting question is to see if this MSR dogma can support multiple clients! We deal with this in Chapter 3. Secondly, constant bandwidths are rarely the case for the heavily loaded Internet connections that are shared by thousands of users. The volatility of the network connections is the key factor for future research. Although, the multi-installment strategy is the way to go, insuring QoS requires that a deployed system assigns and possibly modifies during a session, the document downloading responsibilities, subject to server availability and bandwidth irregularities. We address this in Chapters 5 and 6. Since multiple servers are used, it is obvious to investigate on fault-tolerance, especially under network and/or server failures. These are dealt in Chapter 7. Thus the idea of MSR approach opens up several possibilities to seek best quality of services for high-bandwidth applications via network based service infrastructure.

Bibliographic Notes

There has been an extensive study on many allied problems related to this MSR design. A Video on-Demand(VoD) or Movie on-Demand(MoD) service which is usually offered on hi-speed network based environments is one of the natural candidates [2,10] for the problem presented in this chapter. There has been a continuous effort to optimize the performance of multimedia servers designed for VoD applications [98]. In [19], a multimedia distribution network has been presented. Here, the authors introduce a three tier network architecture to the video distribution problem on networks. Applications such as collaborative video editing and synthesis of multimedia objects and other network based distributed applications can be found in [24, 37, 21, 108]. These essentially focus in optimizing the storage and retrieval of video blocks on the disks [11] and also in the design of servers to maximize the number of customers. Depending on the popularity of the movies in a networking domain, physical placement of movies on particular server sites is important in optimizing the monetary cost incurred for viewing that movie [18]. In order to optimize the monetary costs, clever placement of movies at strategic locations on the network is carried out [19]. Discussions on appropriate admission control and some scheduling algorithms can be found in [89, 108, 79].

A novel technique, referred to as pyramid broadcasting, is proposed in [109], as a means of serving a large pool of customers in Metropolitan Area Networks(MANs). This technique typically supports services like VoD or MoD on MANs. Another closely related theme can be found in a study by Candan et al. [24], in which retrieval schedules are generated based on the availability of the network and other necessary resources with flexible presentation requirements. The influence of the network service providers and on the buffer resources at the client site are also addressed in this study. A slight variant of this service architecture was proposed in the study on multimedia presentation planning in [53]. The study presented in [105] is one of the first attempts to introduce MSR to the multimedia literature.

Chapter 3

SUPPORTING MULTIPLE CLIENTS: CHANNEL PARTITIONING APPROACH

3.1. Tuning MSR Scheme for Multiple Clients: Issues and Challenges

In the last chapter, we have introduced the importance and advantage of using multiple server technology. The strategies (single and multi-installment) clearly offer a *win-win* situation for both the clients and the service providers [1]. While both strategies have been treated with a detailed analysis and a thorough performance study, we have not explored how these technologies could be adapted to efficiently handle several concurrent clients. This chapter deals primarily with this question and exposes the complete design of a scheduler which can support multiple clients. Specifically, we address the underlying design issues and elicit key points to consider in the design of such a system. All these issues are captured in an actual design that is described in Chapter 8.

In the previous chapter, we have shown that by partitioning the video and retrieving the parts from several servers, we can dramatically reduce a client's access time. While this technique seems promising, a more practical and intriguing question to ponder over is whether this scheme would work with multiple clients. The problem becomes overly complex as server bandwidths are finite and have to be catered among client requests. Further, for supporting multiple clients, the design of MSR strategy must take into account the individual playback rates [2] and available server bandwidth at the servers at the time of requests. Clearly, this is a duel between these quantities and must be accommodated in

---

[1] Clients get an inproved Quality of Service (QoS), while the service providers can maximize the number of customers they can serve and leverage their IT investment.

[2] These rates could be time varying quantities depending on a user's interactive commands such as fast-forward, rewind, multiple speeds with the forward and rewind operations, pause, etc.

the scheduler design. Thus a top level synthesis must reflect these estimates of the server bandwidths to react to the varying playback demands from the clients, while the low-level implementation issues capture these in retrieval and timely delivery (transmission). In this chapter, we expose one such design of a scheduler that generates the schedule of events and prescribes optimal media portions to be retrieved from a heterogeneous[3] cluster of servers. The key idea is to partition the aggregate server bandwidth, referred to as a *channel*, available among the servers for handling multiple clients. This approach has yet another significance - it is naturally built-in with an admission control mechanism that controls the admission of requests, taking into account the QoS for the pool of clients currently being serviced. Thus we refer to this approach, in general, as a *Channel Partitioning approach*. Note that this approach basically employs data partitioning on top of a channel partitioning method.

In most of the existing literature and technology, a VoD system is usually conceived as a system having a single video server [4]. However, with an increase in the user access rates, the network bandwidth becomes a natural bottleneck, especially for a network based multimedia service. A decentralized (and distributed) approach would rather handle this increased access rates more elegantly. This is typical of a requirement on Internet like networks, where access rates may be significantly large.

In this chapter, we present a generic version of the problem of using multiple servers to retrieve multiple movies (serving multiple requests) in a coordinated fashion with the objective of minimizing the access times of the movies, block rates and buffer space requirement at the client sites. The analysis presented in this chapter serves for a number of purposes. Firstly, the analysis derives individual media portions to be retrieved from each server depending on its bandwidth. This also reflects in the number of potential clients with their respective playback rates to be supported. This in turn quantifies the amount of buffers to be in place at the clients to support this retrieval and playback. We observe the performance of the SSRS and the MSR strategies by means of a rigorous simulation study employing different access profiles of movies and important system dependent parameters such as buffer availability, retrieval bandwidths, movie playback rates, etc.

---

[3] These refer to a set of servers with non-identical bandwidths.
[4] Most of the times these VoD servers are dedicated, sophisticated pieces of equipment. More often than not they are even realized as clusters of machines that appear as a single virtual entity. We also treat such cases as single servers since they all share the specific bandwidth of a single outgoing connection. In the text we simply use the term "server" to refer to any of these cases.

3.2.   System Model

As before, we now present the underlying system model we are considering for the VoD service. We consider a generic VoD architecture consisting of a high speed network and a set of servers and clients. The network, in general, can be a LAN or a WAN. The main idea employed in the design of this MSR strategy is that whenever a client requests a movie, a pool of servers will cooperate to retrieve the entire movie by employing a strategic schedule. Thus, each server will supply a portion of the entire movie, which is disjoint from others in a particular sequence generated by a scheduler, to the client sites. Further, because of distinct differences in the popularities of various movies, popular movies usually exist in several servers simultaneously. This fact serves as a good precondition in employing a MSR scheme.

3.2.1   Retrieval process

Figure 3.1 explains the retrieval process of a possible MSR strategy. Our approach is a server-push one, however a client-pull could work equally well. The whole process can be described as follows: When a server receives a request for a movie, it forwards the request details to the *Task Generation and Scheduling* (TGS) server in order to obtain an optimal delivery schedule. The bandwidth information (e.g. available bandwidth amount) of the servers is also relayed to the TGS server for the purpose of scheduling. Further, all the servers will not begin to transmit any media data before they receive the schedule from the TGS server. We shall now see how the TGS server does the scheduling and introduce some terminology used throughout this chapter.

3.2.2   About the TGS server

For the design of MSR strategy, the proposed architecture has some special features. Every server on the network, including the TGS server is the same, except that the TGS server keeps additionally, a task generator, a scheduler and a movie directory facility (see Figure 3.2). The task generator allocates the total available server retrieval bandwidth (resource) in a certain manner among the requested movies and organizes the requests/movies into groups, referred to as *scheduling tasks*. The scheduler makes use of some efficient scheduling strategies to determine the retrieval order and the amount of every playback portion for every task, respectively. The movie directory facility has the information about the available movies stored in various servers, e.g., the playback rates and the lengths (duration of playback) of the respective movies. The information is used by the task generator and the scheduler. In effect, the task generation is the process of allocating the total available server bandwidth (resource) among the requested movies. Of course, once the movie allocation among servers changes, the updated movie list information will be transmitted

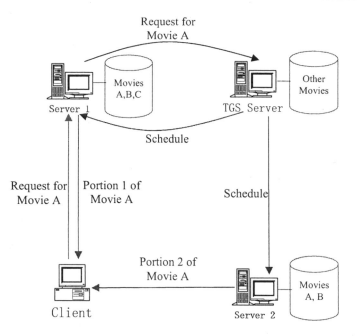

Figure 3.1. A motivating example for showing the retrieval process of a MSR strategy. The process of retrieving the movie A can be described as follows: (1) The client sends the request for movie A to a neighboring server, e.g., Server 1. (2) Server 1 forwards the request to the Task Generation and Scheduling (TGS) server. (3) TGS server carries out task generation and retrieval scheduling. Subsequently, it multicasts the schedule (i.e., scheduling result) to Server 1 and Server 2. (4) Server 1 and Server 2 deliver the different parts of movie A to the client according to schedule, respectively.

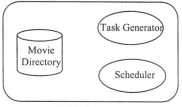

TGS Server

Explanation for the components in the diagram:
1. The **movie directory** provides the information about movies, e.g., the storage location, playback rate and length of every movie.
2. The **task generator** generates scheduling tasks. Its main function is to aggregate retrieval bandwidth and to partition the channels for every movie.
3. The **scheduler** generates the retrieval schedule for every scheduling task.

Figure 3.2. System components in the TGS server

to the TGS server. In order to avoid any resource usage conflicts, the functionality of scheduling cannot be distributed across the servers, as it may incur severe overhead in synchronizing the information and then producing a best schedule. Hence, in the proposed architecture, TGS server predominantly determines the scheduling scheme.

Our MSR strategy dictates that each portion is retrieved with a certain bandwidth within a specific time period. For the sake of description simplicity, we may consider the retrieval of each portion of a movie as being carried out using a *channel*. Here, a **channel** is defined as a certain amount of server bandwidth that is used for a single portion retrieval. Thus, the retrieval of a single movie is carried out with several channels, say, channel 1, channel 2,..., channel N. Thus, N may be different for different retrievals, however N must be at least 2 for the MSR scheme ($N = 1$ for SSRS). For retrieving a movie, we need to choose the required bandwidth to form N channels. After the retrieval of a portion of a movie in a channel is completed, the bandwidth of this channel is released. Thus, for the subsequent retrievals, we have more bandwidth available. In general, the bandwidth in the channels cannot be used until the completion of the previous retrievals that are making use of relative bandwidth. Thus, the time instant at which the available bandwidths can be used is referred to as *allowed start time*. This is denoted as AST_j ($AST_j \geq 0$), where j is the channel index, $j \in [1, N]$. If we use an already free (unused) bandwidth to form a channel, AST_j of that channel is assumed to be zero.

Figure 3.3 shows the typical flow chart of the retrieval process in the TGS server. Upon receiving the requests, the TGS directs these requests to its task generator module that will allocate bandwidth from respective servers to form channels for the retrieval of the movies. The movies sharing the same group of channels constitute one task. In other words, a scheduling task consists of some channels and some movies that share these channels. Thus, the result of partition is the tasks to be scheduled. In next phase, we carry out retrieval scheduling. The net output of scheduling will be the sizes, α_{ij} of the portions of the movies to be retrieved and the start times of the transmissions, ST_{ij} ($i = 1, ..., M, j = 1, ..., N$, where M is the number of movies and N is the number of channels in a task) of every playback portion of the movies, at the respective servers. Finally, server TGS multicasts the resulting schedule to the respective servers. According to the schedule generated by the scheduler, the respective servers will then start transmitting the movies to the users.

Thus, the challenge is in designing efficient strategies of task generation and retrieval scheduling. Good strategies should promise an overall better performance of the entire VoD system. We will present the design of these strategies in more detail in Sections 3.3.1 and 3.3.3.

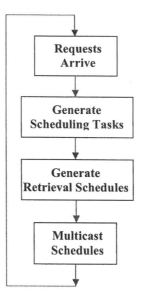

Figure 3.3.   Flow chart of retrieval process in TGS server

3.2.3   Some terminology and performance metric

For reader's convenience, we summarize the key notations used in this chapter in Table 3.1.

The design of our VoD system attempts to address the following question. *Without under-utilizing the network and server resources, how to minimize the access times of the movies and the block rate[5] while satisfying the available buffer space limit ?*.

While considering a single playback portion, referring to Figure 3.4 (a) and (b), the *buffer space requirement* at the client site, m_{ij} is calculated as follows[6].

$$m_{ij} = \alpha_{ij}(1 - min(\frac{BW_j}{R_i}, \frac{R_i}{BW_j}))$$ (3.1)

Figure 3.4 (a) shows the case when the playback rate is more than the retrieval bandwidth. In this case, the playback must be started after retrieving some portion so that the continuity in the playback is maintained thereafter. Figure

---

[5]This is also referred to as block probability by some authors.
[6]Capital letters are used for BW to differentiate the channel bandwidth from the connection bandwidth bw used elsewhere in our text.

Table 3.1. Some common parameters in the VoD system

System Parameters	Symbol	Unit
Playback rate of movie i	R_i	MB/sec
Retrieval bandwidth of channel j in a single schedule	BW_j	MB/sec
Number of channels in a single scheduling task	N	
Number of movies in a single scheduling task	M	
The length of movie i	L_i $S_i = L_iR_i$	min GB
Size of the movie i retrieved from channel j in a single schedule	α_{ij}	GB
Buffer space requirement of retrieving single α_{ij}	m_{ij}	GB
Start time of retrieving α_{ij}	ST_{ij}	sec.
Allowed start time of retrieving α_{1j}	AST_j	sec.

3.4 (b), on the other hand, shows the case when the playback rate is less than the retrieval bandwidth. In this case, the playback can start almost simultaneously with retrieval. The buffer requirement is then computed using (3.1). In (3.1), less difference between R_i and BW_j leads to less buffer space requirements. Besides, when $R_i \neq BW_j$, less α_{ij} value also leads to less buffer space requirement. In fact, in some cases, because the subsequent portions may arrive at the client before the previous portions complete their playback, more buffer space is needed. This problem will be discussed in Section 3.3.3.

Access time, in general, is the time duration between the instant at which a request is placed and the time instant at which the requested movie/video starts playing at the client side. Without loss of generality, we shall ignore the overheads incurred by the scheduler (or can be considered as a constant) and the transmission delay. In a scheduling task, if the first playback portion α_{i1} of a movie i with playback rate R_i is retrieved using a bandwidth of BW_1 (the bandwidth of channel 1), then the access time of movie i, as shown in Figure 3.5, is given by,

$$AT_i = AST_1 + \frac{\sum_{k=1}^{i-1} \alpha_{k1}}{BW_1} + \begin{cases} \alpha_{i1}(\frac{1}{BW_1} - \frac{1}{R_i}) & \text{for } R_i > BW_1 \\ 0 & \text{for } R_i \leq BW_1 \end{cases} \quad (3.2)$$

Block rate is defined as the ratio between the number of requests that are not served successfully (i.e., blocked) and the total number of requests. The strategy we have used in the design of the scheduler tries to minimize the waiting time in

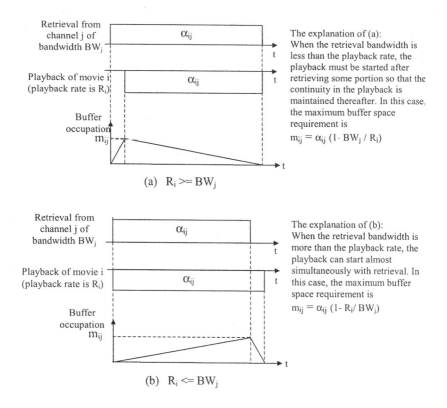

Figure 3.4. Calculation of buffer space requirement

the best possible way. However, because of shortage of resources (bandwidth), some requests may wait for a long time. So, the scheduler defines a bound on the maximum time that a user can wait until he/she receives his/her service. This, in a way, serves as an admission control policy, which determines whether or not the servers will intake all the submitted requests. This is also an issue to be considered while implementing the actual system, as the waiting time of the clients may be prohibitively annoying. Thus, the meaning of "success" of a request in this context is that the access time for that requested movie is less than or equal to the allowed maximum access time.

Now, we shall present a brief comparison between the SSRS that is commonly found in the existing literature and the MSR scheme with respect to effective resource utilization and load balancing.

Resource utilization: In SSRS, suppose if the server has not enough idle time to

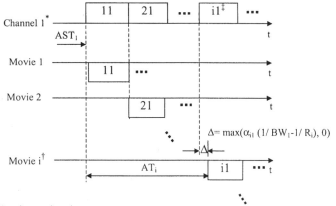

Notation explanation

* "Channel 1" means the retrieval from channel 1; the retrieval bandwidth is BW_1
† "Movie i" means the playback of movie 1 at the client; the playback rate is R_i
‡ "i1" refers to α_{i1} (i.e., index i refers to movie index and index 1 refers to channel index)

Figure 3.5. Calculation of a movie's *i* access time.

support a long length movie retrieval, or if it has inadequate retrieval bandwidth capacity that leads to a considerable delay in the access time, these server resources will be discarded. However, in the MSR strategy, such low bandwidth servers can also participate by carefully considering them during the scheduling process.

Dynamic load balancing: In SSRS, a single retrieval uses only one server. Hence, the server that ensures the minimum access time for that retrieval is not necessarily the server with lighter load. In MSR strategy, since the access time is only with respect to the first retrieved portion and the first retrieval channel, we minimize the access time in channel 1 of MSR strategy and also consider to balance the load in other channels.

Benefiting from the above advantages, our MSR approach can obtain much smaller access times, block rates and buffer space requirements than the SSRS scheme. These will be demonstrated in a simulation experiment in Section 3.4.

3.3. Design of the TGS Server

As a first step, we shall now present the design and functionality of the task generator module in Section 3.3.1. In Section 3.3.3 we shall present the analysis of scheduling strategies for the cases when single and multiple movies are retrieved from multiple channels. We assume that the task generation as

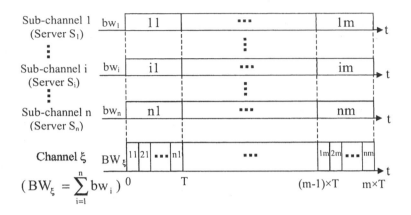

Figure 3.6. Aggregate retrieval bandwidth and concurrent retrieval. Each of n servers renders a part of the portion ξ of the movie in m installments. The order in which these retrieved portions are presented is: block 11, block 21, ..., block n1, block 12, block 22, ..., block n2,...,block 1m, block 2m,..., block nm. N sub-channels can be equivalently treated as channel ξ at every time instant $t = ixT, i = 1, \ldots, m$.

well as generating the retrieval schedules costs little calculation time, and we do not include it in the overall access time calculations.

3.3.1 Task generation strategy

As we mentioned above, while dealing with the requests, the task generator obtains all the server bandwidth information from the respective servers and the information about the movies, such as the length and playback rates from its movie directory repository. Using these information, a group of scheduling tasks are generated. In general, we will allocate several (≥ 2) channels for every movie. In Section 3.3.1.1 we introduce the usage of aggregate retrieval bandwidth to form a single channel. This technique will be used in generating channel 1. Then, we introduce the channel partition algorithm (See Table 2) for every movie as described in Section 3.3.1.2.

3.3.1.1 Aggregate retrieval bandwidth

Usually, we choose the bandwidth from a single server for one channel. However, for fully utilizing the resource available from every server, we aggregate the bandwidth from a pool of servers for retrieving one portion of a movie requested. Figure 3.6 shows a scenario in which a pool of servers from a server cluster $S_1, \ldots, S_n$ retrieve one portion ξ of a movie, in a concurrent fashion. It may be observed that m blocks of the movie are retrieved from each server concurrently, i.e., blocks labeled $11, 12, 13, ..., 1m$ are retrieved from S_1, and $i1, i2, ..., im$ are retrieved from server S_i, and so on. Note that each server renders a part of the portion ξ of the movie in m installments. The order in which these retrieved portions are presented is block 11, block 21, ..., block $n1$, block 12, block 22, ..., block $n2$,...,block $1m$, block $2m$,..., block nm. It may be noted that a single installment is of duration T secs, and the amount of data retrieved from each server in each installment is different. Further, the value of the parameter T is usually kept small, e.g., $T = 1sec$ and it is related with the compression scheme of the movies and trade-off benefits between the available aggregate bandwidth and the computational overheads. This is purely an implementation issue that is beyond the scope of this chapter to discuss[7]. Thus, in the above figure, all the blocks constitute the portion ξ of movie, which is retrieved by a pool of servers. As shown in Figure 3.6, we let the retrieval of every block in the same installment begin and end at the same time instant. So, the sum of the bandwidth from every server, i.e., $\sum_{k=1}^{n} bw_k$ (where bw_k is the retrieval bandwidth of server S_k, $k = 1, ..., n$) can be treated as the retrieval bandwidth of channel ξ (i.e., BW_ξ) at every time instant $t = iT, i = 1, ..., m$. Once we know the size of the portion ξ of movie, e.g., S_ξ (it will be calculated in the Section 3.3.3), we can obtain the $m = \lceil S_\xi / (T \times \sum_{k=1}^{n} bw_k) \rceil$ and the individual size of every block constituting the first portion of the movie, i.e., $\beta_{ij} = bw_i \times T, i = 1, ..., n, j = 1, ..., m$.

Theoretically, the idea of aggregate retrieval bandwidth can be used even for other channels (i.e., channel 2, channel 3, ...) as well as channel 1. Here, an aggregate channel bandwidth is formed using a set of channels with identical start times. However, in general, different channels may have different start times. To form an aggregate bandwidth using the channels with different start times, we may need to devise an alternate strategy. This is one possible future work as an extension to the strategy presented in this chapter. However, in this approach, similar to the case with channel 1, for channels 2, 3,..., aggregate bandwidth can be used provided these aggregate bandwidths are formed using a set of servers whose bandwidths are available at identical start times.

3.3.1.2 Channel partition algorithm

We propose the *Channel Partition Algorithm* for partitioning channels for every movie (see Table 3.2). Some important details of the algorithm will be explained below.

(a) Strategy for forming Channel1

---

[7]In Chapter 8 we show how this can be taken care of in a practical system.

Table 3.2. Channel Partition Algorithm

A request for a movie τ arrives.

Step 1. Choice of channel 1
1.   Determine an aggregate (unused) bandwidth BW of servers that have movie τ;
2.   Determine $BW_\tau^{min} = R_\tau - BS_\tau/L_\tau$ of movie τ, where BS_τ is maximum usable (or available) buffer space for retrieving the movie τ. Note that BW_τ^{min} is derived from (3.1).

3.   Calculate the maximum allowed bandwidth $BW_\tau^{max} = R_\tau + BS_\tau/L_\tau$ of movie τ.

4.   **IF**$(BW \geq BW_\tau^{min})$
         The assigned free bandwidth for movie τ is $min(BW, BW_\tau^{max})$.
         ELSE
         {

5.   Among those channels that are currently in use (for these, $AST_j \neq 0$) or have been allocated to other movies, choose those channels with bandwidth greater than R^* and decrease it to R^*. Note R^* is the maximum playback rate of movies which are using or will use the channel. The reduction in the bandwidth for these channels can provide more bandwidth for the current retrieval, and at the same time it does not affect the continuity constraints. This tuning of the bandwidth is carried out until the free bandwidth reaches BW_τ^{min} or there are no channels with extra bandwidth to be extruded.
         }
6.   **IF**$(BW < BW_\tau^{min})$
         The movie τ will share the Channel 1 with other movies. In one case, the movie τ attempts to use the channel that is currently in use for retrieving a movie. In the other case, the movie τ shares the channel 1 with other movie(s) which have been allocated channels, but not used so far. Thus, together with movie τ, all the movies will share the allocated channels. In this latter case, the movie τ, in fact, becomes a member of the group with the previously channel-allocated movie(s).

Step 2. We use the following rules for choosing other retrieval channels
1.   We use servers with lighter loads (for load balancing);
2.   When choosing channels from a single server, we choose those channels with the minimum AST_j, for shortening the retrieved portion in channel 1 as explained before.

With channel 1, we transmit the first portion of the movie(s) and hence, channel 1 determines the access times of the movie(s). However, it may happen that the free bandwidth (i.e., $AST = 0$) from a single server may not guarantee allowed minimum access times. For minimizing the access times, according to (3.2) we adopt aggregate retrieval bandwidth available from a pool of servers. Another strategy for the minimization of access times is by choosing a smaller AST_2 for the second channel. From (3.2), smaller size of the first retrieved portion (i.e., α_{i1}) of movies probably leads to smaller access time. Also, from equations (3.3)-(3.6) (presented in the Subsection 3.3.2), the smaller difference between AST_2 and AST_1 aids to decrease the size of the portion α_{11}. So, we should choose as small AST_2 as possible for the second channel.

(b) Strategy for forming other channels

It may be noted that another objective in this chapter is to minimize the block rate. Besides efficient utilization of resources, to achieve this goal, we try to balance the total load among the servers. The basic idea is to choose other channels (except channel 1) in servers with the lightest load. The total number of channels in retrieving the movies is not strictly limited. However, two channels are at least needed. Channel 1 is used to realize the goal of minimizing the access times and the second channel aids in balancing the server load.

(c) Buffer space requirement

Through the MSR method, we retrieve a portion of a movie (not the whole movie) in a channel, so, we should use the length of that portion in the calculation of BW_τ^{min} and BW_τ^{max}. However, before scheduling, we do not know the length of these portions. Hence, we use the entire length of movie τ (i.e., L_τ) in the algorithm. Although the calculation of BW_τ^{min} and BW_τ^{max} is approximate, any available bandwidth between BW_τ^{min} and BW_τ^{max} can ensure that the actual buffer space requirement is less than the maximum usable buffer space. This is proven in Section 3.3.3.2.

(d) Generation of scheduling tasks

Following the channel partitioning, if one movie shares the same set of channels with other movies, the scheduling task is of type I, referred to as multiple channels and multiple movies, otherwise it is of type II, referred to as multiple channels and single movie. Thus, we are now confronted with the problem of retrieving the movie(s) belonging to each task in an optimal manner.

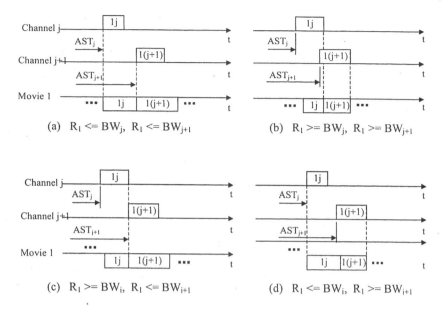

Figure 3.7. Timing diagram of the first playback portion in every channel

3.3.2 Constraints imposed by the allowed start times of retrieval

We now derive recursive relationships among the playback rate of the first movie R_1, the bandwidths and the allowed start times, for all j.

1. $R_1 \leq BW_j$ and $R_1 \leq BW_{j+1}$ (Figure 3.7(a))
This is the case when the playback rate is less than the transmission rate.

$$AST_{j+1} - AST_j \leq \frac{\alpha_{1j}}{R_1}, \text{ for } j = 1, ..., N - 1 \qquad (3.3)$$

2. $R_1 \geq BW_j$ and $R_1 \geq BW_{j+1}$ (Figure 3.7(b))
This is the case when the playback rate is greater than transmission rate.

$$AST_{j+1} - AST_j + \frac{\alpha_{1(j+1)}}{BW_{j+1}} \leq \frac{\alpha_{1j}}{BW_j} + \frac{\alpha_{1(j+1)}}{R_1}, \text{ for } j = 1, ..., N - 1 \quad (3.4)$$

3. $R_1 \geq BW_j$ and $R_1 \leq BW_{j+1}$ (Figure 3.7(c))
This is the case when the jth channel has less transmission rate than the playback rate and the $(j + 1)$th channel has greater transmission rate than the playback rate.

$$AST_{j+1} - AST_j \leq \frac{\alpha_{1j}}{BW_j}, \text{ for } j = 1, ..., N - 1 \qquad (3.5)$$

4. $R_1 \leq BW_j$ and $R_1 \geq BW_{j+1}$ (Figure 3.7(d))
This is the case when the jth channel has greater transmission rate than the playback rate and the $(j+1)$th channel has less transmission rate than the playback rate.

$$AST_{j+1} - AST_j + \frac{\alpha_{1(j+1)}}{BW_{j+1}} \leq \frac{(\alpha_{1j} + \alpha_{1(j+1)})}{R_1}, \text{ for } j = 1, ..., N-1 \quad (3.6)$$

We observe that the continuity relationships during presentation are inherently captured in the above set of equations, involving BW_j, R_1, and AST_j, for all j values, respectively. Further, to determine a minimum (optimum) amount of buffer space required at the client sites, we use the equality relationship in the above set of equations. In other words, we solve the above constraint recursive relationships using equality relationships to obtain the optimal sizes of the disjoint portions of the respective movies.

Recursive relationship of α_{ij}

With the causal precedence relationships, the playback continuity constraints and different combinations of R_i and BW_j, we derive the following recursive equations (see Figure 3.8 - 3.11) while minimize the buffer space requirement and ensure the continuous playback of movies.

1. $R_i \leq BW_j$ and $R_i \leq BW_{j+1}$ (Figure 3.8)
(a). $R_{i+1} \leq BW_j$ and $R_{i+1} \leq BW_{j+1}$.

$$\frac{\alpha_{ij}}{R_i} + \frac{\alpha_{i(j+1)}}{BW_{j+1}} = \frac{\alpha_{ij}}{BW_j} + \frac{\alpha_{(i+1)j}}{R_{i+1}}, \text{ for } i = 1, ..., (M-1), j = 1, ..., (N-1)$$
$$(3.7)$$

(b). $R_{i+1} \geq BW_j$ and $R_{i+1} \leq BW_{j+1}$

$$\frac{\alpha_{ij}}{R_i} + \frac{\alpha_{i(j+1)}}{BW_{j+1}} = \frac{\alpha_{ij}}{BW_j} + \frac{\alpha_{(i+1)j}}{BW_j}, \text{ for } i = 1, ..., (M-1), j = 1, ..., (N-1)$$
$$(3.8)$$

(c). $R_{i+1} \leq BW_j$ and $R_{i+1} \leq BW_{j+1}$

$$\frac{\alpha_{ij}}{R_i} + \frac{\alpha_{i(j+1)}}{BW_{j+1}} + \frac{\alpha_{(i+1)(j+1)}}{BW_{j+1}} = \frac{\alpha_{ij}}{BW_j} + \frac{\alpha_{(i+1)j}}{R_{i+1}} + \frac{\alpha_{(i+1)(j+1)}}{R_{i+1}}, \quad (3.9)$$

for $i = 1, ..., (M-1), j = 1, ..., (N-1)$.

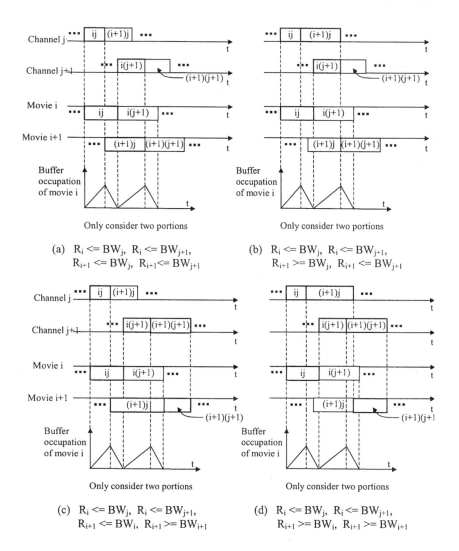

Figure 3.8. Timing diagram of adjacent playback portions (when $R_i \leq BW_j$ and $R_i \leq BW_{j+1}$)

(d). $R_{i+1} \geq BW_j$ and $R_{i+1} \geq BW_{j+1}$,

$$\frac{\alpha_{ij}}{R_i} + \frac{\alpha_{i(j+1)}}{BW_{j+1}} + \frac{\alpha_{(i+1)(j+1)}}{BW_{j+1}} = \frac{\alpha_{ij}}{BW_j} + \frac{\alpha_{(i+1)j}}{BW_j} + \frac{\alpha_{(i+1)(j+1)}}{R_{i+1}}, \quad (3.10)$$

for $i = 1, ..., (M-1), j = 1, ..., (N-1)$.

2. $R_i \geq BW_j$ and $R_i \geq BW_{j+1}$ (Figure 3.9)

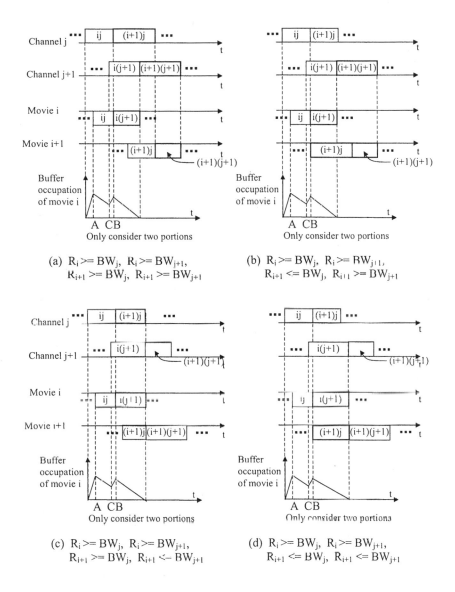

Figure 3.9. Timing diagram of adjacent playback portions (when $R_i \geq BW_j$ and $R_i \geq BW_{j+1}$)

(a). $R_{i+1} \geq BW_j$ and $R_{i+1} \geq BW_{j+1}$

$$\frac{\alpha_{(i+1)j}}{BW_j} + \frac{\alpha_{(i+1)(j+1)}}{R_{i+1}} = \frac{\alpha_{i(j+1)}}{R_i} + \frac{\alpha_{(i+1)(j+1)}}{BW_{j+1}}, \tag{3.11}$$

for $i = 1, ..., (M-1), j = 1, ..., (N-1)$.

(b). $R_{i+1} \leq BW_j$ and $R_{i+1} \geq BW_{j+1}$

$$\frac{\alpha_{(i+1)j}}{R_{i+1}} + \frac{\alpha_{(i+1)(j+1)}}{R_{i+1}} = \frac{\alpha_{i(j+1)}}{R_i} + \frac{\alpha_{(i+1)(j+1)}}{BW_{j+1}}, \tag{3.12}$$

$for i = 1, ..., (M-1), j = 1, ..., (N-1)$.

(c). $R_{i+1} \geq BW_j$ and $R_{i+1} \leq BW_{j+1}$

$$\frac{\alpha_{(i+1)j}}{BW_j} = \frac{\alpha_{i(j+1)}}{R_i}, \text{ for } i = 1, ..., (M-1), j = 1, ..., (N-1) \tag{3.13}$$

(d). $R_{i+1} \leq BW_j$ and $R_{i+1} \leq BW_{j+1}$

$$\frac{\alpha_{(i+1)j}}{R_{i+1}} = \frac{\alpha_{i(j+1)}}{R_i}, \text{ for } i = 1, ..., (M-1), j = 1, ..., (N-1) \tag{3.14}$$

3. $R_i \geq BW_j$ and $R_i \leq BW_{j+1}$ (Figure 3.10)
(a). $R_{i+1} \geq BW_j$ and $R_{i+1} \leq BW_{j+1}$

$$\frac{\alpha_{(i+1)j}}{BW_j} = \frac{\alpha_{i(j+1)}}{BW_{j+1}}, \text{ for } i = 1, ..., (M-1), j = 1, ..., (N-1) \tag{3.15}$$

(b). $R_{i+1} \leq BW_j$ and $R_{i+1} \leq BW_{j+1}$

$$\frac{\alpha_{(i+1)j}}{R_{i+1}} = \frac{\alpha_{i(j+1)}}{BW_{j+1}}, \text{ for } i = 1, ..., (M-1), j = 1, ..., (N-1) \tag{3.16}$$

(c). $R_{i+1} \geq BW_j$ and $R_{i+1} \geq BW_{j+1}$

$$\frac{\alpha_{(i+1)j}}{BW_j} + \frac{\alpha_{(i+1)(j+1)}}{R_{i+1}} = \frac{\alpha_{i(j+1)}}{BW_{j+1}} + \frac{\alpha_{(i+1)(j+1)}}{BW_{j+1}}, \tag{3.17}$$

for $i = 1, ..., (M-1), j = 1, ..., (N-1)$.

(d). $R_{i+1} \leq BW_j$ and $R_{i+1} \geq BW_{j+1}$

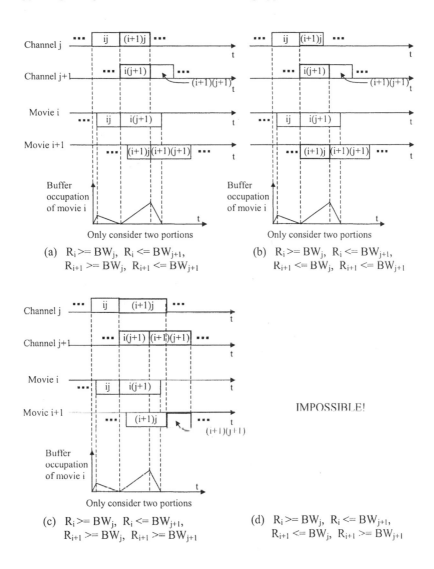

Figure 3.10. Timing diagram of adjacent playback portions (when $R_i \geq BW_j$ and $R_i \leq BW_{j+1}$)

Since $R_{i+1} \leq BW_j$ and $R_{i+1} \geq BW_{j+1}$ can lead to $BW_j > BW_{j+1}$ while $R_i \geq BW_j$ and $R_i \leq BW_{j+1}$ can lead to $BW_{j+1} > BW_j$, the case is impossible.

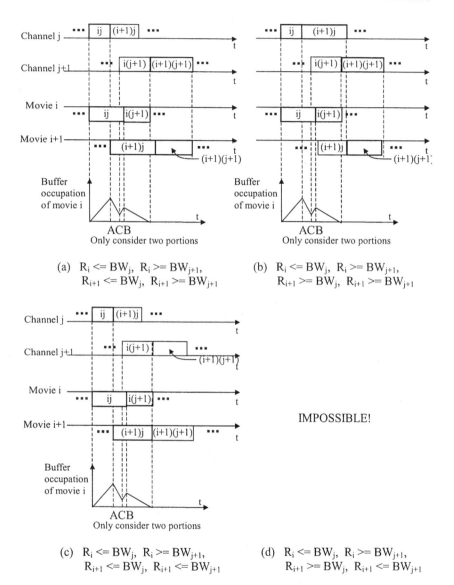

Figure 3.11. Timing diagram of adjacent playback portions (when $R_i \leq BW_j$ and $R_i \leq BW_{j+1}$)

4. $R_i \leq BW_j$ and $R_i \geq BW_{j+1}$ (Figure 3.11)

(a). $R_{i+1} \leq BW_j$ and $R_{i+1} \geq BW_{j+1}$

$$\frac{\alpha_{ij}}{BW_j} + \frac{(\alpha_{(i+1)j} + \alpha_{(i+1)(j+1)})}{R_{i+1}} = \frac{\alpha_{(i+1)(j+1)}}{BW_{j+1}} + \frac{(\alpha_{ij} + \alpha_{i(j+1)})}{R_i}, \quad (3.18)$$
$$\text{for } i = 1, ..., (M - 1), j = 1, ..., (N - 1)$$

(b). $R_{i+1} \geq BW_j$ and $R_{i+1} \geq BW_{j+1}$

$$\frac{\alpha_{ij}}{BW_j} + \frac{\alpha_{(i+1)j}}{BW_j} + \frac{\alpha_{(i+1)(j+1)}}{R_{i+1}} = \frac{\alpha_{(i+1)(j+1)}}{BW_{j+1}} + \frac{(\alpha_{ij} + \alpha_{i(j+1)})}{R_i}, \quad (3.19)$$
$$\text{for } i = 1, ..., (M - 1), j = 1, ..., (N - 1)$$

(c). $R_{i+1} \leq BW_j$ and $R_{i+1} \leq BW_{j+1}$

$$\frac{\alpha_{ij}}{BW_j} + \frac{\alpha_{(i+1)j}}{R_{i+1}} = \frac{(\alpha_{ij} + \alpha_{i(j+1)})}{R_i}, \quad (3.20)$$
$$\text{for } i = 1, ..., (M - 1), j = 1, ..., (N - 1) \quad (3.21)$$

(d). $R_{i+1} \geq BW_j$ and $R_{i+1} \leq BW_{j+1}$ is impossible because of similar reason with 3(d).

3.3.3 Movie retrieval scheduling strategy

The problem we are precisely attacking at this juncture can be described as follows. We are given that there are M movies requested by the respective users and there are N channels that can be used to retrieve these movies. Every channel have an AST_j (i.e., allowed start time of retrieval). The problem is to determine the exact (optimal) sizes of the portions to be retrieved from the respective servers in such a way that the buffer space requirement is a minimum while ensuring the continuous playback of movies. To achieve this goal, we propose the *Multiple Channels Retrieval Scheduling Algorithm*

Multiple Channels Retrieval Scheduling Algorithm

Step A. Sort the channels (except channel 1) in the order of increasing AST_j values. The channels with the least AST_j value will be scheduled earlier.

Step B. Sort the movies in the order of importance (e.g., some users have special requirements for the access times of some movies). If all the requests have the same importance, the movies with the shorter length will be scheduled earlier (*shortest movie first (SMF)*).

Step C. Derive the schedule constraints. These mainly include, (i) The temporal constraints imposed by the availability of channel bandwidths, namely the AST_j values; (ii) The temporal constraints between adjacent playback portions; (iii) The movie length constraints. A detailed description can be found in Subsection 3.3.2 and Section 3.3.3.1, respectively.

Step D. Calculate α_{ij}, $i = 1, ..., M, j = 1, ..., N$ using the derived equations in Step C. We will discuss the analysis in detail in Section 3.3.3.1.

Step E. Once we obtain α_{ij} values, we can calculate the start times ST_{ij} using (3.22) below.

$$ST_{ij} \geq AST_j + \frac{\sum_{k=1}^{i-1} \alpha_{kj}}{BW_j}, \text{ for } i = 1, ..., M, j = 1, ..., N \qquad (3.22)$$

The start time of transmitting every playback portion obtained from the above step are then notified to the respective servers. Without under-utilizing the bandwidth resource, we use the equality relationship in (3.22). Also we can calculate the access times of the movies by (3.2). If the access time is less than allowed maximum access time, the movie will be retrieved according to the schedule, otherwise it will be blocked.

Some important details of the above algorithm are discussed in the following sections.

3.3.3.1   Derivation of scheduling constraints

Three kinds of scheduling constraints are needed for computing the optimal sizes of the portions of the movies, i.e., constraints imposed by AST_j values, constraints between adjacent playback portions, and movie length constraints. The continuity relationships during presentation between adjacent playback portions are used to derive the first two kinds of constraints mentioned above. Further, we should also fully utilize the available bandwidth. The details of the derivation can be found in Subsection 3.3.2. The movie length constraints are given by,

$$\sum_{j=1}^{N} \alpha_{ij} = S_i, \text{ for } i = 1, ..., M \qquad (3.23)$$

Thus, on the whole, we have, the number of constraint relationships resulting from AST_j values is $N - 1$, and these are obtained from the combination of equations (3.3), (3.4), (3.5) and/or (3.6), the constraint relationships between adjacent playback portions due to equations (3.7)-(3.21) (these are $(M - 1) \times (N - 1)$ in number), and finally, we have M movie length constraints. Thus, we have a total of $M \times N$ equations involving $M \times N$ unknowns (α_{ij} values), which can be solved to yield optimal sizes of the portions of the movies.

Table 3.3. Known parameters (before calculation) in Example 1

Parameter	Value (MB/sec)	Parameter	Value (min)
BW_1	0.40	AST_1	0
BW_2	0.35	AST_2	10
BW_3	0.45	AST_3	40
R_1	0.42	L_1	110
R_2	0.38	L_2	140

Now we shall demonstrate all the above theoretical findings through a numerical example presented below. Example 1 clarifies all the calculations in detail and is presented for the ease of understanding.

Example 1. Assume that there are requests for 2 movies and we have 3 channels. Their parameters are listed in Table 3.3. Then, we can obtain $6(= 2 \times 3)$ constraint equations as follows.

(1). Since $R_1 > BW_1$, $R_1 > BW_2$, we choose (3.4). Thus, we have,

$$AST_2 - AST_1 + \frac{\alpha_{12}}{BW_2} = \frac{\alpha_{11}}{BW_1} + \frac{\alpha_{12}}{R_1} \qquad (3.24)$$

(2). Since $R_1 > BW_2$, $R_1 < BW_3$, we choose (3.5). Thus, we have,

$$AST_3 - AST_2 = \frac{\alpha_{12}}{BW_2} \qquad (3.25)$$

(3). Since $R_1 > BW_1$, $R_1 > BW_2$, $R_2 < BW_1$, $R_2 < BW_2$, we choose (3.14). Thus, we have,

$$\frac{\alpha_{21}}{R_2} = \frac{\alpha_{12}}{R_1} \qquad (3.26)$$

(4). Since $R_1 > BW_2$, $R_1 < BW_3$, $R_2 < BW_2$, $R_2 < BW_3$, we choose (3.16). Hence, we have,

$$\frac{\alpha_{22}}{R_2} = \frac{\alpha_{13}}{BW_3} \qquad (3.27)$$

(5). The length constraint of movie 1 is given by,

$$\alpha_{11} + \alpha_{12} + \alpha_{13} = L_1 \times R_1 \qquad (3.28)$$

(6). Similarly, the length constraint of movie 2 is given by,

$$\alpha_{21} + \alpha_{22} + \alpha_{23} = L_2 \times R_2 \qquad (3.29)$$

Table 3.4. Optimal sizes of the portions for Example 1

Parameter	α_{11}	α_{12}	α_{13}	α_{21}	α_{22}	α_{23}
Value (MB)	309	684	1779	619	1502	1071

Table 3.5. Detailed results for Example 1

Parameter	Value (MB)	Calculation Eq.	Parameter	Value (min)
m_{11}	15	(3.31)	ST_{11}	0
m_{12}	114	(3.1)	ST_{12}	10
m_{13}	119	(3.1)	ST_{13}	40
m_{21}	31	(3.1)	ST_{21}	13
m_{22}	119	(3.1)	ST_{22}	43
m_{23}	167	(3.1)	ST_{23}	106
m_1	119	(3.34)	AT_1	0.6
m_2	167	(3.34)	AT_2	12.9

Using the above set of equations, we obtain the optimal sizes (see Table 3.4) of the portions of the movies to be retrieved and other parameters (see Table 3.5). In Table 3.5, AT_i and ST_{ij} ($i = 1, 2$ and $j = 1, 2, 3$) are calculated using (3.2) and (3.22), respectively. Thus, the entire timing diagram is as shown in Figure 3.12.

If we use SSRS, i.e., movie 1 and 2 are retrieved from channel 1 and channel 2 respectively. The results for this case are $m_1 = 132MB$, $m_2 = 252MB$, $AT_1 = 5.5min$ and $AT_2 = 22min$. From the comparison of results, we see that the MSR strategy in general, is better than SSRS. The subsequent simulation experiments will further demonstrate this fact.

3.3.3.2   Analysis of buffer space requirement

In Section 3.2.3, we induct the equation of minimum buffer space requirement for a single portion, (3.1). Here, we will induct the equation of minimum buffer space requirement for two consecutive (adjacent) portions in one movie. Thus, we can calculate the actual buffer space requirement.

1. $R_i \leq BW_j$ and $R_i \leq BW_{j+1}$(Figure 3.8)

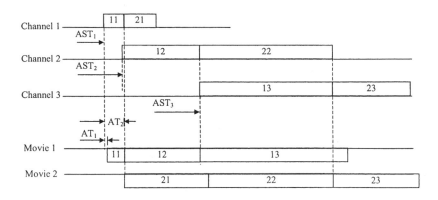

Figure 3.12. The timing diagram for Example 1

In this case, only after the playback of α_{ij} finishes, the retrieval of $\alpha_{i(j+1)}$ begins. So, the buffer space requirement of α_{ij} has no relationship with that of $\alpha_{i(j+1)}$. Thus we can calculate individually the buffer space requirement of every portion using (3.1).

2. $R_i > BW_j$ and $R_i > BW_{j+1}$(Figure 3.9)
In this case, when the retrieval of $\alpha_{i(j+1)}$ begins before the playback of α_{ij} begins, the buffer space requirement will be larger than the calculated value from (3.1). The actual buffer space requirement is,

$$m_{ij} = RHS \ of \ equation(3.1) + max(0, |CB| - |CA|)BW_{j+1} \quad (3.30)$$

where, $|CB|, |CA|$ are time length as shown in Figure 3.9. Hence,

$$m_{ij} = \alpha_{ij} - \frac{\alpha_{ij}BW_j}{R_i} + K_{max}, \quad (3.31)$$

where $K_{max} = max(0, \frac{\alpha_{i(j+1)}}{BW_{j+1}} - \frac{\alpha_{i(j+1)}}{R_i} - \frac{\alpha_{ij}}{R_i})BW_{j+1}$.

3. $R_i \geq BW_j$ and $R_i \leq BW_{j+1}$(Figure 3.10)
Because of the same reason as case 1, the buffer space requirement is given by (3.1).

4. $R_i \leq BW_j$ and $R_i \geq BW_{j+1}$(Figure 3.11)
In this case, when the retrieval of $\alpha_{i(j+1)}$ begins before the retrieval of α_{ij} finishes, the buffer space requirement will be larger than the calculated value from (3.1). The actual buffer space requirement is,

$$m_{ij} = RHS \ of \ equation((3.1) + max(0, |CB| - |CA|)BW_{j+1} \quad (3.32)$$

where, $|CB|$, $|CA|$ are time length as shown in Figure 3.11. Hence,

$$m_{ij} = \alpha_{ij} - \alpha_{ij}\frac{R_i}{BW_j} + P_{max},\qquad(3.33)$$

where, $P_{max} = max(0, \frac{\alpha_{i(j+1)}}{BW_{j+1}} - \frac{\alpha_{i(j+1)}}{R_i} - (\frac{\alpha_{ij}}{R_i} - \frac{\alpha_{ij}}{BW_j}))BW_{j+1}$.

When $j = N$, for the calculation of m_{ij}, we use (3.1). Once we obtain all the buffer requirements for every portion of a single movie, we use

$$m_i = max_{j=1,\dots,N}(m_{ij})\qquad(3.34)$$

as the maximum size of the buffer required. In the channel partition algorithm, we determine the allowed retrieval bandwidth BW_τ^{min} and BW_τ^{max} with α_{ij} assigned the whole length of movie $L_\tau \times R_\tau = S_\tau$ in the buffer space equation (3.1). In fact, the actual buffer space requirement should be calculated according to four cases (i.e., refer to Figure 3.8 - 3.11) discussed above with α_{ij}. Although the calculation of BW_τ^{min} and BW_τ^{max} is approximate, the bandwidth between BW_τ^{min} and BW_τ^{max} can ensure that the actual buffer space requirement is less than the maximum usable buffer space. Following theorems testify these facts.

Theorem 1: In MSR strategy, any available bandwidth between BW_i^{min} and BW_i^{max} can ensure that the actual buffer space requirement is less than the maximum usable buffer space BS_i.

Proof. Let the retrieval bandwidth be denoted as BW_i during a particular retrieval phase of a movie i. Also, assume that $BW_i^{min} \leq BW_i \leq BW_i^{max}$ holds. BW_i^{min} and BW_i^{max} are calculated from (3.1), and hence,

$$L_i \times R_i(1 - min(\frac{BW_i}{R_i}, \frac{R_i}{BW_i})) \leq BS_i\qquad(3.35)$$

The actual buffer space requirement is determined by four cases, i.e., (3.31), (3.33) or (3.1). In the following we prove that (3.31) (Figure 3.9) is less than BS_i.

Firstly, consider the case when $\frac{\alpha_{i(j+1)}}{BW_{j+1}} - \frac{\alpha_{i(j+1)}}{R_i} - \frac{\alpha_{ij}}{R_i} > 0$. This implies that,

$$\frac{\alpha_{ij}}{R_i}(R_i - BW_j) + max(0, \frac{\alpha_{i(j+1)}}{BW_{j+1}} - \frac{\alpha_{i(j+1)}}{R_i} - \frac{\alpha_{ij}}{R_i})BW_{j+1} \quad (3.36)$$

$$= \frac{\alpha_{ij}}{R_i}(R_i - BW_j) + (\frac{\alpha_{i(j+1)}}{BW_{j+1}} - \frac{\alpha_{i(j+1)}}{R_i} - \frac{\alpha_{ij}}{R_i})BW_{j+1} \quad (3.37)$$

$$\leq \alpha_{ij}(1 - \frac{BW_j}{R_i}) + \alpha_{i(j+1)}(1 - \frac{BW_{j+1}}{R_i}) \quad (3.38)$$

$$\leq (\alpha_{ij} + \alpha_{i(j+1)})(1 - \frac{min(BW_j, BW_{j+1})}{R_i}) \quad (3.39)$$

$$\leq L_i \times R_i(1 - \frac{BW_i}{R_i}) \leq BS_i \quad (3.40)$$

Secondly, consider the case, when $\frac{\alpha_{i(j+1)}}{BW_{j+1}} - \frac{\alpha_{i(j+1)}}{R_i} - \frac{\alpha_{ij}}{R_i} \leq 0$. This means that,

$$\frac{\alpha_{ij}}{R_i}(R_i - BW_j) + max(0, \frac{\alpha_{i(j+1)}}{BW_{j+1}} - \frac{\alpha_{i(j+1)}}{R_i} - \frac{\alpha_{ij}}{R_i})BW_{j+1} \quad (3.41)$$

$$= \alpha_{ij}(1 - \frac{BW_j}{R_i}) \leq L_i \times R_i(1 - \frac{BW_i}{R_i}) \leq BS_i \quad (3.42)$$

So, if we use bandwidth BW_i, the buffer requirement calculated from (3.31)(see Figure 3.9) is not more than usable buffer space BS_i. Using similar method, we can prove that (3.33)(see Figure 3.11) can also be satisfied. Besides, for Figure 3.8 and 3.10,

$$\alpha_{ij}(1 - min(\frac{BW_j}{R_i}, \frac{R_i}{BW_j})) \leq L_i \times R_i(1 - min(\frac{R_i}{BW_i}, \frac{BW_i}{R_i})) \leq BS_i$$
$$\quad (3.43)$$

Thus, we prove that *only if* BW_i satisfies $BW_i^{min} \leq BW_i \leq BW_i^{max}$, the actual buffer space requirement is less than the maximum usable buffer space BS_i. □

Theorem 2: The buffer space requirement of SSRS is greater than or equal to that of the MSR strategy.

Proof. In MSR scheme, actual buffer space requirement is determined by the buffer space requirement equations of two consecutive portions case (one of (3.31), (3.33) and (3.1)). In SSRS, actual buffer space requirement is determined by (3.1) while α_{ij} is assigned the whole length of the movie. In Theorem 1, we have proved that the amount of bandwidth derived from (3.1) must ensure that the buffer space requirement of two consecutive portions is less than the maximum usable buffer space. Hence, if we use the same retrieval bandwidth, the buffer space requirement of SSRS is certainly not less than that of the MSR strategy. □

3.3.3.3   Remarks

As far as the time complexity of the entire MSR process is concerned, the following can be observed. In the channel partition phase, the worst time complexity is $O(A \times N)$ (where A is the total number of requests) and for generating the retrieval schedule, the time complexity is $O(M \times N)$. Thus, each phase has a polynomial time complexity.

3.4.   Performance Study

In this section, we compare the performance of SSRS and MSR strategies on several system dependent parameters. The SSRS used in our simulation can be described as follows. We choose the maximum value between available bandwidth and maximum usable bandwidth calculated from buffer utilization limit, as retrieval bandwidth. Then we calculate the access time. If the access time is less than the maximum allowed access time, this request is accepted, otherwise this request is blocked. Table 3.6 shows the system parameters (constant and varying) and Table 3.7 introduces some common equations used in the simulation study. In the simulation, we will explore the effect of the following parameters: θ_r and T_{max}. In Table 3.6, R_0 can be an arbitrary value, e.g., $0.42 MB/sec$ (MPEG-II) since the concrete value of R_0 will not effect the performance comparison.

For the purpose of simulation, we restrict the number of movies that can be stored in a server. Of course, in reality, one must have adequate memory to store the movies, and without loss of generality, we assume that the servers have sufficient storage capacity to store the same number of movies. Further, in the simulation study, the movie length is a parameter that is uniformly distributed. In the case of dynamic access rates, the access rates for movies changes with time. In the case of static access rate, the access rate does not change. Obviously, the dynamic access rate is reasonable model for a real situation. We generate dynamic access rate through the change of the arrival rate during one day. The arrival rate of the requests is assumed to follow a Gaussian distribution. The arrival rate varies with respect to the time interval for every minute. Using the above distribution, we calculate the arrival rate λ_i for every minute time interval. In other words, we assume that the arrival rate is non-homogeneous.

The expected access rates of the movies and the relative loads on the servers are assumed to follow a Zipf-like distribution[8]. The hot set parameter θ_e or θ_r reflects the extent to which the distribution is skewed. The higher the value of θ_e or θ_r are, the greater the difference between the access rates of the movies or relative loads on the servers are, respectively.

---

[8]Reader may refer to details of this distribution and significance of all the parameters in [68].

Table 3.6. Parameters in the VoD system simulation

System Parameters	Symbol	Parameter Values
Number of different movies	M^s	200
Number of servers	N^s	20
Per-server disk size (in number of movies)	B	10
The length of movie	L	uniform in [90 - 150min]
Playback rate	R	uniform in $[0.5 - 2.0]R_0$
Total requests in 24 hrs	A	2000
Peak time	μ	240min
Std. dev. of arrival rate	σ	30
Maximum usable buffer space of retrieving movie i	BS_i	$60R_0$ (in MB)
Maximum access time	T_{max}	0.5,1.0,...,5min
Bandwidth of every server	BW	$3BR_0$
Expected hot-set factor of movie access rate	θ_e	30/5(Very Sharp, value is 0.0355) 20/5(sharp, value is 0.022), 10/5(moderately sharp, value is 0.0085), 5/5(Flat, value is 0)
Hot-set factor of actual server load	θ_r	30/5(Very Sharp, value is 0.355), 20/5(sharp, value is 0.22), 10/5(moderately sharp, value is 0.085), 5/5(Flat, value is 0)

3.4.1 Simulation experiments

We store M^s movies in N^s servers according to an *expected access rate* of every movie. The algorithm is as follows:

Movie Copy Placement Algorithm:
count ← 1;
FOR i=1 to M^s

Table 3.7. Commonly used equations in VoD system simulation

Relation	Equation
Determine the request arrival rate (per min)	$\lambda_i = \frac{A}{\sigma\sqrt{2\pi}} e^{-(i-\nu)^2/2\sigma^2}$, $i = 1, ..., 1440$
Determine the expected access rates of movies from θ_e	probability of accessing movie i, $P_i = \frac{e^{-\theta_e i}}{T}$, $T = \sum_{i=1}^{M^s} e^{-\theta_e i}$, ($i$ is the movie index, T is a normalization constant), $\sum_{i=1}^{M^s} P_i = 1$
Determine the relative load of servers from θ_r	load of accessing server j, $a_j = \frac{e^{-\theta_r j}}{T}$, $T = \sum_{j=1}^{N^s} e^{-\theta_r j}$, ($i$ is the server index, T is a normalization constant), $\sum_{j=1}^{N^s} a_j = 1$

```
{
    copy[i] ← ⌊Nˢ × B × Pᵢ/ ∑ᵢ₌₁ᴹˢ Pᵢ⌋; /*The number of copies of movie i*/
    FOR j=1 to copy[i]
    {
        Server (mod(count − 1, Nˢ) + 1) is assigned a copy of movie i;
        count ← count + 1;
    }
}
```

In the above algorithm, firstly, we calculate the optimal number of copies of every movie according to the expected access rates. The movies with higher expected access rates probably have several replications; the movies with less expected access rates may not be stored in any servers. Thus, the overall availability of a movie in the system matches the demand profile (though it is an expected quantity). Secondly, we determine the strategic locations (servers) of movies. In the above algorithm, it may be noted that we avoid placing the copies of the same movie in the same server to the maximum possible extent. This is in view of the fact that dispersed placement of the same movies makes the dynamic access adjustment much easier. Thus, even if the access rates of movies change drastically, depending on the access adjustment algorithms such as *dancing algorithm* proposed by Wolf et al., in 1995 [112], the load to be accessed from every server can be balanced to some extent and the available server bandwidth is utilized fully. Obviously, if we know more about the dynamic relations between the access rates of different movies, a better placement algorithm can be designed. Alternatively, one could attempt to propose an approach to dynamically reconfigure the VOD system so as to alter the number of copies of each movie maintained on the server as the access demand for these movies fluctuates. This approach is also attempted in the literature.

Requests arrive with arrival rate λ_i, $i = 1, ..., 1440$. In general, in a single day, the parameter λ_i is a function of time (in minute). For every movie, the number of accesses is controlled by the *actual access rate* of every movie. In the simulation, we will measure the difference between actual access rate and expected access rate with parameter θ_r. When $\theta_r = 0$, it means that the expected access rates are the same as the actual access rates. The method of generating the number of times movie i $(i = 1, ..., M^s)$ is actually accessed is as follows.

(a). From the actual load to be accessed from server j, denoted as a_j $(j = 1, ..., N^s)$, we can determine the actual access rates of movies in the servers using (3.44).

$$q_i = \sum_{j-1}^{N^s} \eta_{ij} \frac{a_j}{B}, \ i = 1, ..., M^s \tag{3.44}$$

where, $\eta_{ij} = 1$ only if there is movie i copy in server j, otherwise $\eta_{ij} = 0$. Note that (3.44) cannot be used to calculate the actual access rates of movies which have so small expected access rates that they do not be uploaded to any server. For these movies, we assume actual access rates are the same as expected access rates.

(b). After the calculation of actual access rates, we calculate the number of times the movie i is accessed, A_i with

$$A_i = \frac{A q_i}{\sum_{i=1}^{M^s} q_i} \tag{3.45}$$

The effect of VCR control and caching strategy on the performance of single and multiple movies retrieval strategies are almost identical and hence, we will not consider them in the simulation experiments.

3.4.2 Performance comparison

We now present some interesting simulation results for comparison between SSRS and MSR schemes. We compare block rates, access times, buffer space requirement and bandwidth utilization. Figures 3.13 and 3.14((a), (b) and (c)) show the comparison of average access times, block rates and buffer space requirements of SSRS and MSR schemes, respectively. Further, Figure 3.13(d) and Figure 3.14(d) shows the difference in bandwidth utilization of SSRS and

MSRS. And every point in the curve is calculated using

$$\int_{t=1}^{1440} (BW_{MSRS}(t) - BW_{SSRS}(t))dt \qquad (3.46)$$

where, $BW_{MSRS}(t)$, $BW_{SSRS}(t)$ are the amount of bandwidth used with respect to time in the respective strategies. Both Figure 3.13 and Figure 3.14 show the following common features.

From these figures, we see that, the average access time, block rate and buffer space requirement of the MSR strategy are significantly lower than that of SSRS. This performance improvement is mainly caused by: the optimal choice of shorter playback portion derived through the set of equations presented in the earlier section, an efficient utilization of the available server bandwidths using the aggregate retrieval bandwidth, and balancing of the total load in a careful manner among the qualified servers.

A. Performance under a variation of expected access rates with respect to the actual access rates

In the simulation, we use $T_{max} = 5\ min$. Since we use θ_r (i.e., hot-set factor of actual server loads) to tune the difference between actual access rates and expected access rates, θ_r is our choice of the x-axis parameter in Figure 3.13. From Figure 3.13(a), the average access time of SSRS is threefold the access time of the MSR scheme. However, for strategies SSRS and MSR, the difference between the expected access rates and the actual access rates has no obvious effect on the access time. It may be noted that when the difference between the expected access rates and the actual access rates increases, the effect of load balancing is weakened. Thus, the difference of block rate value between these two strategies decreases. Because of the same reason, the difference in the utilization of bandwidth between these strategies also decreases, as demonstrated in Figure 3.13(d). It may be noted that the buffer space requirement, in general, at a client site is determined by the retrieval bandwidth. The decrease in the buffer requirements as θ_r increase is mainly due to the use of less server bandwidth resource for retrieval. This effect also manifests in Figure 3.13(b), as the block rate increases.

When the difference between the expected access rates and the actual access rates increases, it leads to a situation wherein some servers will be kept busy while some other servers remain idle. Thus, the bandwidth available from idle servers is wasted and more requests submitted at the busy servers are blocked. In such a case, the MSR scheme has less bandwidth "tuning" space. In other words, the effect of load balancing is "weakened". It may be noted that the load balancing ability of MSR approach is the key reason behind the improvement

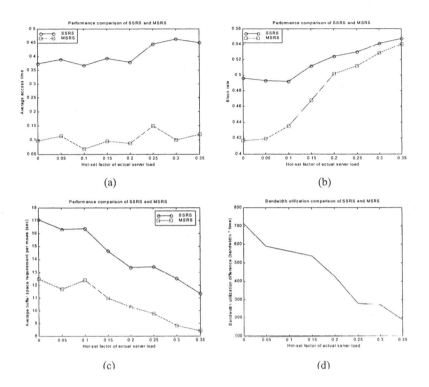

Figure 3.13. Performance comparison of SSRS and MSR strategies under a variation of expected access rates with respect to the actual access rates

of block rates and not the access times. Hence, the difference in the block rates between SSRS and MSR strategies becomes smaller when the difference between the expected access rates and the actual access rates increases. On the other hand, the performance improvement of the access time in the MSR strategy is mainly due to a full utilization of the available bandwidth resource. The requests that lead to larger access times will be blocked (i.e., they will not be included in the calculation of average access time), and hence, the block rate does not greatly affect the average access time. Thus, the load balancing function has no strong relationship with the improvement of average access time. Hence, with respect to average access time in Figure 3.13(a), the performance of MSR approach beats the performance of SSRS significantly.

B. Performance under different allowed maximum access times

In the simulation, we use $\theta_r = 0$. When allowed maximum access time T_{max}

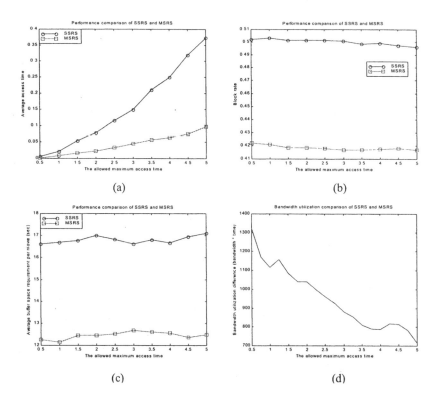

Figure 3.14. Performance comparison of SSRS and MSR strategies for different allowed maximum access time

increases, the average access time increases for both MSR and SSRS schemes. However, the rate at which the average access time of MSRS increases is slower than that of SSRS. As the scope of the parameter T_{max} ($0.5\ min - 5.0\ min$) is much smaller than the entire movie length, the increase of T_{max} has very little effect on the block rate for both the schemes. When T_{max} increases, smaller retrieval bandwidth can be used, and thus more buffer space is required.

3.5.   Concluding Remarks

In this chapter we have extended the idea of employing multiple servers for long duration multimedia document (mainly non-stream object) retrieval presented in Chapter 2 to a more realistic multiple client scenario. We have considered several system dependent parameters such as, server bandwidths, movie lengths, playback rates and the available buffer spaces at the client sites, in the design of MSR approach.

A systematic design of a MSR strategy for retrieving the movies has been carried out with the goal of minimizing the client access times and the block rates. A two-step hierarchical approach has been followed to attack the problem. In the first step (allocate bandwidth), we strategically partition the available server bandwidths for minimizing the access time and the block rate. In the second step (scheduling phase), we determined the exact size of the individual disjoint portions that need to be retrieved from each of the servers, which also decides the amount of buffer space required at the client site. In each tier, sufficient care is taken to design the algorithms considering the access rates, movie lengths, playback rates, retrieval bandwidths, and the available buffer space at the client site. The solution satisfying the system of equations generated also has the inherent property of satisfying the continuity relationships while presenting the movies to the users. The two-tier approach guarantees a timely retrieval of movies and utilizes the available bandwidth efficiently. This approach provides a general method of implementing MSR strategies for both static access rate and dynamic access rate cases.

It may be noted that the TGS server designed in this chapter attempts to group the requests into tasks for scheduling. There may be two possible cases - static and dynamic. The static case refers to a predefined a number of movies in a group, however, the grouping method chapter does not limit the number of movies (i.e., requests) and hence, it is dynamic. The grouping depends on current bandwidth resource availability. In other words, whenever the required amount of bandwidth can be derived from a pool of servers, the allocation of one movie in one task can always be carried out. Thus, the requests will have shorter access time.

It may be noted that in the strategy we present in this chapter, a playback is not triggered until the corresponding movie portion is downloaded completely by the client. While this guarantees that there are no hiccups during the playback, one can still initiate the playback as soon as a client is "adequately" filled with video data to circumvent any data starvation at a later time. In fact, commercial players use this technique. This is studied in the next chapter in which we present an alternate way of implementing this multiple server scheduling technology which may even deliver better performance, whenever possible.

Bibliographic Notes

A lot of research has been devoted to design several retrieval scheduling strategies, e.g., retrieval scheduling for disk (single and arrays of disks) [80, 110] and tape cartridges [62], for minimizing the access time of a requested document, while maximizing the number of concurrent streams and minimizing the client buffer requirements. In [58], multiple channels retrieval is researched for minimizing the number of tardy frames in end-to-end delivery of multimedia data. These scheduling strategies are tightly related with the type of storage media. In [55] a MOD service (server) architecture consisting of multiple processors (nodes) connected by an interconnection network is proposed. The objective of the study presented in this work is to maximize the throughput (the number of video streams that this server can supply). The problem is to assign streams to the interface node (the nodes that actually supplies the requested video streams) from a set of potential storage nodes in such a way that the throughput and the resource utilization are maximized. This is done by carefully balancing the load on the processors. Five different allocation polices are designed and analyzed. This paper also considers the file replication problem (in the view of improving the performance).

In [12, 13], the video streaming problem for a group of users (clusters) is considered and the optimal solution for achieving a minimum average bandwidth is discussed. Further, it is argued that for dynamic interactive situations (using VCR control functions), this problem is *isomorphic* to the Rectilinear Steiner Minimal Arborescence (RSMA) problem. Since the latter problem is known to be NP-complete, heuristic schemes are suggested and their performance is evaluated. In [13], implementation details are provided. In [60] the authors consider the interactive functions under a failure and overloading situations in VOD server systems. The authors proposed an analytical model that takes into account failure and overload server conditions and performs rigorous recoverability analysis. In [28], the authors extend and generalize the treatment followed in [105] for the case of multiple servers and multiple clients and also carry out load balancing across the servers.

Also, there are scheduling methods used in broadcasting like the Pyramid Broadcasting [109], Permutation-Based Pyramid Broadcasting [3] and Skyscraper Broadcasting [51]. In these schemes, basically, the idea is that each movie is partitioned into several segments and broadcasted periodically, towards the goal of achieving a minimum access time. However, broadcasting schemes have inherent disadvantages of making the client wait through the entire broadcast batch to get his/her choice [41], while requiring high-end client capabilities. An excellent compilation and comparison of various VoD techniques proposed in the literature until 1997 appears in [41]. However, all these works are limited to a single video server.

A recent work in [85] considers employing multiple servers to retrieve MM documents, however, from a different objective. In this work, the authors design a scheduling scheme, referred to as *application layer broker*, at the client's site. In this work, buffer utilization is the only performance metric. It presents an algorithm (referred to as application-layer broker (ALB)) that postpones buffer overflow optimally. In other words, the retrieval from a server is delayed to prevent buffer overflows at the client end, in advance. In general, the problem addressed in [25] can be described as follows. A collection of objects $O_1, O_2, ..., O_n$ should be available in the client buffer before certain time t. Object O_i can be retrieved from server j with retrieval bandwidth $r_{ij}(t)$. When $\sum_{j=1}^{n} b_j \geq B_{max}$ (where b_i is the size of object i and B_{max} is maximum available buffer size in client end), the authors propose a method to generate an optimal retrieval schedule that postpones the buffer overflow as much as possible. Also, this study assumes the retrieval bandwidth of every server is known beforehand and based on this assumption the design of a scheduling strategy to maximize client buffer utilization is carried out.

While this work is about retrieval scheduling, the contents of this chapter are concerned with the retrieval of various disjoint portions of the movies from several servers. Moreover, with the problem formulation presented in this chapter, knowing the amount of bandwidth required to retrieve a movie and the bandwidth currently available with the servers, one can carefully balance the requests such that the available bandwidth is catered among the requests and the access times are minimized for the respective movies. We had also shown how to determine the exact amount of buffer size required at the client end. An interesting merge of this work with the work in [85], would be to invoke the ALB algorithm after determining the buffer size at the client end with the scheme in this chapter. As before, we can even consider average access time, block rate as well as buffer utilization, as performance metrics.

Chapter 4

AN ALTERNATIVE RETRIEVAL STRATEGY: A PLAY-WHILE-RETRIEVE APPROACH

In this chapter, we consider designing an alternate efficient movie retrieval strategy that minimizes the access times of movies. The main difference between the strategy to be introduced in this chapter and the previous ones depends on when the playback is initiated without suffering any hiccups for data. Most commercial media players (software) practice this idea to minimize the waiting time delays of the client. However, with existing VoD service architectures, whenever the underlying network experiences long delays, the players at the client end are bound to starve for data and result in presentation discontinuities. Especially with connectionless oriented services, the effect of waiting times amidst an ongoing presentation, due to unpredictable delays are significant. In this chapter, we follow the idea of an "early start" strategy. However, as seen in the earlier chapters, the underlying network architecture continues to use MSR technology. While we remain in the MSR domain, we attempt to minimize the access delays by initiating the playback of the first portion before the entire portion is downloaded. One significant advantage during implementation of this scheme is that whenever networks delays are sensed, the system can react in advance by slowing down the retrieval from that channel and allow other faster channels to transfer more data in the future[1]. Thus, MSR residing at the backbone, continues to play a crucial role in quality control and hence this scheme is clearly a welcome one! In Chapter 8, we will discuss a practical prototype that is designed and we specifically follow the strategy to be introduced in this chapter in the design of that prototype.

In this chapter we investigate the following issues:

---

[1] Also, when client buffer spaces are not adequate, this strategy adapts and does the load sharing automatically.

- We first attempt to design and analyze a *play-while-retrieve* (PWR) playback strategy for a multi-server environment. For this strategy, we use both the single installment and multi-installment retrieval strategies to analyze the performance of the system.

- For the above mentioned retrieval strategies, we explicitly derive closed-form expressions for a minimum access time.

- For the case of multi-installment retrieval strategy, since the retrieval follows several rounds of installments, we derive the ultimate performance bounds (asymptotic performance analysis) that quantify the limiting performance of PWR strategy. We demonstrate the presence or impact of a large scale network as well as the impact of indefinitely increasing the number of installments with the PWR strategy, thus quantifying the performance of such a multi-server service architecture.

- We then address the problem of buffer management at the client site, which is one of the closely related issues that has a significant influence on the performance of the strategy. We derive relationships that quantify the minimum amount of buffer expected at the client site to have a smooth presentation with this multi-server service structure. We do this for both the single installment and multi-installment retrieval strategies.

- Finally, in order to test all the theoretical findings, we present some interesting simulation experiments. In the experiments, we compare the performance of the PWR strategy with that of the Play-After-Retrieval (PAR) strategy and discuss certain important points that are crucial for implementing a real-life working multi-server service system.

4.1.   Service Model and Preliminary Remarks

As usual, we first present the problem more formally, describe the network architecture that is considered, and introduce the necessary definitions, notations and terminologies. We envisage the underlying network as shown in Figure 4.1. In the network architecture shown, each server serves its respective local customers along with customers situated at other sites. The request for viewing a movie is individually initiated by local customers/clients on each server. Upon an arrival of a request, the server first seeks the requested movie locally. If this movie is available locally, then it is retrieved and presented to the user. However, if the requested movie is not available locally, this original server can obtain the information about the requested movie from other servers by employing look up services, such as the directory service. Then the requested movie can be retrieved from one or more servers employing the PWR proposed strategy. In the following, we describe the basic retrieval mechanism employed in this PWR strategy.

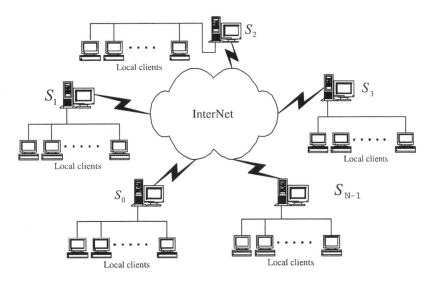

Figure 4.1. Architecture of a multi-server VoD system

4.1.1 Description of the strategy

We now describe the details of the PWR strategy. Consider a scenario in which a requested movie is not available locally at the original server, denoted as, S. Without loss of generality, we assume that the requested movie is present at servers S_0, S_1 and S_2. Let the total size of the requested movie be L, measured in *bits*. The connection bandwidths of channels from other servers(in this case S_0 to S_2) to the local server(in this case server S) are denoted as bw_i, $i = 0, 1, 2$, measured in *bits per second*. Let the playback rate at the client site be R_p, measured in *bits per second*. *Please note that in the other chapters both bw_i and R denote the inverse of the corresponding parameters and are usually expressed in s/MB.* Once locating the respective servers having the requested movie, server S starts retrieving the requested movie from these servers. Since the design of the Service Module supports multiple servers, the movie will be streamed from all available servers concurrently using separate connections. This implies that the movie data will be partitioned into multiple portions and streamed from each of these servers. In this running example, a portion of the entire movie, denoted as m_i, $i = 0, 1, 2$, is retrieved from each server and is collected by S in a particular order. Upon receiving the first portion of the movie from S_0, the playback may start at the user terminal, when retrievals from other servers are underway. As mentioned before, the presentation continuity is a major Quality of Service (QoS) requirement for a multimedia presentation. Thus, in order to start the playback when retrievals from other servers are underway, the size of the portion retrieved must be such that there should not be any data starvation for playback. In other words, the size of the portion retrieved must guarantee the presentation continuity. Now, the retrieval strategy must be such that before the playback of this portion comes to an end, the next portion of the requested movie data should be made available from S_1. This retrieval process continues until all the movie is retrieved from the set of servers.

The above example describes the PWR retrieval strategy in which server S only retrieves one portion of the movie from each server. This strategy can also be referred to as *single installment* retrieval strategy. On the other hand, the retrieval process may be such that server S may retrieve movie portions from each server in multiple installments. Thus, each server participates in the retrieval process more than once. In subsequent sections, we will describe these strategies in detail. In the basic retrieval strategy introduced in Chapter 2, a client is allowed to start the playback only after the client has received the entire portion from the first server(S_0, in the example above). However, in PWR retrieval strategy, this mode of operation is relaxed and we design a strategy which allows an *early start* of the playback and at the same time guarantees presentation continuity. Thus, as soon as the *critical size*, defined below, of the first portion has been retrieved, the playback can be initiated on the client site. In other words, the client can start play this portion while the remaining portion is being retrieved and hence the name of *PWR*. The *critical size*, denoted as cs_i, $i = 0, 1, 2$, is the minimum size of movie that a client should retrieve before the playback of this portion could be started so as to avoid data starvation and hiccups during playback. This critical size depends on the available connection bandwidth of the channels and the playback rate of the movie at the client site. Hence, this is somewhat a dynamic quantity and must be recomputed every time before fetching the data. For every portion that is to be retrieved from a server, PWR strategy recommends a critical size that should be retrieved in order to avoid data starvation. Figure 4.2 shows the whole process of the above example.

4.1.1.1   Determination of critical size

We now describe on how this critical size can be computed. This will be used later in the analysis of PWR strategy. Consider a scenario in which a portion of the movie of size m is to be retrieved from a server using a connection bandwidth of bw demanding a playback rate of R_p at the client site. The client can safely start playing the portion after the critical size cs of this portion has been retrieved. Figure 4.3 shows this concept. From the figure, we observe that in order to guarantee a continuous playback, the time to retrieve the remaining

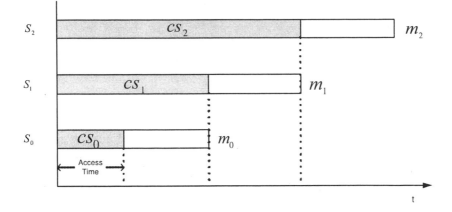

Figure 4.2. Example of PWR strategy

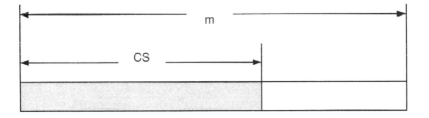

Figure 4.3. Critical size

portion $(m - cs)$ must be not greater than the entire playback duration of the portion m. In other words,

$$\frac{m}{R_p} \geq \frac{m - cs}{bw} \tag{4.1}$$

Thus, by satisfying this condition (4.1), we ensure that the retrieval of the remaining portion will not affect the continuity of the playback at any time instant. Further, when sufficiently large amount of bandwidth is available (high bandwidth networks), i.e., whenever $bw \geq R_p$, we note that the playback can almost start instantaneously, which is consistent with the PWR strategy. This means that we avoid buffering the data. However, in reality, due to numerous reasons, such as the constrains of the admission control mechanism and the network bandwidth available between remote servers and this client, most remote VoD servers other than S cannot support each client with a connection bandwidth that is higher than the playback rate, for example, 1.5Mbps for MPEG1. Hence, without loss of generality, we assume $R_p > bw$ hereafter. We have,

$$cs \geq \frac{(R_p - bw)m}{R_p} \qquad (4.2)$$

As soon as cs of one portion has been retrieved, we can start playing the portion safely and the rest of the portion can be retrieved continuously while the playback is underway. From (4.2), we can see that the critical size bears a linear relationship with the movie size for a given bandwidth and playback rate.

4.1.2   Some basic definitions

We will recapture certain definitions stated earlier for the sake of continuity and introduce few additional definitions used throughout this chapter.

1.*Retrieval schedule distribution*: This is defined as an N ordered tuple m given by,

$$m = (m_0, m_1, \ldots, m_{N-1}) \qquad (4.3)$$

where m_i is the portion of the movie retrieved from server S_i, $i = 0, 1, 2, \ldots, N-1$. Further,

$$\sum_{k=0}^{N-1} m_k = L \qquad (4.4)$$

and

$$0 \leq m_i \leq L, \quad i = 0, 1, 2, \ldots, N-1 \qquad (4.5)$$

The set of all such retrieval schedule distributions is denoted as Γ.

2.*Critical size distribution*: This is defined as an N ordered tuple cs given by

$$cs = (cs_0, cs_1, \ldots, cs_{N-1}) \qquad (4.6)$$

where cs_i is the critical size of corresponding portion m_i, $i = 0, 1, 2, \ldots, N-1$. Using equality relation in (4.2), we have,

$$cs_i = \frac{(R_p - bw_i)m_i}{R_p} \qquad (4.7)$$

3.*Access Time*: This is defined as the time between the instant at which the servers start transmitting their portions and the instant at which the presentation starts. This is denoted as, $AT(m)$. According to the scheme motioned before, together with a practical perspective, we have,

$$AT = \frac{max\{cs_0, \delta\}}{bw_0} \qquad (4.8)$$

where bw_0 is the connection bandwidth of the established communication channel from S_0 to S (supposing the first portion is retrieved from S_0). δ is introduced in (4.8) to present the minimum size that a video player needs to initiate a playback. δ depends on the video stream, i.e. the codec used, but it can also depend on player being used. Because the value of δ only affects the access time, regardless of the retrieval strategy, without loss of generality, we set $\delta = 0$ hereafter.

4.*Minimum access time*: This is defined as ,

$$AT^*(m^*) = min_{m \in \Gamma} AT(m) \qquad (4.9)$$

where, $m^* = (m_0^*, ..., m_{N-1}^*) \in \Gamma$ denotes an optimal retrieval schedule distribution of the entire movie.

Thus, from above set of definitions and the strategy, the key objective is to minimize the access time by determining the optimal sizes of the portions of the movie to be retrieved from different servers involved in the retrieval process.

4.2. Design of Movie Retrieval Strategies

In this section, we shall attempt using single installment and multi-installment retrieval strategies in the design of PWR and determine the optimal sizes of various portions retrieved from all the N servers in order to achieve minimum access time.

4.2.1 Single installment strategy

The movie portions are retrieved in a specific order from the servers. We will assume without loss of generality that this order is S_0 to S_{N-1}. Each server participates in the retrieval process only once for a client and hence the name *single installment* strategy. We now derive a closed-form solution for the minimum access time following this strategy. In Figure 4.4 we show the retrieval process using a directed flow graph comprising communication nodes (retrieval) and playback nodes. The arrows capture the precedence relationships in the retrieval and playback portions. For example, portion i can be played after portion $(i - 1)$ and after receiving its critical size. Note that the weights of the nodes are indeed the communication and playback durations of the respective nodes. From this figure, we can derive a relationship between the retrieval of portion i and $(i + 1)$ and the playback time of the portion m_i with the use of causal precedence relation and continuity constraint as,

$$\frac{cs_i}{bw_i} + \frac{m_i}{R_p} \geq \frac{cs_{i+1}}{bw_{i+1}} \qquad (4.10)$$

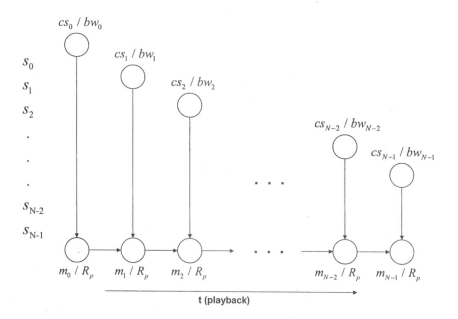

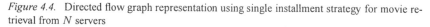

Figure 4.4. Directed flow graph representation using single installment strategy for movie retrieval from N servers

By using (4.7) in (4.10), we can get

$$\frac{(R_p - bw_i)m_i}{R_p bw_i} + \frac{m_i}{R_p} \geq \frac{(R_p - bw_{i+1})m_{i+1}}{R_p bw_{i+1}} \tag{4.11}$$

Further

$$m_{i+1} \leq \frac{R_p bw_{i+1} m_i}{(R_p - bw_{i+1})bw_i} \tag{4.12}$$

Let us denote $R_p bw_{i+1}/(R_p - bw_{i+1})bw_i = \rho_i$. Rewriting (4.12),we have,

$$m_{i+1} \leq m_i \rho_i, \quad i = 0, 1, \ldots, N - 2. \tag{4.13}$$

This equation means that the amount of a portion could be determined, given the information of the previous portion and servers' bandwidths. Then, the above equation represents a set of recursive equations that can be solved under equality conditions. Note that the use of equality relationships in (4.12) and (4.13) results in the *maximum* size of all the portions other than m_0. Hence, using (4.4) we obtain a *minimum* value for m_0, equivalently the minimum cs_0. In other words, we obtain a minimum access time. Thus, we have a recursive set of $(N - 1)$ equations with equality relations from (4.13). Each m_i can be expressed in terms of m_0 as ,

$$m_i = m_0 \prod_{k=0}^{i-1} \rho_k, \quad i = 1, 2, \ldots, N - 1. \tag{4.14}$$

Thus, the above set of $(N - 1)$ equations given by (4.14) together with (4.4) are solved to obtain the individual disjoint portions of the requested movie. Substituting each m_i from (4.14) into (4.4), we obtain,

$$m_0 = \frac{L}{1 + \displaystyle\sum_{p=1}^{N-1} \prod_{k=0}^{p-1} \rho_k} \tag{4.15}$$

Substituting (4.15) in (4.14), we obtain the individual sizes of the portions as,

$$m_i = \frac{L \displaystyle\prod_{k=0}^{i-1} \rho_k}{1 + \displaystyle\sum_{p=1}^{N-1} \prod_{k=0}^{p-1} \rho_k}, \quad i = 1, 2, \ldots, N - 1. \tag{4.16}$$

Thus, the access time is given by,

$$AT^*(m^*) = \frac{cs_0}{bw_0} = \frac{(R_p - bw_0)m_0}{R_p bw_0} = \frac{L(\frac{1}{bw_0} - \frac{1}{R_p})}{(1 + \displaystyle\sum_{p=1}^{N-1} \prod_{k=0}^{p-1} \rho_k)} \tag{4.17}$$

It may be noted that only when $R_p > bw_0$ PWR strategy becomes meaningful. This is because of the fact that in the case of high bandwidth connections (more than the playback rate would demand), employing a pool of servers has no tangible effect on the access time.

4.2.1.1 Homogeneous channels

We consider a network with identical connection bandwidths among servers , i.e., $bw_i = bw$, for all $i = 0, 1, \ldots, N - 1$. In this case, using (4.15) and (4.16), the individual sizes of the portions retrieved from the servers S_i are given by,

$$m_0 = \frac{L(\rho - 1)}{\rho^N - 1} \tag{4.18}$$

$$m_i = \frac{L(\rho - 1)\rho^i}{\rho^N - 1}, \quad i = 1, 2, \ldots, N - 1. \tag{4.19}$$

Hence, the access time is given by,

$$AT^*(m^*) = \frac{cs_0}{bw} = \frac{L(\rho - 1)}{\rho(\rho^N - 1)bw} \qquad (4.20)$$

Remarks on the effect of sequencing: The strategy described above, assumes that the retrieval follows a *fixed sequence*, i.e., from S_0 to S_{N-1}. However, it may be noted that given a set of N servers, we have $N!$ retrieval sequences possible. Following the steps described in Chapter 2, even for the PWR single installment strategy, we can show that the access time remains independent of the retrieval sequence. Below we present a Lemma and a theorem that proves this claim.

Lemma 1. Let the access time of a requested movie file by the server S be denoted as $AT(m, \sigma(k, k+1))$, where $\sigma(k, k+1)$ (this sequence is given by S_0 to S_{N-1} in that order[2]), denotes the sequence in which the requested movie file is retrieved from the servers. Then, for a sequence $\sigma'(k, k+1)$ (See the order below.[3]), the access time $AT(m', \sigma'(k, k+1))$ is equal to $AT(m, \sigma(k, k+1))$ where, $\sigma'(k, k+1)$ denotes a retrieval sequence in which the adjacent channels k and $k+1$ are swapped, i.e., portion from server S_{k+1} is retrieved first and then from server S_k.

Proof. The denominator of (4.17) can be written as :

$$denom(m) = 1 + \rho_0 + \rho_0\rho_1 + \rho_0\rho_1\rho_2 + \ldots = 1 + \rho_0(1 + \rho_1(1 + \rho_2(\ldots))) \quad (4.21)$$

We can distinguish two cases depending on whether the first server S_0 is involved or not. If S_0 is not involved, when a switch is made between two successive servers, the new denominator is different from the original one in three ρ terms. This difference can be written as:

$$denom(m') - denom(m) = \sum_{j=0}^{i-1} \rho_j$$

$$[\frac{\rho_i bw_i}{bw_{i-1}}(1 + \frac{\rho_{i-1}bw_{i-1}}{bw_{i+1}}(1 + \frac{\rho_{i+1}bw_{i+1}}{bw_i}(1 + \rho_{i+3}(\ldots))))$$

$$- \rho_{i-1}(1 + \rho_i(1 + \rho_{i+1}(1 + \rho_{i+3}(\ldots)))))] \quad (4.22)$$

With little algebraic manipulation, the above equation returns zero. In the second case, where the first two servers S_0 and S_1 are switched, the difference

---

[2]$(S_0, S_1, \ldots, S_{k-1}, S_k, S_{k+1}, S_{k+2}, \ldots S_{N-1})$ is the sequence.
[3]$(S_0, S_1, \ldots, S_{k-1}, S_{k+1}, S_k, S_{k+2}, \ldots S_{N-1})$ is the sequence.

in access time is,

$$AT(m) - AT(m') = \frac{L(\frac{1}{bw_0} - \frac{1}{R_p})}{denom(m)} - \frac{L(\frac{1}{bw_1} - \frac{1}{R_p})}{denom(m')}$$

$$= L\frac{(\frac{1}{bw_0} - \frac{1}{R_p})denom(m') - (\frac{1}{bw_1} - \frac{1}{R_p})denom(m)}{denom(m)denom(m')} \quad (4.23)$$

By using (4.21)($denom(m)$ and $denom(m')$ differ in two ρ-terms, ρ_0 and ρ_1), the numerator of the above fraction becomes equal to

$$(\frac{1}{bw_0} - \frac{1}{R_p})(1 + \frac{R_p bw_0}{(R_p - bw_0)bw_1}(1 + \frac{R_p bw_2}{(R_p - bw_2)bw_0}(1 + \rho_2(...))))$$

$$-(\frac{1}{bw_1} - \frac{1}{R_p})(1 + \frac{R_p bw_1}{(R_p - bw_1)bw_0}(1 + \frac{R_p bw_2}{(R_p - bw_2)bw_1}(1 + \rho_2(...))))$$

$$(4.24)$$

which in turn can be immediately proven to be equal to zero. $\square$

Therefore, one can easily conclude that the order in which the portions are downloaded only affects the respective size distribution, but not the access time when the retrieval order is changed. We prove this claim in general for the case of N servers, as follows.

Theorem 1. *Given a pool of N video servers capable of rendering the requested movie file, using the PWR single installment strategy, the access time is independent of the retrieval sequence used.*

Proof. One can easily prove the theorem with the aid of Lemma 1. Any valid sequence of servers can be derived from a single sequence by switching the positions between adjacent servers. Lemma 1 guarantees that these operations do not affect access time. $\square$

4.2.2 Multi-installment strategy

In this section, as opposed to the idea of retrieving the movie portions from each server in one installment, we attempt to design a strategy in which each server takes part in the retrieval process for more than one installment. This strategy is referred to as *multi-installment* strategy.

Thus, starting from server S_0 to S_{N-1}, the individual portions retrieved in the first installment are, $m_{0,0}, \ldots, m_{N-1,0}$, in the second installment we have, $m_{0,1}, \ldots, m_{N-1,1}$, and so on, until the n-th installment, given by, $m_{0,n-1}, \ldots,$

$m_{N-1,n-1}$, respectively. Similar to the single installment strategy, the continuity of the presentation must be guaranteed during playback using this multi-installment strategy.

4.2.2.1 Recursive equations and solution methodology

Figure 4.5 shows the entire process of this retrieval strategy. Let $m_{i,j}$ represents a portion of the total movie retrieved from server S_i during the j-th installment, where $j = 0, 1, \ldots, n - 1$. Thus, there are a total of Nn portions of the movie that are retrieved from servers S_0 to S_{N-1} in n installments. Further,

$$\sum_{i=0}^{N-1} \sum_{j=0}^{n-1} m_{(i,j)} = L \tag{4.25}$$

Let $cs_{i,j}$ denote the critical size of the corresponding portion $m_{i,j}$. Similar to (4.7), we have,

$$cs_{i,j} = \frac{(R_p - bw_i)m_{i,j}}{R_p} \tag{4.26}$$

It can be deducted from Figure 4.5 that the causal precedence relations and the continuity relationships impose the following inequalities:

$$\frac{cs_{k,0}}{bw_k} + \frac{m_{k,0}}{R_p} \geq \frac{cs_{k+1,0}}{bw_{k+1}}, \quad k = 0, 1, \ldots, N - 2. \tag{4.27}$$

For $i = 1, 2, \ldots, n - 1$, we have,

$$\frac{\displaystyle\sum_{p=k+1}^{N-1} m_{p,i-1} + \sum_{p=0}^{k-1} m_{p,i}}{R_p} \geq \frac{cs_{k,i}}{bw_i}, \quad k = 0, 1, \ldots, N - 1. \tag{4.28}$$

The *minimum* size of $m_{0,0}$, which determines the minimum critical size can be obtained by seeking the *maximization* of all other $m_{i,j}$. This goal can be achieved by using the equality relationships in (4.27) to (4.28) together with (4.25). We obtain,

$$m_{i+1,0} = m_{i,0} \left(\frac{R_p bw_{i+1}}{(R_p - bw_{i+1})bw_i} \right), \quad i = 0, 1, \ldots, N - 2. \tag{4.29}$$

For $i = 1, 2, \ldots, n - 1$, we have,

$$m_{k,i} = \left(\sum_{p=k+1}^{N-1} m_{p,i-1} + \sum_{p=0}^{k-1} m_{p,i} \right) \frac{bw_k}{R_p - bw_k}, \quad k = 0, 1, \ldots, N - 1. \tag{4.30}$$

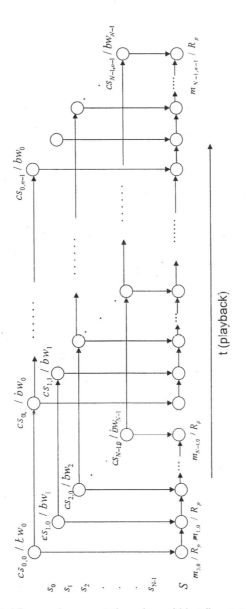

Figure 4.5. Directed flow graph representation using multi-installment strategy for movie retrieval from N servers

Since access time is now a function of both the number of servers (N) and the number of installments (n) used, we denote the access time produced by the multi-installment strategy, as $AT(N, n)$. The access time is given by

$$AT(N,n) = \frac{max\{cs_{0,0}, \delta\}}{bw_0} \qquad (4.31)$$

where $cs_{0,0}$ can be obtained by solving the recursive equations (4.29) to (4.30) together with (4.25) above. Note that the complexity of this procedure is $O(Nn)$.

4.2.2.2   Homogeneous channels

Although the generic case posed above is too complex to solve in order to obtain a closed-form solution, for the case of identical connection bandwidths we attempt to derive an expression for the access time given by the multi-installment strategy. Thus, the above set of recursive equations ((4.29) and (4.30)) can be rewritten as,

$$m_{k,0} = m_{k-1,0}\frac{R_p}{R_p - bw}, \quad k = 1, 2, \ldots, N - 1. \qquad (4.32)$$

Then, for $i = 1, 2, \ldots, n - 1$, we have,

$$m_{k,i} = \left(\sum_{p=k+1}^{N-1} m_{p,i-1} + \sum_{p=0}^{k-1} m_{p,i}\right)\frac{bw}{R_p - bw}, \quad k = 0, 1, \ldots, N - 1. \qquad (4.33)$$

Denoting $bw/(R_p - bw)$ as σ, we have,

$$m_{k,0} = m_{k-1,0}(1 + \sigma), \quad k = 1, 2, \ldots, N - 1. \qquad (4.34)$$

For $i = 1, 2, \ldots, n - 1$, we have,

$$m_{k,i} = \left(\sum_{p=k+1}^{N-1} m_{p,i-1} + \sum_{p=0}^{k-1} m_{p,i}\right)\sigma, \quad k = 0, 1, \ldots, N - 1. \qquad (4.35)$$

Now, each of the $m_{k,0}, k = 1, 2, \ldots, N - 1$ from (4.34) can be expressed as a function of $m_{0,0}$ as,

$$m_{k,0} = m_{0,0}P(\sigma, k) \qquad (4.36)$$

where, $P(\sigma, k) = (1 + \sigma)^k$. We define a transformation $k = i(n - 1) + jN$ and denote the portions of the movie retrieved from $S_0, S_1, \ldots, S_{N-1}$ in n installments as $Q_k, k = 0, 1, \ldots, Nn - 1$, where k is as defined above. Thus, with this transformation and using (4.34) and (4.35), we generate the following

$m_{i,j}$	k	j							
		0	1	2	3	4	5	6	7
0,0	0	1	0	0	0	0	0	0	0
1,0	1	1	1	0	0	0	0	0	0
2,0	2	1	2	1	0	0	0	0	0
3,0	3	1	3	3	1	0	0	0	0
0,1	4	0	3	6	4	1	0	0	0
1,1	5	0	2	8	10	5	1	0	0
2,1	6	0	1	8	17	15	6	1	0
3,1	7	0	0	6	22	31	21	7	1

Table 4.1. Coefficients table for multi-installment strategy

Table 4.1. We have shown the table for $N = 4$ and $n = 2$ case. The entries in each row of the table are the coefficients of the respective powers of σ. Thus, the maximum number of columns and rows will be 7, i.e., $(Nn \quad 1)$. As an example, $m_{1,1}$ corresponds to the row Q_5, given by (4.35) as $m_{0,0}(2\sigma + 8\sigma^2 + 10\sigma^3 + 5\sigma^4 + \sigma^5)$, and the entries in the table are precisely these coefficients of the various powers of σ. Thus, generalizing this idea, we have the following (boundary) conditions and a recursive definition to generate a particular entry $E(i, j)$ in the table for arbitrary N and n. The boundary conditions that generate entries for the first installment $n = 0$ are given by,

$$E(k, 0) - 1, \quad \forall k - 0, 1, \ldots, N - 1, \tag{4.37}$$

$$E(k, 0) = 0, \quad \forall k - N, \ldots, Nn - 1, \tag{4.38}$$

$$E(k, j) - 0, \quad \forall j > k, \text{ and } k, j - 0, 1, \ldots, Nn - 1, \tag{4.39}$$

$$E(k, j) = E(k - 1, j - 1) + E(k - 1, j), \quad \forall k = 1, 2, \ldots, N - 1 \tag{4.40}$$

Note that the first entry $E(0, 0)$ is always assumed to be equal to 1, for normalization purposes. Now, for the remaining rows, $Q_N, Q_{N+1}, \ldots, Q_{Nn-1}$, $\forall k = N, N + 1, \ldots, Nn - 1$, $j = 1, 2, \ldots, Nn - 1$, we have,

$$E(k, j) = \sum_{p-k-N+1}^{k-1} E(p, j - 1), \tag{4.41}$$

Thus, in the example, we have for $Q_5 = m_{1,1} = m_{0,0}(E(5, 0) + E(5, 1)\sigma + \ldots + E(5, 4)\sigma^4 + E(5, 5)\sigma^5)$. This is the polynomial shown above. Following this notion, we can write $m_{i,j}$ as,

$$m_{i,j} = Q_k = m_{0,0} \sum_{i=0}^{k} E(k,i)\sigma^i, \quad \forall k = 1, 2, \ldots, Nn - 1, \qquad (4.42)$$

We have a total of Nn unknowns with $(Nn - 1)$ equations. As in the previous section, together with the normalizing equation,

$$m_{0,0} \sum_{i=0}^{Nn-1} \sum_{j=0}^{i} E(i,j)\sigma^j = L \qquad (4.43)$$

we have a total of Nn equations to solve for all the unknowns. Note that each of the $m_{i,j}$ can be expressed in terms of $m_{0,0}$, by using (4.43), we obtain,

$$m_{0,0} = \frac{L}{\displaystyle\sum_{i=0}^{Nn-1} \sum_{j=0}^{i} E(i,j)\sigma^j}, \qquad (4.44)$$

where, $E(i,j)$ is generated by using (4.37) to (4.41). Thus, given a set of N video servers having identical connection bandwidths, we obtain the optimal sizes of the movie portions to be retrieved from each server by using (4.37) to (4.44).

4.2.2.3   Asymptotic analysis

It is of natural interest to examine the impact of using a large number of servers and large number of installments, as both these parameters influence the performance. It may be noted that the parameter n is software-tunable, and hence the system designers can use this parameter to improve the performance by increasing the number of installments whenever there are fewer servers available for servicing. At the same time, when the system is large, the number of installments that can be used may be small. Thus, the flexibility of tuning the parameters (N and n) of the system serves as a QoS assurance to the client by the service provider. Finally, we will attempt to derive asymptotic performance bounds when the number of installments tends to be large (infinity) and the number of servers in the system is large (theoretically tending to infinity). These bounds serve as invaluable measures in quantifying the performance of the system. That is, we want to obtain:

$$AT(N, \infty) = \lim_{n \to \infty} AT(N, n) \qquad (4.45)$$

$$AT(\infty, n) = \lim_{N \to \infty} AT(N, n) \qquad (4.46)$$

Using (4.37) through (4.41), we can rewrite (4.43) as,

$$m_{0,0}\Gamma = L \tag{4.47}$$

where Γ is given by,

$$\Gamma = \left[\sum_{i=0}^{Nn-1} E(i,0) + \sigma \sum_{i=0}^{Nn-1} E(i,1) + \ldots + \sigma^{Nn-1} \sum_{i=0}^{Nn-1} E(i, Nn-1) \right]$$

Equation (4.47) can be written as

$$m_{0,0} \left(\sum_{j=0}^{Nn-1} R(j)\sigma^j \right) = L \tag{4.48}$$

where,

$$R(j) = \sum_{i=0}^{Nn-1} E(i,j) \tag{4.49}$$

and is defined as the coefficient of σ^j in (4.48). In order to evaluate (4.45), we need to compute,

$$\lim_{n \to \infty} m_{0,0} = \lim_{n \to \infty} \left(\frac{L}{\sum_{j=0}^{Nn-1} \sigma^j R(j)} \right) \tag{4.50}$$

From (4.41),

$$\lim_{n \to \infty} R(j) = \sum_{i=0}^{\infty} E(i-1, j-1) + \sum_{i=0}^{\infty} E(i-2, j-1)$$

$$+ \ldots + \sum_{i=0}^{\infty} E(i-N+1, j-1) \tag{4.51}$$

which, upon using (4.37) through (4.40), reduces to:

$$\lim_{n \to \infty} R(j) = (N-1) \lim_{n \to \infty} R(j-1) \tag{4.52}$$

However, from (4.37) we know that,

$$R(0) = N \tag{4.53}$$

Hence,

$$\sum_{j=0}^{\infty} \sigma^j \left(\lim_{n \to \infty} R(j) \right) = N + N(N-1)\sigma + N(N-1)^2\sigma^2$$
$$+ \quad N(N-1)^3\sigma^3 + \ldots \tag{4.54}$$

The above equation can be further simplified depending on the condition we impose on the factor $(N-1)\sigma$. The following are the two different cases which may arise.

Case 1: $(N-1)\sigma < 1$
For this case, it can be readily seen that (4.54) can be written as

$$\sum_{j=0}^{\infty} \sigma^j \lim_{n \to \infty} R(j) = \frac{N}{1-(N-1)\sigma} \tag{4.55}$$

Thus,

$$\lim_{n \to \infty} m_{0,0} = \frac{(1-(N-1)\sigma)}{N} L \tag{4.56}$$

Case 2: $(N-1)\sigma \geq 1$
For this case, it is obvious that (4.54) will not converge to a finite value. Thus, it can be seen that

$$\lim_{n \to \infty} m_{0,0} = 0 \tag{4.57}$$

Now, we shall evaluate (4.46). From (4.37) through (4.41), we observe that as $N \to \infty$, $\sum_{i=0}^{Nn-1} \sum_{j=0}^{i} E(i,j)\sigma^j \to \infty$. This means that,

$$\lim_{N \to \infty} m_{0,0} = 0 \tag{4.58}$$

Summarizing the results, we have,

$$AT(N,\infty) = \frac{1-(N-1)\sigma}{(1+\sigma)Nbw} L, \quad if \ (N-1)\sigma < 1 \tag{4.59}$$
$$= 0, \quad \text{otherwise} \tag{4.60}$$
$$AT(\infty,n) = 0, \tag{4.61}$$

Further, (4.59) can be rewritten as,

$$AT(N,\infty) = \left(\frac{R_p - Nbw}{NbwR_p} \right) L \tag{4.62}$$

Now, when the number of installments is chosen to be sufficiently large and for a given bw, in order to obtain a specified (user defined or guaranteed by the service provider) access time, we can derive the minimum number of servers required as:

$$N_{min} = \left\lceil \frac{R_p L}{(R_p AT + L)bw} \right\rceil \tag{4.63}$$

On the other hand, when N is fixed, the minimum bandwidth needed to achieve a desired access time is given by,

$$bw_{min} = \left\lceil \frac{R_p L}{(R_p AT + L)N} \right\rceil \tag{4.64}$$

We shall testify the above theoretical findings through simulation tests later in this chapter.

4.3.   Buffer Management at Client Sites

The client's system requirements have always been considered as one of the most important concerns during the design and implementation of the system. The main reason for the concern lies in the fact that any successful commercial application should always assume minimum requirements at the client site for the service to be attractive.

By and large, one of the most important requirements at the client site refers to the minimum amount of buffer size expected. The buffer space requirements include the space to store the incoming stream under normal conditions, the buffer space needed to prevent overflow situations under abnormal conditions, and the buffer space that the local media-player[4] requires for implementing its VCR-like control functions such as rewind, fast-forward, pause, stop, etc.

4.3.1   Analysis on buffer occupancy

The client buffer size demanded by the PWR single installment strategy, B_{single}, can be derived as follows. Since the buffer occupancy is different at

---

[4]Different media-players may impose different requirements for a smooth playback

different intervals of retrieval durations, we have:

$$
\begin{aligned}
B_{single} \;&= \tag{4.65}\\[4pt]
&= \sum_{i=0}^{N-1} bw_i t, \text{ if Condition A1}\\[4pt]
&= \sum_{i=0}^{N-1} bw_i t - \alpha R_p(t - AT_{single}), \text{ if Condition B1}\\[4pt]
&= m_0 + \sum_{i=1}^{N-1} bw_i t - \alpha R_p(t - AT_{single}), \text{ if Condition C1}\\[4pt]
\cdots \\[4pt]
&= \sum_{i=0}^{j-1} m_i + \sum_{i=j}^{N-1} bw_i t - \alpha R_p(t - AT_{single}), \text{ if Condition D1}\\[4pt]
\cdots \\[4pt]
&= \sum_{i=0}^{N-2} m_i + bw_{N-1}t - \alpha R_p(t - AT_{single}), \text{ if Condition E1}\\[4pt]
&= \sum_{i=0}^{N-1} m_i - \alpha R_p(t - AT_{single}), \text{ if Condition F1}
\end{aligned}
$$

where, the conditions $A1$ to $F1$ are as follows.

Condition A1: Condition A1: $0 \le t < AT_{single}$

Condition B1: $AT_{single} \le t < \dfrac{m_0}{bw_0}$

Condition C1: $\dfrac{m_0}{bw_0} \le t < \dfrac{m_1}{bw_1}$

Condition D1: $\dfrac{m_{j-1}}{bw_{j-1}} \le t < \dfrac{m_j}{bw_j}$

Condition E1: $\dfrac{m_{N-2}}{bw_{N-2}} \le t < \dfrac{m_{N-1}}{bw_{N-1}}$

Condition F1: $\dfrac{m_{N-1}}{bw_{N-1}} \le t \le (\dfrac{L}{R_p} + AT_{single})$

In the above equations AT_{single} denotes the access time achieved by the PWR single-installment strategy. α is a parameter controlling the buffer occupancy, either, by flushing the buffer that is currently consumed ($\alpha = 1$), or, by retaining the retrieved data without flushing until the end of the presentation ($\alpha = 0$). The former case is typical of an application such as *pay-per-view* kind of movie services and the latter is typical of an application such as *interactive* movie viewing services on networks. Thus, any value of $0 \leq \alpha \leq 1$, is a measure of the extent to which interactivity is provided by the service provider. Hence, depending on the current network and server loading conditions, the service provider may vary the value of α for clients, thus exercising different levels of interactivity with the server systems. This may also be a measure of QoS and hence the pricing for users may be varied as per a client's interactive requirements.

When $\sum_{i=0}^{N-1} bw_i \leq \alpha R_p$, the minimum buffer size[5] expected of single installment retrieval strategy would be,

$$B_{single}^{min} = \sum_{i=0}^{N-1} \frac{bw_i}{bw_0} cs_0 \qquad (4.66)$$

However, when $\sum_{i=0}^{N-1} bw_i > \alpha R_p$, B_{single} will increase until portion m_j has been totally retrieved from server S_j, where $\sum_{i-j}^{N-1} bw_i \geq \alpha R_p$ and $\sum_{i-j+1}^{N-1} bw_i < \alpha R_p$. Then, B_{single}^{min} would be

$$B_{single}^{min} = \sum_{i=0}^{j} m_i + \sum_{i=j+1}^{N-1} \left(\frac{bw_i}{bw_j} m_j \right) - \alpha R_p (\frac{m_j}{bw_j} - AT_{single}) \qquad (4.67)$$

---

[5]We denote this as B_{single}^{min}.

Similarly, the size of buffer space demanded by the PWR multi-installment strategy B_{multi}, is given by,

$$B_{multi} = \qquad\qquad (4.68)$$

$$= \sum_{i=0}^{N-1} bw_i t, \text{ if Condition A2}$$

$$= \sum_{i=0}^{N-1} bw_i t - \alpha R_p(t - AT_{multi}), \text{ if Condition B2}$$

$$= \sum_{i=0}^{n-1} m_{(0,i)} + \sum_{i=1}^{N-1} bw_i t - \alpha R_p(t - AT_{multi}), \text{ if Condition C2}$$

$$\cdots$$

$$= \sum_{j=0}^{k-1}\sum_{i=0}^{n-1} m_{j,i} + \sum_{i=k}^{N-1} bw_i t - \alpha R_p(t - AT_{multi}), \text{ if Condition D2}$$

$$\cdots$$

$$= \sum_{j=0}^{N-2}\sum_{i=0}^{n-1} m_{j,i} + bw_{N-1} t - \alpha R_p(t - AT_{multi}), \text{ if Condition E2}$$

$$= \sum_{j=0}^{N-1}\sum_{i=0}^{n-1} m_{j,i} - \alpha R_p(t - AT_{multi}), \text{ if Condition F2}$$

where, the conditions $A2$ to $F2$ are as follows.

Condition A2: $0 \le t < AT_{multi}$

Condition B2: $AT_{multi} \le t < \dfrac{\sum_{i=0}^{n-1} m_{0,i}}{bw_0}$

Condition C2: $\dfrac{\sum_{i=0}^{n-1} m_{0,i}}{bw_0} \le t < \dfrac{\sum_{i=0}^{n-1} m_{1,i}}{bw_1}$

Condition D2: $\dfrac{\sum_{i=0}^{n-1} m_{k-1,i}}{bw_{k-1}} \le t < \dfrac{\sum_{i=0}^{n-1} m_{k,i}}{bw_k}$

Condition E2: $\dfrac{\sum_{i=0}^{n-1} m_{N-2,i}}{bw_{N-2}} \le t < \dfrac{\sum_{i=0}^{n-1} m_{N-1,i}}{bw_{N-1}}$

Condition F2: $\dfrac{\sum_{i=0}^{n-1} m_{N-1,i}}{bw_{N-1}} \le t \le \left(\dfrac{L}{R_p} + AT_{multi}\right)$

In the above equations AT_{multi} denotes the access time achieved by the PWR multi-installment strategy. Now, in the case of $\sum_{i=0}^{N-1} bw_i \leq \alpha R_p$, the minimum

of buffer size demanded by multi-installment retrieval strategy[6] would be

$$B_{multi}^{min} = \sum_{i=0}^{N-1} \frac{bw_i}{bw_0} cs_{0,0} \qquad (4.69)$$

In the case of $\sum_{i=0}^{N-1} bw_i > \alpha R_p$, B_{multi} will increase until portion $m_{j,n-1}$, the

last portion from server S_j, has been totally retrieved, where $\sum_{i=j}^{N-1} bw_i \geq \alpha R_p$

and $\sum_{i=j+1}^{N-1} bw_i < \alpha R_p$. Then, B_{multi}^{min} would be,

$$
\begin{aligned}
B_{multi}^{min} &= \sum_{i=0}^{j}\sum_{k=0}^{n-1} m_{i,k} + \sum_{i=j+1}^{N-1} \left(\frac{bw_i}{bw_j} \sum_{k=0}^{n-1} m_{j,k} \right) \\
&\quad - \alpha R_p \left(\frac{\sum_{k=0}^{n-1} m_{j,k}}{bw_j} - AT_{multi} \right) \qquad (4.70)
\end{aligned}
$$

4.3.2 Buffer size availability constraints

As the buffer size is of fixed-size in any commercially available client machine, it will be wiser if the pre-allocated space during system initialization for this VoD application can be reused without further invoking a memory allocation service from the operating system. Clearly, if the OS renders a smaller than appropriate buffer space an overflow will be caused resulting in jitters during presentation. On the other hand, a larger than required buffer will not improve system performance. As far as the performance of this strategy is concerned, an important question to address is as follows: *Given a buffer size of B bits at the client site, can we expect a continuous presentation by using the PWR multi-installment strategy?* To answer this question, we need to consider both the buffer occupancy and the access time. For the ease of analysis, we only consider the case of homogeneous channels and set $\alpha = 1$. Note that $\alpha = 1$

---

[6]We denote this as B_{multi}^{min}.

implies that the system is of *pay-per-view* kind of service framework.

In order to compute the minimum buffer size expected at the client site, we need to determine exactly the time instants at which these servers finish transferring their last installments to the client. When $\sum_{i=0}^{N-1} bw_i < \alpha R_p$, from (4.62) and (4.69), we deduce

$$\lim_{n \to \infty} B_{multi}^{min} = \left(\frac{R_p - Nbw}{R_p} \right) L \qquad (4.71)$$

However, when $\sum_{i=0}^{N-1} bw_i \geq \alpha R_p$, it is complex to determine the time instants at which these servers finish transferring their last movie portion except from the last server. To clarify this aspect, we now consider an example that allows us to explicitly derive the equations that govern the time instants at which these servers finish transferring their last installments.

Example 1. Consider a scenario in which the requested movie is supplied by 3 servers, S_0, S_1 and S_2 by using multi-installment strategy. From (4.35) we have,

$$\begin{aligned} m_{2,i} &= \sigma(m_{1,i} + m_{0,i}) \\ m_{1,i} &= \sigma(m_{0,i} + m_{2,i-1}) \\ m_{0,i} &= \sigma(m_{2,i-1} + m_{1,i-1}), \quad i = 0, 1, \ldots, n-1 \end{aligned} \qquad (4.72)$$

Further, (4.72) can be rewritten as,

$$\begin{aligned} \sum_{i=0}^{n-1} m_{2,i} &= \sigma \left(\sum_{i=0}^{n-1} m_{1,i} + \sum_{i=0}^{n-1} m_{0,i} \right) \\ \sum_{i=0}^{n-1} m_{1,i} &= \sigma \left(\sum_{i=0}^{n-1} m_{0,i} + \sum_{i=0}^{n-2} m_{2,i} \right) \\ \sum_{i=0}^{n-1} m_{0,i} &= \sigma \left(\sum_{i=0}^{n-2} m_{2,i} + \sum_{i=0}^{n-2} m_{1,i} \right) \end{aligned} \qquad (4.73)$$

Note that when we divide the left sides of each of the above expressions by the connection bandwidth bw, we can compute the time instants at which the last installment will be completed. Now, we have,

$$\frac{\sum_{i=0}^{n-1} m_{2,i}}{\sum_{i=0}^{n-1} m_{1,i}} = (1+\sigma) - \sigma \left(\frac{\sum_{i=0}^{n-2} m_{2,i}}{\sum_{i=0}^{n-1} m_{1,i}} \right) \tag{4.74}$$

Further,

$$\frac{\sum_{i=0}^{n-1} m_{1,i}}{\sum_{i=0}^{n-2} m_{2,i}} = \sigma(1+\sigma \left(1 + \frac{\sum_{i=0}^{n-2} m_{1,i}}{\sum_{i=0}^{n-2} m_{2,i}} \right)) \tag{4.75}$$

When the number of installments tends to be large (infinity), $n \to \infty$, we realize that

$$\frac{\sum_{i=0}^{n-1} m_{k,i}}{\sum_{i=0}^{n-1} m_{j,i}} = \frac{\sum_{i=0}^{n-2} m_{k,i}}{\sum_{i=0}^{n-2} m_{j,i}} \tag{4.76}$$

This means that the ratio of the sizes of the loads between different servers remains more-or-less identical when a very large number of installments is considered. Thus, by using (4.75) and (4.76) in (4.74), we have,

$$\frac{\sum_{i=0}^{\infty} m_{2,i}}{\sum_{i=0}^{\infty} m_{1,i}} = (1+\sigma) - \left(1 + \sigma(1 + \frac{\sum_{i=0}^{\infty} m_{1,i}}{\sum_{i=0}^{\infty} m_{2,i}}) \right)^{-1} \tag{4.77}$$

Similarly we have,

$$\frac{\sum_{i=0}^{\infty} m_{1,i}}{\sum_{i=0}^{\infty} m_{0,i}} = (1+\sigma) - \left(1 + \frac{\sum_{i=0}^{\infty} m_{2,i}}{\sum_{i=0}^{\infty} m_{1,i}} \right)^{-1} \tag{4.78}$$

From (4.77) and (4.78) we conclude,

$$\frac{\sum_{i=0}^{\infty} m_{2,i}}{\sum_{i=0}^{\infty} m_{1,i}} = \frac{\sum_{i=0}^{\infty} m_{1,i}}{\sum_{i=0}^{\infty} m_{0,i}} \tag{4.79}$$

Equation (4.79) means that the loads on these 3 servers, from S_0 to S_2, form a geometric progression. In fact, this holds true for using any number of servers. Now denoting the ratio between the loads on the adjacent servers as γ, we can express,

$$\sum_{i=0}^{\infty} m_{j,i} = \gamma^j \sum_{i=0}^{\infty} m_{0,i} \tag{4.80}$$

Further,

$$\sum_{i=0}^{\infty} m_{N-1,i} = \gamma^{N-1} \sum_{i=0}^{\infty} m_{0,i} = \frac{bwL}{R_p} \tag{4.81}$$

Thus solving equation (4.81) we obtain the value of γ. Together with (4.70), we have:

$$\lim_{n \to \infty} B_{multi}^{min} = \left(\sum_{i=0}^{N-M-1} \left(\frac{bw}{R_p} \gamma^{i-N+1} \right) - \frac{Mbw}{R_p} \gamma^{-M} - \gamma^{-M} \right) L \tag{4.82}$$

where,

$$M = \left\lfloor \frac{R_p}{bw} \right\rfloor \tag{4.83}$$

The minimum buffer size required by the PWR multi-installment strategy is derived under the assumption that the number of installments is very large ($n \to \infty$). Thus, in reality when the number of installments is finite, the client needs at least a buffer size equal to B_{multi}^{min} obtained from either (4.71) or (4.82). Otherwise, when the available amount of buffer at the client site is less than the required amount, the client will not be able to handle the incoming data. In this case, the client is not qualified to request the servers to transmit movie data. This problem could be considered as a part of the admission control mechanism.

4.4.   Performance Evaluation of PWR: Single and Multi-installment Strategies

In this section, we evaluate the performance of the PWR single installment and multi-installment retrieval strategies through a number of simulation studies. In the simulation experiments to be presented later in this chapter, we consider the case when the connection bandwidths are identical, i.e., $bw_i = bw$

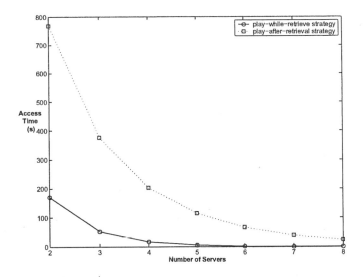

Figure 4.6.   Access time vs. number of servers using PWR and PAR: single installment strategy

for all the channels. The movie size L is assumed to be 2Gbits, and the playback rate R_p is 1.5Mbps.

4.4.1   Behavior of access time

We first see the performance of the single installment strategy. As it is evident from the closed-form solution, the access time decreases monotonically as we tend to utilize more and more number of servers. Figure 4.6 shows this behavior of the access time with respect to the number of servers utilized. The connection bandwidth bw is 1Mbps. In the figure, we have shown the plots using both PWR single installment strategy and PAR single installment strategy, respectively. As expected, the access time decreases because the requested movie is available on more servers. From these plots we observe that the PWR single installment strategy remarkably outperforms the PAR single installment strategy on minimizing the access time. Typically, when using 3 servers, the access time of PAR single installment strategy is 376.16 seconds. However, the access time of PWR single installment strategy is 52.51 seconds. Thus, we gain a significant decrease of 86.04% in this case.

In the case of the multi-installment strategy, we have two parameters, the number of servers and the number of installments, to control the retrieval procedure. First, we see the influence of the number of servers on the access time. Figure 4.7 shows the behavior of the access time with respect to the number of

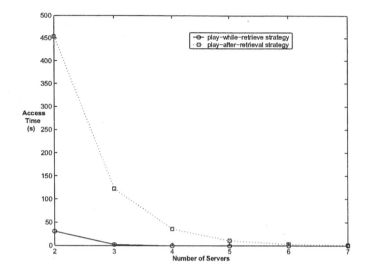

Figure 4.7. Access time vs. number of servers with $n = 2$ using PWR and PAR: multi-installment strategy

servers, while in the simulation experiments the number of servers is varied from 2 onwards. The connection bandwidth bw is 1Mbps. In this figure, we have shown the plots using both PWR and PAR multi-installment strategies corresponding access times when $n = 2$. From these plots we observe that the PWR multi-installment strategy also outperforms the PAR multi-installment strategy. For example, when using 3 servers, the access time of PAR multi-installment strategy is 122.19 seconds. However, the access time of PWR multi-installment strategy is 2.42 seconds. Thus, we gain a striking reduction of 98.02%. Comparing the performance shown in Figure 4.7 with Figure 4.6, we observe that there is a significant reduction on the access time between PWR multi-installment and single installment strategies. Typically, in the case of using 3 servers, we gain a reduction of 95.39%.

The effect of the number of installments on the access time is shown in Figure 4.8. The number of servers considered in this experiment is 3 while the number of installments is varied from 2 onwards. Further, in order to evaluate the effect of the connection bandwidth on the access time, we use two different connection bandwidths, 0.45Mbps and 0.6Mbps, respectively. From the results, we observe that when the number of installments is increased the access time using both PWR and PAR multi-installment strategies tend to decrease at first. Then the access time using either strategy tends to quickly saturate to a value when

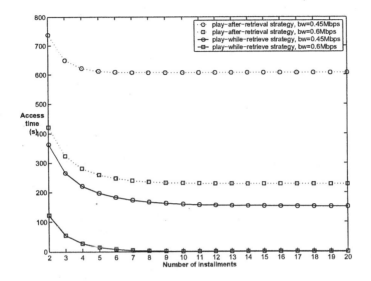

Figure 4.8. Access time vs. number of installments using PWR and PAR: multi-installment strategy

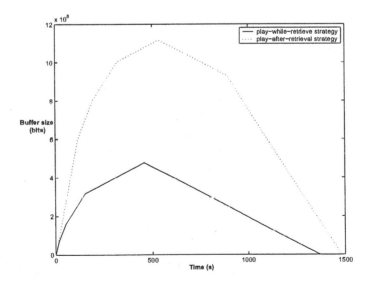

Figure 4.9. Client buffer occupancy using PWR and PAR: single installment strategy

the number of installments is increased indefinitely. Also, it may be observed that the saturation of the access time is quick in the case of the PAR strategy when compared with the PWR strategy. The plots also reveal the fact that even with smaller connection bandwidths the PWR strategy has a clear advantage of yielding a minimum access time when compared with the PAR strategy with higher connection bandwidths. Further, using the PWR strategy, in the case of $Nbw \geq R_p$, the saturation value of the access time is 0, otherwise, this value is given by (4.62).

4.4.2   Quantifying client buffer requirements

We now evaluate the buffer requirements at the client site. We set $\alpha = 1$. First, we consider the single installment retrieval strategy employing 5 servers S_0 to S_4 with connection bandwidths of 1Mbps. Figure 4.9 shows the behavior of buffer occupancies at the client site with respect to time t, using both the PWR and the PAR single installment strategies.

As expected, the buffer requirement using the PWR single installment strategy is much less than that of the PAR single installment strategy. In simulation experiments, the maximum buffer space expected by the former strategy is 457Mbits and for the latter it is 1.041Gbits. Thus, we have a reduction of 57.13% on buffer requirement. The influence of α on buffer requirements can be seen by varying α in the range [0,1], as shown in Figure 4.10. Thus we observe that regardless of the α value, the buffer requirement imposed by the PWR single installment strategy is smaller than that of the PAR single installment strategy. Typically, when $\sigma = 1$, we gain a significant reduction of 57.13% on the buffer requirement. Even at $\alpha = 0.5$, we also gain a reduction of 30.35% on the buffer requirements. Now we consider the multi-installment retrieval strategy employing 5 servers S_0 to S_4 using connection bandwidths of 0.3Mbps and the number of installments of 4. The behavior of buffer requirement using multi-installment retrieval strategy is demonstrated by Figure 4.11. In this figure, we show the buffer occupancies at the client site with respect to time t using both the PWR and the PAR multi-installment strategies. From the results, the maximum buffer needed by PWR strategy is 215.6Mbits, while the maximum buffer needed by the PAR strategy is 317.8Mbits. Thus, we have a decrease of 32.16% on the buffer requirement. While this behavior is somewhat identical to the single installment strategy, the behavior becomes interesting if we take the effect of connection bandwidth into consideration. We show the effect of the connection bandwidth on the buffer requirement in Figure 4.12. In this experiment, the connection bandwidth is varied from 0.1Mbps onwards. We observe that the buffer requirement reaches a minimum value at a point where the cumulative connection bandwidth becomes equal to the playback rate of the movie. Afterwards, the buffer requirement trend seems to increase for

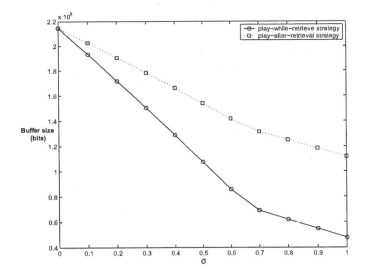

Figure 4.10. Client buffer size vs. α using PWR and PAR: single installment strategy

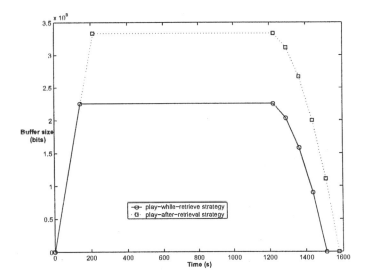

Figure 4.11. Client buffer occupancy using PWR and PAR: multi-installment strategy

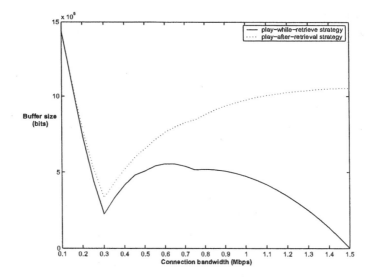

Figure 4.12. Client buffer occupancy vs. connection bandwidth using PWR and PAR: multi-installment strategy

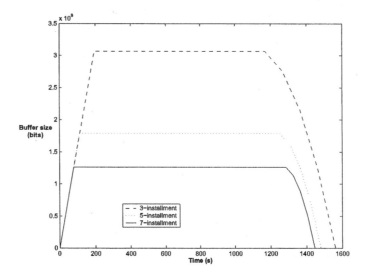

Figure 4.13. Client buffer occupancy vs. number of installments using PWR multi-installment strategy

both the strategies although the PWR strategy clearly wins the race. Another observable effect is that for large connection bandwidth magnitudes, the buffer requirement tends to decrease faster for PWR while the requirement continues to increase in the case of the other strategy. This is due to the fact that in the PWR multi-installment strategy, as the connection bandwidth approaches the playback rate, the access time approaches zero and the video stream storage requirements diminish.

The effect of the number of installments on the buffer requirements is shown on Figure 4.13 for the PWR strategy. The number of servers considered is 5 with connection bandwidths of 0.3Mbps. Clearly, using a larger number of installments minimizes the buffer requirements at the client site. Typically, we obtain a reduction of 58.82% in buffer requirement between 3-installment strategy (292.6Mbits) and 7-installment strategy (120.5Mbits) are used.

4.4.3 Effect of load balancing

From our earlier experiments, we observed that the server loads (uploading duties) are not identical and hence it would be interesting to quantify the ratios of the amount of loads rendered by adjacent servers with respect to different connection bandwidths. First, we consider the PWR single installment strategy. We define the ratios as $R_i = m_i/m_{i-1}$, $i = 1, ..., 4$. The connection bandwidth in this experiment is varied from 0.3Mbps onwards. Figure 4.14 shows the ratios of loads on adjacent servers using PWR single installment strategy. From the results, we observe that $R_i = R_j$, $\forall i \neq j$, for a given bandwidth. Also, the sizes of the portions rendered by different servers, S_0 to S_{N-1}, form a geometric progression.

Now, we consider the PWR multi-installment strategy. Figure 4.15 shows the ratios of loads on adjacent servers using PWR multi-installment strategy with connection bandwidths of 0.5Mbps. As in the previous experiment, we define the ratios as $R_i = \sum_{j=0}^{n-1} m_{i,j} / \sum_{j=0}^{n-1} m_{i-1,j}$,
$i = 1, ..., 4$. As the number of installments increases, the ratios of loads rendered by adjacent servers become identical, i.e., $R_i = R_j$, $\forall i \neq j$, and even in this case, as testified by the theoretical findings earlier, we observed that the sizes of the portions rendered by different servers, S_0 to S_{N-1}, form a geometric progression.

From the above experiment, we know that the ratios of loads rendered by adjacent servers become identical by using a relative large number of installments. Our next experiment aims to examine the impact of connection bandwidths on the load ratios, by varying the connection bandwidths starting at 0.1Mbps onwards. Figure 4.16 shows the ratios of loads on adjacent servers using the PWR multi-installment strategy. We observe that the ratio remains at 1 when

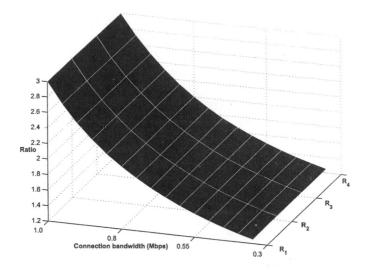

Figure 4.14. Loads on servers vs. connection bandwidth using PWR single installment strategy

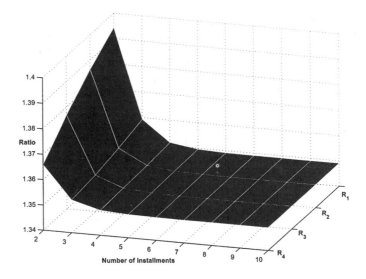

Figure 4.15. Loads on servers using PWR multi-installment strategy

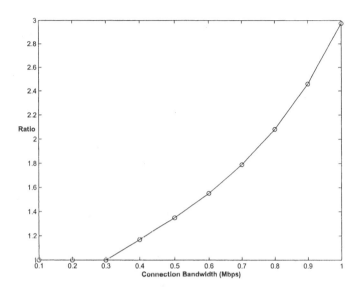

Figure 4.16. Loads on servers vs. connection bandwidth using PWR multi-installment strategy

$Nbw \leq R_p$. Afterwards, the ratio increases when the connection bandwidth is increased. Further, comparing Figure 4.14 with Figure 4.16, we observe that the ratio of the PWR multi-installment strategy is slightly smaller than the PWR single installment strategy one, at a given connection bandwidth.

4.5. Concluding Remarks

In this chapter, we have presented a generalized approach to the theory of retrieving a long-duration movie requested by a client using a network based multimedia service infrastructure. For a network based environment, we have designed and analyzed an efficient PWR playback strategy to minimize the access time of the movie. The analysis clearly highlights the advantages of the strategy when compared to a PAR approach. Further, with the novel design, we have shown that both the playback strategies (PWR and play after retrieve(PAR)) can in turn choose to retrieve the movie portions using either single installment or multi-installment retrieval strategies. Thus playback strategies are basically concerned about *how* and *when* to initiate the playback while retrieval strategies are concerned about *how* to retrieve the movie data from the servers. The use of PWR or PAR depends on the application requirements. For instance, for a pay-per-view kind of multimedia service, PWR is suitable as it is also shown to expect a minimum buffer requirement, given by (4.71) or (4.82), at the client site. However, when an interactive service is to be provided, PAR is the natural choice, although the client is expected to have a bigger buffer size compared to the PWR strategy, as shown in the simulation experiments. Furthermore, for the pay-per-view service with the PWR strategy, depending on server availabilities, one may tune the number of installments to suit client buffer availability. This is clearly evident from the results shown in Figure 4.13. Of course, when the availability of servers is somewhat constrained in the system, using the multi-installment strategy may not be possible. In such situations, the single installment strategy may be meaningful, despite the larger buffer space consumption and the longer access time.

For the PWR strategy, we have derived closed-form solutions for the access time using both single installment and multi-installment retrieval strategies. Further, we have derived a closed-form expression for the *critical size* that must be retrieved prior to kick-starting the movie presentation. Also, for the PWR playback strategy employing the multi-installment retrieval strategy, we have conducted an asymptotic performance analysis. Such an asymptotic analysis elicits performance bounds on the strategies and serves as a valuable measure for tuning the system performance. For instance, together with simulation experiments, the choice on the minimum number of installments can be made depending on the saturation level of the access time. Also, the choice on the number of servers to be utilized for a given number of installments can also be quantified. The analysis presented in this chapter, followed by experimental support, clearly renders clues on client buffer management and also on tuning the servers to meet the buffer availability at the client site. Thus, the service can be attractive even to clients with low buffer space, by tuning the number of installments.

4.5.1   Some open-ended issues

There are some important issues that need careful consideration if a real-life system is to be developed on the basis of the PWR strategy. First, the transmission rates between the servers and the client should be known a-priori if the delivery schedule is to be calculated. This translates to the need to perform transmission tests in order to accurately estimate these bandwidths before any strategy is decided upon. Of course, this will consume additional time and generate more network traffic. An alternative approach might be to use the data of the requested movie in the tests, so as to compensate for such extra work. But this definitely complicates the retrieval strategy and requires some sort of schedule adaptation while the actual delivery is happening. Such techniques are discussed in Chapter 6. Chapter 6 also addresses the second concern, which is that the bandwidths must remain constant throughout the uploading procedure. Otherwise, the presentation continuity could be compromised. A third concern relates to the use of other techniques such as batching, patching, and caching, with the PWR strategy. Such a merge can lead to the conservation of the server and network resources, possibly allowing for higher system availability. Further, taking into account the available bandwidth and buffer sizes at both the server and client sides, it would become more meaningful to combine the problem of admission control and retrieval strategy. This is a very critical problem when handling multiple client requests.

In practice, most of the commercial players exercise software control for interactivity. While the interactions of Play/Stop, /Pause/Resume can be easily incorporated in our PAR/PWR schemes, other interactions, such as Fast Forward/Rewind, Fast Search/Reverse Search and Slow motion, are major challenges to be considered.

Bibliographic Notes

Following are the published papers somewhat closer to the context of this chapter. Most of the contributions in this chapter appear in [71]. In the design of parallel server architectures, the concepts of using a *concurrent push* [67] or a *pull-based* [65] scheme have been proposed. In the pull-based design shown in [65], the need for inter-server synchronization is completely eliminated and also by a careful design of admission control algorithm the loads across the serves are carefully balanced. There is also a third approach that incorporates a proxy at the client site [66]. With this scheme, a proxy located at the client machine is responsible for requesting and processing data, thus avoiding further network communications. There are some differences between the service model employed in [66, 67, 65] and the model adopted in this chapter. In the former model, the video data is basically partitioned and stored (striped) across many servers, and hence, each server can render only the portions that are stored with it. Also, the data that is stored across these servers are of uniform sized stripes. However, the model adopted in the design of MSR strategies, in general, assumes that the entire movie is available at some servers (just as in conventional video rental stores) and each server is *scheduled* to retrieve only a portion of the movie. Also, the MSR strategies allow non-uniform sized portions to be retrieved from the servers in view of minimizing the access time on a highly delay-sensitive networked environment. Thus, the model in the latter study explicitly accounts for any non-zero communication delays in the process of minimizing the access time, while the studies in [66, 67, 65] are more suited when communication delays are negligible[7]. In fact, [28] extends

---

[7]Distributing the data across the servers/disks is very similar to the striping employed by RAID (see section 1.3

and generalizes the treatment followed in [105] for the case of multiple servers and multiple clients and also carries out load balancing across the servers.

Apart from the recent attempts employing multiple servers in the literature mentioned in Chapters 2 and 3, there are a lot of studies in the literature focused on the design methodologies for different aspects of a VoD system. Techniques such as batching [2, 27], chaining [94, 95] patching [22, 50] and piggybacking [42, 43] have been investigated. Some of these techniques can be also combined to improve the efficiency further [38, 64, 77]. The effects of different techniques to reduce the aggregate bandwidth requirements are evaluated in [76], while providing interactivity for a VoD system. These techniques include server replication, program caching in intermediate nodes and user sharing of video streams and caches. Further, an excellent compilation and comparison of various multicast VoD techniques and implementations proposed in the literature until 2001 appears in [73].

There is also a lot of research devoted in designing retrieval scheduling strategies for broadcasting. These include, pyramid broadcasting [109], permutation-based pyramid broadcasting [3] and skyscraper broadcasting [51]. In these schemes, basically, the idea is to partition each movie into several segments and broadcast them periodically, towards a goal of achieving a minimum access time. However, broadcasting schemes have the inherent disadvantage of making the client wait through the entire broadcast batch to get his/her choice [41] and they usually require high-end client capabilities.

Furthermore, the problem of data organization and storage is well studied in the literature [78, 88, 113]. Some studies also focus on the design of movie buffer caching strategies for effectively utilizing the memory and reducing disk I/O overheads [26] and dynamic network resource allocation for improving transmission rates with low jitter variation in media streams [32]. The work in [85] considers employing multiple servers to retrieve multimedia objects, but from a different objective. In this work, the authors design a scheduling scheme, referred to as an *application layer broker*(ALB), at the client site. Typically, a client negotiates with a group of servers and identifies the best server to retrieve an object. This scheme attempts to minimize the buffer space requirements at the client site.

Chapter 5

SCHEDULING OVER UNRELIABLE CHANNELS

5.1.   Nothing Is Certain But Death And Taxes!

The main problem associated with the deployment of the methods described in the previous chapters is their dependence on fixed, a-priori-known parameters about the state of the network, that do not change for the duration of the data upload process. While this can be relatively safely assumed about the availability of the servers, it cannot be assumed, at least given the current state of affairs on the public Internet, about the bandwidth parameters bw_i.

In this chapter we explore ways of relaxing the scheduling constraints that stem from the constant system parameters. We still assume that bandwidths bw_i are constant in order to be able to derive a closed-form solution to the partitioning, scheduling and playback problems, but our model incorporates the features necessary to statistically address this deficiency in a systematic manner.

This chapter presents the modified system model and associated derivations, while Chapter 6 addresses the issue of how to use the new model capabilities towards adapting to network variability.

5.2.   A Refined Model

The changes made to the system model aim at providing not only an even more realistic approach at describing the target process, but also at facilitating the flexibility to adjust the schedule in response to network problems such as packet losses.

The communication cost for each server S_i is assumed to be equal to $bw_i \cdot m_i \cdot L + o_i$, where o_i is a constant overhead, bw_i is the (inverse of the) bandwidth and m_i the percentage of the L-sized data that S_i needs to upload. A number of factors can contribute to a server's o constant, such as the communication round-trip-time (RTT), setup costs, the cost of establishing a connection or any other fixed cost activities. The overhead o_i can also be utilized to indicate when server S_i becomes available for contributing to the delivery of a document. This feature is used in Chapter 6 to accommodate network variability in the derived schedules.

This model has been shown to provide adequate accuracy in many cases [7] while at the same time being more true-to-life than the simpler linear one used in the previous chapters. In the sections that follow, a server's communication characteristics are noted as the pair $S_i(bw_i, o_i)$.

Any communication over the Internet (TCP or UDP based) involves the breakup of the message into packets. Each packet contains additional routing and other information resulting in an increase of the actual transmitted data. The analysis that follows is based on the assumption that each server's bandwidth relates to how fast the "bare" document can be communicated, effectively allowing us to ignore the overhead associated with packaging.

In order to cater for the unreliable nature of the communication media, the upload schedule that is computed for each server is extended so that it allows the transmission of additional data. In particular, each server is "clocked" for the transmission of $c\, m_i\, L$, where c is the *relaxation parameter* satisfying $c \geq 1$. Effectively, each server is allowed to utilize its connection for $c - 1$ percent more time (see Fig. 5.1(a)). The implications of this policy are the following:

- If packet losses or other causes, delay the delivery of the m_i portion of the document, more download time is available *without any disturbance* to the playback schedule.

- The additional data could overlap with the ones delivered by another server, e.g. S_{i+1}, a technique that has been suggested in [92] for parallel FTP access. For example, the $(c - 1)\, m_i\, L$ portion of the data could be identical with the last portion of the data delivered by server S_{i+1}. If traffic prevents the timely delivery of part m_{i+1}, the data delivered by S_i could prevent the appearance of interruptions in the playback. This possibility is well worth investigating, but it is not studied further in this book.

Obtaining the packet loss probability can be accomplished by monitoring previous transfers, while prediction can also be performed via Markov-chain models [63]. It should be noted that although, we assume fixed values for all the problem parameters, the proposed partitioning and delivery scheme can be used in a completely adaptive fashion, regularly modifying the delivery schedule in response to network/server state changes. Dynamic schedule adaptation is explicitly treated in Chapter 6.

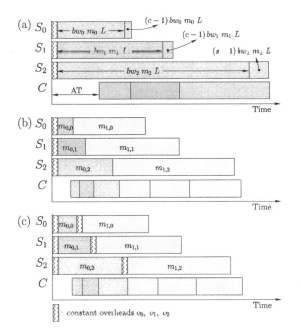

Figure 5.1. Example of delivering a document to a client C by 3 servers, using (a) a single installment strategy, (b) two-installments with a single overhead per server and (c) two-installments with multiple overheads. Figure (a) features a breakdown of the time costs involved, including the extra time provided for transmission (e.g. $(c-1)\,bw_0 m_0 L$ for S_0). Colour indexing associates the downloaded parts with portions of the play-back operation.

The playback can start while the data are being downloaded (same as the PWR strategy of Chapter 4). The only constraint is that playback has to finish -at least- δ time units after the download ends. δ is a consequence of the fact that current video encoding standards organize the data stream into Groups Of Pictures (GOP) that have to be decoded in a certain order. For a video stream that consists only of intra-coded (I) and predicted (P) frames δ is equal to the time needed to download one frame. If bidirectional (B) frames are utilized, the delay has to be extended to the time needed to download a GOP. In practice, we can, either, use a fixed delay of a few seconds (e.g. 1-10), or, use the time that would be required by the slowest link to download a GOP.

Thus, for a single server, the continuity constraints under the model used in this chapter, would be expressed as follows if AT is the access time (a.k.a. initiation latency [39]) and R is the playback rate of the document (expressed for convenience in sec/MB as bw):

$$AT + R\,L \geq c\,bw + o + \delta \tag{5.1}$$

In a direct analogy to the use of parameters o_i for scheduling currently busy servers (see discussion in Sections 6.3 and 5.3.2.1), we can manipulate δ to accommodate interrupt-free scheduling of Variable-Bit-Rate (VBR) documents as shown in section 5.4.

The conditions and relationships that should be satisfied for this approach to work for a Constant-Bit-Rate (CBR) document, are presented in the following section. The model used in this chapter can be considered a refinement of the one used in Chapter 4, although no critical size is identified for each server. Instead, parameter δ and the continuity inequalities discussed in the next section, guarantee interrupt free playback.

An overview of the cases examined in the following sections is presented in Fig. 5.1 in the form of simple examples. Both single and multi-installment strategies are examined for CBR content, while section 5.4 extends these for Variable Bit Rate (VBR) content.

For convenience, we summarize the notations used in this Chapter in Table 5.1.

5.3. CBR Case

5.3.1 Single-Installment Case

Although a single installment approach has been shown to yield inferior results [105], we present the associated analysis here for completeness. Additionally, as it is shown in Chapter 6, the single-installment strategy can be the basis of a robust dynamic scheduling scheme that adapts to changing system conditions effectively.

An example of a single-installment strategy is shown in Fig. 5.1(a). Based on this and the discussion on δ of the previous section, we can deduce that the following inequalities should hold for each of the N servers:

$$AT + m_0\,R\,L \geq c\,m_0\,L\,bw_0 + o_0 + \delta \tag{5.2}$$

$$AT + (m_0 + m_1)\,R\,L \geq c\,m_1\,L\,bw_1 + o_1 + \delta \tag{5.3}$$

$$AT + (m_0 + m_1 + m_2)\,R\,L \geq c\,m_2\,L\,bw_2 + o_2 + \delta \tag{5.4}$$

$\cdots$

Table 5.1. Notations

bw_i	the inverse of the bandwidth of the connection between server S_i and client C	mp_i	percent of movie downloaded by server S_i that has been played back
bw_C	the inverse of the bandwidth of the client's connection (sec/MB)	N	number of servers
c	schedule relaxation parameter	o_i	overhead associated with starting a download from S_i
CP	percent confidence on the delivery schedule	p_i	packet loss probability for server S_i connection
D_i	equal to $c\,bw_i - R$	R	the inverse of the playback rate of the requested movie (sec/MB)
$G_{j,i}$	equal to $\frac{m_{j,i}L}{sz\,p_i}$	sz	payload of each packet
L	size of requested document (MB)	v	upper limit of fraction $\frac{X_{j,i}-\mu}{\sigma}$
m_i	percent of document to be delivered by server S_i for a single installment schedule	$X_{j,i}$	random variable describing how many packets from server S_i are dropped during installment j
$m_{j,i}$	percent of document, scheduled to be delivered by server S_i during installment j	δ	time delay introduced in the schedule to accommodate out-of-order frame decoding
md_i	percent of movie downloaded by server S_i	μ	mean of normal distribution followed by $X_{j,i}$
M	number of installments	σ^2	variance of normal distribution followed by $X_{j,i}$

$$AT + (m_0 + m_1 + \cdots + m_{N-1})\,R\,L \geq c\,m_{N-1}\,L\,bw_{N-1} + o_{N-1} + \delta \quad (5.5)$$

It is obvious that in order to obtain the minimum AT, inequalities (5.2) to (5.5) must be solved by using the equal sign. The result is the following formula that connects the portions assigned to successive pairs of servers:

$$m_i = m_{i-1}\frac{c\,bw_{i-1}}{c\,bw_i - R} + \frac{o_{i-1} - o_i}{L(c\,bw_i - R)} \quad (5.6)$$

where $i = 1, \ldots, N - 1$. Eq. (5.6) opens the road to expressing each m_i $\forall\, i : 0, \ldots, N - 1$ as a function of m_0:

$$m_i = m_0 \frac{c^i \prod_{k=0}^{i-1} bw_k}{\prod_{k=1}^{i}(c\, bw_k - R)} +$$

$$\frac{1}{L} \sum_{k=0}^{i-1} \frac{c^{i-1-k}(o_k - o_{k+1}) \prod_{j=k+1}^{i-1} bw_j}{\prod_{j=k+1}^{i}(c\, bw_j - R)} \quad (5.7)$$

where it is assumed that $\prod_{n_1}^{n_2} \cdots = 1$ and $\sum_{n_1}^{n_2} \cdots = 0$ if $n_1 > n_2$.

Thus, finding m_0 becomes only a matter of using the normalization equation, i.e.

$$\sum_{i=0}^{N-1} m_i = 1 \quad (5.8)$$

which yields:

$$m_0 = \frac{1 + \frac{1}{L} \sum_{n=1}^{N-1} \sum_{i=0}^{n-1} \frac{c^{n-1-i}(o_{i+1}-o_i) \prod_{j=i+1}^{n-1} bw_j}{\prod_{j=i+1}^{n}(c\, bw_j - R)}}{1 + \sum_{n=1}^{N-1} \frac{c^n \prod_{i=0}^{n-1} bw_i}{\prod_{i=1}^{n}(c\, bw_i - R)}} \Rightarrow$$

$$m_0 = \frac{1 + \frac{1}{L} \sum_{n=1}^{N-1} \frac{c^n \prod_{j=0}^{n-1} bw_j}{\prod_{j=1}^{n}(c\, bw_j - R)} \left(\sum_{i=0}^{n-1} \frac{(o_{i+1}-o_i) \prod_{j=1}^{i}(c\, bw_j - R)}{c^{i+1} \prod_{j=0}^{i} bw_j} \right)}{1 + \sum_{n=1}^{N-1} \frac{c^n \prod_{i=0}^{n-1} bw_i}{\prod_{i=1}^{n}(c\, bw_i - R)}}$$

$$(5.9)$$

Access time can then be computed from Eq.(5.2):

$$AT = \delta + o_0 + (c\, bw_0 - R)L\, m_0 \quad (5.10)$$

The above equations provide for an $O(N)$ time complexity solution of the partitioning problem, given a fixed, pre-determined server order. The order here refers to the fact that the downloading of the individual portions from the servers follow a specific sequence. A typical sequence could be, S_4, S_0, S_2, S_1, S_3, assuming that there are 5 servers in the system. This means that the first portion is downloaded from server S_4, the second portion from S_0, and so on. The problem of optimally ordering the servers is addressed in Section 5.5.

A similar derivation to the above can yield the solution when a different 're-laxation' constant c is used for each server, i.e. c_i. This would be desirable when each server connection exhibits different loss characteristics. In this case, Eq. 5.9 becomes:

$$m_0 = \frac{1 + \frac{1}{L}\sum_{n=1}^{N-1} \frac{\prod_{j=0}^{n-1} c_j \, bw_j}{\prod_{j=1}^{n}(c\,bw_j - R)}\left(\sum_{i=0}^{n-1} \frac{(o_{i+1} - o_i)\prod_{j=1}^{i}(c\,bw_j - R)}{\prod_{j=0}^{i} c_j \, bw_j}\right)}{1 + \sum_{n=1}^{N-1} \frac{\prod_{i=0}^{n-1} c_i \, bw_i}{\prod_{i=1}^{n}(c\,bw_i - R)}}$$

(5.11)

In order for an *equivalent* server to offer the same AT, the following equation should hold:

$$AT + L\,R = c\,bw_{equiv}L + o_{equiv} + \delta \qquad (5.12)$$

Substituting (5.10) into (5.12) and by using Eq. (5.9), it can be shown that the N servers behave like a single equivalent server with attributes:

$$bw_{equiv} = \frac{bw_0}{1 + B} + \frac{R}{c}\frac{B}{1 + B} \qquad (5.13)$$

and

$$o_{equiv} = o_0 + \frac{c\,bw_0 - R}{1 + B}F \qquad (5.14)$$

where $F = \sum_{n=1}^{N-1} \frac{c^n \prod_{j=0}^{n-1} bw_j}{\prod_{j=1}^{n}(c\,bw_j - R)}\left(\sum_{i=0}^{n-1} \frac{(o_{i+1} - o_i)\prod_{j=1}^{i}(c\,bw_j - R)}{c^{i+1}\prod_{j=0}^{i} bw_j}\right)$.

The buffering requirements of the proposed method, if we assume that the data are discarded once viewed (like using $\alpha = 1$ in Section 4.3), can be computed as follows: At any given time $t \geq AT$, the data that have been displayed and thus removed from the buffers are equal to $\frac{t - AT}{R}$. At time $t = AT$ the maximum volume of data that have been received by the client is:

$$\sum_{i=0}^{N-1} max\left(0, \frac{min\,(AT, o_i + m_i bw_i L) - o_i}{bw_i}\right) \qquad (5.15)$$

where the max function caters for the possibility of $AT < o_i$, while the min function covers the case of $AT > o_i + m_i bw_i L$, guarding against calculating the part uploaded by server S_i in excess of $m_i L$.

After playback has started, the rate that data are buffered, changes only when a server completes its part of the transmission. The buffer requirements are maximized when the links do not suffer any losses, which translates to the following buffer requirements at the end of each S_j server transmission:

$$L\left(\sum_{i=0}^{j} m_i + m_j bw_j \sum_{i=j+1}^{N-1} bw_i^{-1}\right) +$$

$$+ \sum_{i=j+1}^{N-1} \frac{o_j - o_i}{bw_i} - max\left(0, \frac{o_j + bw_j m_j L - AT}{R}\right) \qquad (5.16)$$

for $\forall j : 0, \ldots, N - 1$, where $max\left(0, \frac{o_j + bw_j m_j L - AT}{R}\right)$ are the data that have been already "consumed". The maximum of the $N + 1$ quantities given by Eq. (5.15) and (5.16) produces the maximum buffer requirements for the multi-server distribution. It should be noted that when all servers are identical, Eq. (5.16) reduces to:

$$L\left(\frac{D^{j+1} - 1}{D^N - 1} + \frac{D - 1}{D^N - 1} D^j (N - j - 1)\right) -$$

$$max\left(0, \frac{o + bw \frac{D-1}{D^N-1} D^j L - AT}{R}\right) \qquad (5.17)$$

where $D = \frac{c\,bw}{c\,bw - R}$ and $m_0 = \frac{D-1}{D^N-1}$.

The following lemma shows exactly how much packet loss can be tolerated by our approach without the introduction of playback interrupts.

Lemma 1. *The maximum packet loss percentage any server connection can endure without disturbing the playback is equal to* $\frac{c-1}{c}$.

Proof. If S_i's connection suffers a PL percent packet loss, then its effective bandwidth reduces to $\frac{bw_i}{1-PL}$. Without loss of generality, lets assume that while the client is playing the document part delivered by S_i, it has displayed the $m_0 + m_1 + \ldots mp_i$ portion of the document, where $mp_i \leq m_i$. If at the same time S_i has uploaded $md_i\,L$ data, i.e.

$$AT - \delta - o_i + (m_0 + m_1 + \cdots + m_{i-1})\,R\,L + mp_i\,R\,L =$$

$$= md_i\,L\frac{bw_i}{1 - PL} \qquad (5.18)$$

then ensuring the continuity of the document presentation means that the following should hold:

$$mp_i \leq md_i \Rightarrow mp_i\,L\frac{bw_i}{1 - PL} \leq md_i\,L\frac{bw_i}{1 - PL}$$

which through Eq. (5.18) becomes

$$mp_i \, L\frac{bw_i}{1 - PL} \leq$$
$$AT - \delta - o_i + L\left(m_0 + m_1 + \cdots + m_{i-1}\right)R + mp_i \, L \, R \quad (5.19)$$

By using Eq. (5.5) (substitute i for $N - 1$), Equation (5.19) becomes:

$$mp_i \, L\frac{bw_i}{1 - PL} \leq c \, m_i \, L \, bw_i - m_i \, R \, L + mp_i \, L \, R \Rightarrow$$

$$mp_i \, L\left(\frac{bw_i}{1 - PL} - R\right) \leq m_i \, L \, (c \, bw_i - R) \quad (5.20)$$

Since it is obvious that $mp_i \leq m_i$, inequality (5.20) becomes

$$(1 - PL)^{-1} \leq c \Rightarrow PL \leq \frac{c - 1}{c}$$

$\square$

The equations presented above can be simplified further under special circumstances. In the case of identical servers (i.e. $bw_i \equiv bw$ and $o_i \equiv o$) Eq. (5.9) is reduced to:

$$m_0 = \frac{\frac{c \, bw}{c \, bw - R} - 1}{\left(\frac{c \, bw}{c \, bw - R}\right)^N - 1} \quad (5.21)$$

If only the constant communication overheads are the same, $o_i \equiv o$, Eq. (5.9) and (5.10) become:

$$m_0 = (1 + B)^{-1} \quad (5.22)$$

and

$$AT = \delta + o_0 + L\frac{c \, bw_0 - R}{1 + B} \quad (5.23)$$

where $B = \sum_{n=1}^{N-1} \frac{c^n \prod_{i=0}^{n-1} bw_i}{\prod_{i=1}^{n}(c \, bw_i - R)}$. In this case (i.e. $o_i = o$), if we denote by $AT^{(N)}$ the access time offered by a group of N servers and by $AT^{(0)}$ the one achieved by S_0 only, then

$$AT^{(0)} - AT^{(N)} = L \, (c \, bw_0 - R)\frac{B}{1 + B} \quad (5.24)$$

which is also an indication of the improvement a multi-server distribution can offer in the general case (i.e. when $o_i \neq o$).

5.3.2   Multi-Installment Case

In the single-installment case, it is assumed that each server incurs a start-up overhead before actual data transmission. When a multi-installment strategy is employed, there are two possibilities related to the start-up overhead: (a) one start-up per server and (b) one start-up for each installment. In the following subsections we examine both possibilities:

5.3.2.1   Single Overhead

The overhead in this case can be associated with setup costs, or even denotes a server's *release time*, i.e., the time instant some of its resources are released, allowing the server to service the specific request. An example is shown in Fig. 5.1(b). If for example a server X is expected to become available for uploading data after a time instance t_X^{rel}, by setting $o_X = t_X^{rel}$, we can incorporate server X in the delivery schedule.

In order to guarantee the playback's continuity , the following inequalities should hold for the first installment, where $m_{j,i}$ denotes the j-th installment of the i-th server:

$$AT + m_{0,0}\, R\, L \geq c\, m_{0,0}\, L\, bw_0 + o_0 + \delta \qquad (5.25)$$

$$AT + (m_{0,0} + m_{0,1})\, R\, L \geq c\, m_{0,1}\, L\, bw_1 + o_1 + \delta \qquad (5.26)$$

$$\cdots$$

$$AT + R\, L \sum_{k=0}^{N-1} m_{0,k} \geq c\, m_{0,N-1}\, L\, bw_{N-1} + o_{N-1} + \delta \qquad (5.27)$$

For the second installment we have:

$$AT + R\, L\, m_{1,0} + R\, L \sum_{k=0}^{N-1} m_{0,k} \geq$$
$$c\, (m_{0,0} + m_{1,0})\, L\, bw_0 + o_0 + \delta \quad (5.28)$$

$$AT + R\, L\, (m_{1,0} + m_{1,1}) + R\, L \sum_{k=0}^{N-1} m_{0,k} \geq$$
$$c\, (m_{0,1} + m_{1,1})\, L\, bw_0 + o_1 + \delta \quad (5.29)$$

In general, for M installments and $\forall\, j = 0 \ldots M - 1$, the i-th server during the j-th installment should satisfy:

$$AT + R\,L\,\left(\sum_{k=0}^{i} m_{j,k} + \sum_{n=0}^{j-1}\sum_{k=0}^{N-1} m_{n,k}\right) \geq$$

$$c\,L\,bw_i \sum_{k=0}^{j} m_{k,i} + o_i + \delta \quad (5.30)$$

Minimizing AT suggests solving inequalities (5.25) to (5.30) by using the equality sign. Subtracting the equation governing the j-th installment of S_i server, from the equation governing the j-th installment of S_{i+1}, we obtain $\forall\,i = 0, \ldots, N-2$ and $\forall\,j = 0, \ldots, M-1$:

$$R\,L\,m_{j,i+1} = o_{i+1} - o_i + c\,L\,bw_{i+1} \sum_{k=0}^{j} m_{k,i+1} - c\,L\,bw_i \sum_{k=0}^{j} m_{k,i} \Rightarrow$$

$$m_{j,i+1} =$$

$$\frac{o_i - o_{i+1} + c\,L\,bw_i \sum_{k=0}^{j} m_{k,i} - c\,L\,bw_{i+1} \sum_{k=0}^{j-1} m_{k,i+1}}{L\,(c\,bw_{i+1} - R)} \quad (5.31)$$

Similarly, subtracting the equation governing the j-th installment of S_{N-1} server, from the equation governing the $(j+1)$-th installment of S_0, we get $\forall\,j = 0, \ldots, M-2$:

$$R\,L\,m_{j+1,0} = o_0 - o_{N-1} + c\,L\,bw_0 \sum_{k=0}^{j+1} m_{k,0} - c\,L\,bw_{N-1} \sum_{k=0}^{j} m_{k,N-1} \Rightarrow$$

$$m_{j+1,0} =$$

$$\frac{o_{N-1} - o_0 + c\,L\,bw_{N-1} \sum_{k=0}^{j} m_{k,N-1} - c\,L\,bw_0 \sum_{k=0}^{j} m_{k,0}}{L\,(c\,bw_0 - R)} \quad (5.32)$$

Equations (5.31), (5.32) are complemented by the normalization equation,

$$\sum_{j=0}^{M-1}\sum_{i=0}^{N-1} m_{j,i} = 1 \quad (5.33)$$

to form a set of $N \cdot M$ linear equations. The coefficients of the equations form a band-triangular matrix. A fast method for solving this system of equations is described in the next subsection.

5.3.2.2   Multiple Overheads

Each server S_i incurs a constant overhead o_i at the beginning of each install-ment. An example is shown in Fig. 5.1(c). A scenario that would fit this profile is when each server re-evaluates the strategy of what data to transmit during the excess $(c-1)$ time. Tracing the same steps as in the previous case, we can show that for the i-th server during the j-th installment:

$$AT + RL \left(\sum_{k=0}^{i} m_{j,k} + \sum_{n=0}^{j-1} \sum_{k=0}^{N-1} m_{n,k} \right) \geq$$

$$c\,L\,bw_i \sum_{k=0}^{j} m_{k,i} + (j+1)\,o_i + \delta \quad (5.34)$$

Similarly, the equation governing the j-th installment of S_{i+1} is $\forall\, i = 0, \ldots, N-2$ and $\forall\, j = 0, \ldots, M-1$:

$$m_{j,i+1} = \frac{(j+1)\,(o_i - o_{i+1}) + c\,L\,bw_i \sum_{k=0}^{j} m_{k,i}}{L\,(c\,bw_{i+1} - R)} -$$

$$\frac{c\,L\,bw_{i+1} \sum_{k=0}^{j-1} m_{k,i+1}}{L\,(c\,bw_{i+1} - R)} \quad (5.35)$$

and the equation governing the $j+1$-th installment of S_0 is $\forall\, j = 0, \ldots, M-2$:

$$m_{j+1,0} = \frac{(j+1)\,(o_{N-1} - o_0) - o_0 +}{L\,(c\,bw_0 - R)} +$$

$$\frac{c\,L\,bw_{N-1} \sum_{k=0}^{j} m_{k,N-1} - c\,L\,bw_0 \sum_{k=0}^{j} m_{k,0}}{L\,(c\,bw_0 - R)} \quad (5.36)$$

Again, the normalization equation (5.33) completes the set of $N \cdot M$ linear equations which form a band-triangular matrix.

Unfortunately, the above sets of equations are too difficult to handle in order to produce a closed-form solution to the problem, as in the case of a single installment. Even under the assumption of homogeneity ($bw_i \equiv bw\ and\ o_i \equiv o\ \forall\, i$) seeking a closed-form is difficult.

However, the solution can still be computed very quickly, as the equations are recursive in nature. Moreover, equations (5.31), (5.32), (5.35) and (5.36) can all be shown to produce an affine connection between individual $m_{j,i}$ parts and $m_{0,0}$:

$$m_{j,i} = A_{j,i} m_{0,0} + B_{j,i} \quad (5.37)$$

The constants $A_{j,i}$ and $B_{j,i}$ can only be determined after the calculation of the constants $A_{l,k}$ and $B_{l,k}$, $\forall k < i$ if $j = l$, or $\forall k$ if $l < j$. For both the single and multiple overhead cases, $A_{0,0} = 1$, $A_{0,1} = (c\, bw_0 - R)^{-1}$ and $B_{0,0} = B_{0,1} = 0$.

Calculating the constants $A_{j,i}$ and $B_{j,i}$ for all j, i pairs, requires approximately N steps for the first installment and $2\, j\, N$ steps for each of the other $j = 1, \ldots, M - 1$ installments. Thus, given $O(N \cdot M)$ memory, we need

$$N + 2N \sum_{j=1}^{M-1} j = N + 2N\, M\, \frac{M-1}{2} = O\left(N \cdot M^2\right) \qquad (5.38)$$

computations for computing all $A_{j,i}$ and $B_{j,i}$. An additional $O(N \cdot M)$ operations are required for calculating $m_{0,0}$ from Equation (5.33):

$$m_{0,0} \sum_{j=0}^{M-1} \sum_{i=0}^{N-1} A_{j,i} + \sum_{j=0}^{M-1} \sum_{i=0}^{N-1} B_{j,i} = 1 \qquad (5.39)$$

followed by $O(N \cdot M)$ more operations to complete the calculation of all $m_{j,i}$s via Eq.(5.37).

A natural question that needs to be addressed at this juncture is on the number of installments to be used. This matter is treated extensively in Section 5.7.

It should be noted that if the above set of equations return negative values for the parts $m_{j,i}$, then this means that the document can be delivered faster than it can be played-back, i.e. fewer servers can be used.

5.4. VBR Case

Equations (5.9),(5.7) are based on the assumption that the download rate will be able to keep pace with the playback rate. This may very well not be the case for VBR movies that can have wildly varying rates depending on the scene content. An example is shown in Figure 5.2. Even CBR content is in reality VBR if you consider intra-GOP frame size. Average GOP sizes remain constant though, allowing us to treat this case differently.

As reported in the literature [25], the statistical distribution of the frame sizes is a heavy-tailed one. This presents a difficulty for modeling VBR traffic, but under the problem settings as outlined in this paper, we need only to determine whether the playback time of any movie frame exceeds its expected delivery time.

In such a case, the AT has to be increased by adding a delay δ_{vbr}, i.e.

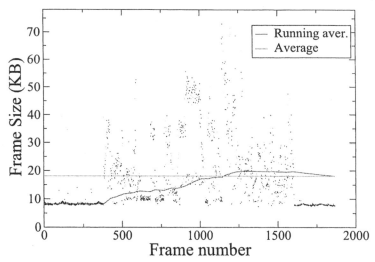

Figure 5.2. Frame sizes over time for the 78sec MPEG-4 coded trailer of the movie *Matrix Revolutions*. The 640x256 movie was coded with the Xvid codec (http://www.xvid.org). The size of the PCM-coded audio is incorporated in the frame sizes.

replacing δ in the Equations of the previous Section with $\delta + \delta_{vbr}$. Since Equations (5.9), (5.7) do not contain a reference to δ, parts $m_0, \ldots, m_{N-1}$ remain unchanged by this modification.

δ_{vbr} needs to satisfy the following:

$$AT + \delta_{vbr} + \frac{i}{fps} \geq deliver(i) \qquad (5.40)$$

where $deliver(i)$ is the expected delivery time of frame $i : 0, \ldots, n-1$, for a movie with n frames and a rate of fps frames per second. $deliver(i)$ can be computed once the delivery schedule is known. Then we can proceed to estimate $deliver(i)$, for $\forall\, i : 0 \ldots n - 1$ as follows:

$$deliver(i) = \mu\, o_j +$$

$$c\, bw_j \left(\sum_{l=0}^{i} fr(l) - L \left(\sum_{l=0}^{k-1} \sum_{\forall\, p \neq j} m_{l,p} + \sum_{l=0}^{j-1} m_{k,l} \right) \right) \qquad (5.41)$$

where S_j is the server delivering the last bytes of frame i, during installment k. where $fr(i)$ is the size of the i-th frame (including audio data). μ is, either, 1 for the single-, or k for the multiple-overhead case. Please note that Equation (5.41) is based on the assumption that the frames are stored within the movie stream in the same order they are played back, which is of course false for B-frames. This is though, a small discrepancy that is in-any-case rectified by the original δ parameter of our model.

The minimum δ_{vbr} that satisfies Equation (5.40) is:

$$\delta_{vbr} = max_{\forall\ i}\left(deliver(i) - AT - \frac{i}{fps}\right) \qquad (5.42)$$

and it has to be computed on-line for each instance of the movie uploading problem.

To avoid having to compute δ_{vbr} on-line, we can calculate a worst-case alternative based on R, i.e. we have to find a value for δ_{vbr} that keeps the running average of the playback rate always below R:

$$\delta_{vbr}^{offline} = max_{\forall\ i}\left(R\sum_{k=0}^{i}fr(k) - \frac{i}{fps}\right) \qquad (5.43)$$

$\delta_{vbr}^{offline}$ yields a pessimistic schedule but since it depends solely on the movie characteristics, it needs to be computed only once.

For the example shown in Figure 5.2, $\delta_{vbr}^{offline}$ is found to be equal to 6.16sec for $R = 2.363s/MB$, $L = 32.95MB$, $fps = 24$ and $n = 1872$. The value of the delay δ_{vbr} for the delivery of the movie through two servers $S_0(10sec/MB, 1sec)$ and $S_1(10sec/MB, 1sec)$ with $p = 0.1$, $sz = 1500$ and a confidence of 95% (see Section 5.6 for more on this issue) is equal to 5.46sec.

To these numbers we should add an extra delay to cater for the download of all the information needed for the decoding of a frame, as has been discussed earlier for δ. For this particular example where the video stream consists only of I and P frames, this additional delay is zero.

5.5. Optimum Server Ordering

In the case of heterogeneous servers, e.g. different o and/or bw attributes, the order that servers are assigned a portion of the movie, influences the access time. This does not contradict the results reported in Chapter 2 and in [105], where it is assumed that $o_i = 0$. Solving the ordering problem for the simplest possible case of having just two servers, offers valuable insight for solving the general problem. For two servers and a single installment, the two possible configurations are shown in Fig. 5.3.

In the following paragraphs, we focus on the single-overhead case but it

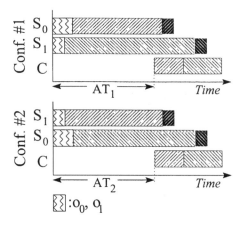

Figure 5.3. The two possible configurations that two servers can be arranged to deliver a document. Inverted patterns depict extra time provided for recovering from network errors.

should be noted that the same results can be shown to apply in the multiple-overheads case as well.

There are only two possible configurations: in configuration #1 S_0 delivers the very first part of the document, while in configuration #2 S_1 does so. For one installment, we can use Equations (5.9) and (5.10) to compute the difference between $AT_1^{(1)}$ and $AT_2^{(1)}$, where the subscript indicates the configuration and the superscript indicates the number of installments:

$$AT_1^{(1)} - AT_2^{(1)} = \frac{(o_0 - o_1)R}{c\,bw_0 + c\,bw_1 - R} \qquad (5.44)$$

For two installments, $m_{0,0}$ and $AT_1^{(2)}$ can be computed from Equations (5.25)-(5.30), by subtracting the formula for $m_{i,1}$ from $m_{i,0}$ $(i = 0, 1)$ and the formula for $m_{j,0}$ from $m_{j-1,1}$ $(j = 1)$. A similar procedure can be applied for $AT_2^{(2)}$. Then, it can be shown that:

$$AT_1^{(2)} - AT_2^{(2)} =$$

$$\frac{(o_0 - o_1)R^3}{c\,bw_0 R^2 + c^2 bw_0^2 (c\,bw_1 - R) + (c\,bw_0 - R)(c\,bw_1 - R)^2} =$$

$$= \frac{(o_0 - o_1)R^3}{c\,bw_0 R^2 + D_1\left[D_0 D_1 + c^2 bw_0^2\right]} \qquad (5.45)$$

where $D_0 = (c\,bw_0 - R)$ and $D_1 = (c\,bw_1 - R)$. In both Eq. (5.44) and (5.45) the difference of ATs has the same sign as the $(o_0 - o_1)$ difference, as the denominator is positive.

If we apply the same procedure for a three-installment situation, it can be proven that:

$$AT_1^{(3)} - AT_2^{(3)} =$$

$$\frac{(o_0 - o_1)R^5}{c\,bw_0R^4 + D_1\left[D_0^2D_1^2 + c^2\,bw_0^2\left[D_0D_1 + R^2\right]\right]} \quad (5.46)$$

Similarly, for four installments:

$$AT_1^{(4)} - AT_2^{(4)} =$$

$$\frac{(o_0 - o_1)R^7}{c\,bw_0R^6 + D_1\left[D_0^3D_1^3 + c^2\,bw_0^2\left[D_0^2D_1^2 + R^2D_0D_1 + R^4\right]\right]} \quad (5.47)$$

and for five installments we have:

$$AT_1^{(5)} - AT_2^{(5)} = \frac{(o_0 - o_1)R^9}{H} \quad (5.48)$$

where

$$H = c\,bw_0R^8 +$$
$$D_1\left[D_0^4D_1^4 + c^2\,bw_0^2\left[D_0^3D_1^3 + R^2D_0^2D_1^2 + R^4D_0D_1 + R^6\right]\right]$$

It is now straightforward from Equations (5.44)-(5.48) that the difference for M installments, in general, is given by:

$$AT_1^{(M)} - AT_2^{(M)} = \frac{(o_0 - o_1)R^{2M-1}}{J} \quad (5.49)$$

where

$$J = c\,bw_0R^{2(M-1)} +$$
$$D_1\left[D_0^{M-1}D_1^{M-1} + c^2\,bw_0^2\sum_{i=0}^{M-2}\left(R^{2(M-2-i)}D_0^iD_1^i\right)\right]$$

The importance of Equation (5.49) is that it shows that the sign of the difference depends only on the $(o_0 - o_1)$ difference as the denominator is always positive. This translates to the following:

Lemma 2. *When two servers are used to deliver a document, the minimum access time is achieved if the servers are in non-decreasing order of their respective overheads o_i.*

Proof. The proof is evident from Equation (5.49).   □

The above relates to the general case of N servers if we consider two consecutive servers S_i and S_{i+1} for $i = 0, \ldots, N - 2$ in the given server order. We can assume without loss of generality, that $o_i \leq o_{i+1}$. Lets also assume that the part of the document that these two servers deliver is a fraction f of the original, i.e. $f \leq 1$. Then, we can derive the following from Equation (5.30) for installment $j = 1, \ldots, M - 1$:

$$AT + R L \left(m_{j,i} + \sum_{k=0}^{j-1}(m_{k,i} + m_{k,i+1}) \right) + T_{i,j} =$$

$$c L\, bw_i \sum_{n=0}^{j} m_{n,i} + o_i + \delta \quad (5.50)$$

$$AT + R L \sum_{k=0}^{j}(m_{k,i} + m_{k,i+1}) + T_{i,j} =$$

$$c L\, bw_{i+1} \sum_{n=0}^{j} m_{n,i+1} + o_{i+1} + \delta \quad (5.51)$$

where $T_{i,j}$ is the duration of the playback of parts delivered by the other servers:

$$T_{i,j} = R L \left(\sum_{n=0}^{j} \sum_{k=0}^{i-1} m_{n,k} + \sum_{n=0}^{j-1} \sum_{k=i+2}^{N-1} m_{n,k} \right) \quad (5.52)$$

Lets also assume that swapping the order of servers S_i and S_{i+1} does not cause a change in the document parts that are assigned to the rest of the servers. That means that the fraction f that is collectively assigned to S_i and S_{i+1} remains the same, i.e.:

$$\sum_{n=0}^{M-1} m_{n,i} + m_{n,i} = f \quad (5.53)$$

Equations (5.50),(5.51), and (5.53) allow the computation of AT as a function of f and the parts assigned to the rest of the servers. For example, the access time for configuration #1 (i.e. S_i precedes S_{i+1}) and 2 installments is:

$$AT_1^{(2)} = o_i + \delta - T_{0,i} +$$
$$D_i \frac{c\,bw_i D_{i+1}(f\,L\,D_{i+1} - o_i + o_{i+1} - \Delta T)}{c\,bw_i R^2 + D_{i+1}\left[D_i D_{i+1} + c^2 bw_i^2\right]} -$$
$$D_i \frac{c\,bw_{i+1}(c\,bw_{i+1} - 2R)(f\,L\,R - \Delta T)}{c\,bw_i R^2 + D_{i+1}\left[D_i D_{i+1} + c^2 bw_i^2\right]} -$$
$$D_i \frac{R^2(o_i - o_{i+1} + f\,L\,R + \Delta T)}{c\,bw_i R^2 + D_{i+1}\left[D_i D_{i+1} + c^2 bw_i^2\right]} \qquad (5.54)$$

where $D_i = c\,bw_i - R$ and $D_{i+1} = c\,bw_{i+1} - R$ and $\Delta T = T_{1,i} - T_{0,i}$. Similarly we can compute $AT_2^{(2)}$ which yields the same results for $AT_1^{(2)} - AT_2^{(2)}$ as Equation (5.45):

$$AT_1^{(2)} - AT_2^{(2)} = \frac{(o_i - o_{i+1})R^3}{c\,bw_i R^2 + D_{i+1}\left[D_i D_{i+1} + c^2 bw_i^2\right]} \qquad (5.55)$$

In general, it can be shown that given a fixed part assignment to the rest of the servers, the rearrangement of S_i and S_{i+1} produces the same change in access time as predicted by Equation (5.49).

The above means that Lemma 2 is also applicable to any pair of consecutive servers:

Lemma 3. *Given any pair of consecutive servers used to deliver a document, the minimum access time is achieved if the servers are in non-decreasing order of their overheads o_i.*

Proof. Lets assume without loss of generality that $o_i \leq o_{i+1}$. Swapping the order of S_i and S_{i+1} can have two possible outcomes:

– The remaining servers get the exact same assignments. Then the lemma is correct.

– The change in server order causes a global redistribution of document delivery parts. Then, the only way that the access time for configuration #2 could be smaller, would be if the rest of the servers were assigned more load, in effect increasing AT, which proves the lemma.

$\square$

With the above we can formulate the *Optimum Server Ordering Theorem*, as follows:

Theorem 1 (Optimum Server Ordering Theorem). *In order to minimize the access time required for delivering a document via N servers $S_0, S_1, \ldots, S_{N-1}$ and M installments, the portions of the document should be assigned so that the servers are sorted in non-decreasing order of their constant communication overheads o_i.*

Proof. The theorem is a direct consequence of Lemma 3. An optimum server ordering has to satisfy the property that any pair S_i, S_{i+1} of consecutive servers must be ordered so as $o_i \leq o_{i+1}$. The only way this could be achieved is by sorting the servers in non-decreasing order of their constant communication overheads. □

If we include the sorting of the servers, the complexity of computing a delivery schedule becomes $O(N \cdot M + N \log N)$. Also, a direct consequence of the above theorem is that in the case where all o_i are the same, the order of the servers does not influence the access time. This matches the result reported in [105] and Chapter 2, where it is assumed that $o_i = 0 \; \forall i$. The above by no means implies that the servers' communication speed does not influence access time. It just states that *their optimum order does not depend on it.*

5.6. Determining the Optimum Relaxation Parameter c

The anticipated packet loss percentage $\frac{c-1}{c}$, has a significant influence on the determination of when the playback will commence. As this percentage cannot be effectively predicted and is not even constant for the duration of a document transmission, setting the value for c is a problem. If a small value is used, there is a danger of introducing playback interruptions. On the other hand if a large value is used, access time can be needlessly increased. The following example is illustrative:

Example: Lets suppose that three servers $S_0(15s/MB, 1s)$, $S_1(20s/MB, 2s)$ and $S_2(12s/MB, 1s)$ are to deliver a 1 GB document with $R = 8s/MB$ to a client with an available bandwidth of $bw_C = 5s/MB$. If we assume that no packet loss occurs, then $c = 1$, while if we assume a 10% probability loss, we have to use $c = 1.1111$. For each of these values and for $M = 1, 2, 3$ the AT will be:

M	AT for $c = 1$	AT for $c = 1.1111$	% increase
1	845.4 sec	1260.0 sec	49
2	114.6 sec	250.7 sec	118
3	20.1 sec	64.5 sec	221

The above example is indicative of how important the choice of c is. In this section we explore how the optimum c can be found given the number of installments M. It is clear that there is a strong relationship between M and c but in this chapter we will assume M to be constant. The algorithm for finding the optimum c is the basis of finding the optimum M in an attempt to adapt to network variability as explained in Chapter 6.

If $m_{j,i}$ is the document portion to be delivered by server S_i during install-ment j and sz is the packet payload, then the multi-server schedule allows for a total of $\lfloor \frac{c\, m_{j,i} L}{sz} \rfloor$ attempted packet deliveries. The packets that can be dropped without playback "hick-ups" are $\lfloor \frac{(c-1)\, m_{j,i}\, L}{sz} \rfloor$.

In the analysis that follows, we assume that the packet-loss probability fol-lows a Bernoulli distribution with a mean of p_i for the path used by server S_i. Packet-loss is usually being modeled by k-order Markov chain models [63]. The Bernoulli is the simplest of these models ($k = 0$), with more sophisticated ones (e.g. Gilbert for $k = 1$ and Extended Gilbert for $k > 1$) providing better prediction accuracy. The sine model, a variation of the Bernoulli model, where the loss probability oscillates with a 24-hour long period between a minimum and maximum value, has been also described by Arai et al. to provide better accuracy than the Gilbert model [6].

Given that we focus not on the duration or length of the loss bursts, but on the total number of lost packets during an installment, the assumption of a Bernoulli distribution is sufficient. Given all the above, the Central Limit Theorem [75] predicts that the random variable $X_{j,i}$ that describes how many packets get dropped, follows a normal distribution with mean $\mu = \left(\frac{c\, m_{j,i} L}{sz} p_i \right)$ and variance $\sigma^2 = \left(\frac{c\, m_{j,i} L}{sz} p_i (1 - p_i) \right)$. Since the ran-dom variable $\left(\frac{X_{j,i} - \mu}{\sigma} \right)$ is standard normal, we can use cumulative distribu-tion tables for obtaining an upper limit of $X_{j,i}$ that would yield a specific percentage of confidence on the robustness of the schedule.

For example, if we require that the probability of not breaching the delivery schedule during uploading $m_{j,i}\, L$, to be 95%, then,

$$P\left(X_{j,i} \leq \frac{(c-1)\, m_{j,i}\, L}{sz} \right) = P\left(\frac{X_{j,i} - \mu}{\sigma} \leq V \right) - 0.95 \rightarrow$$

$$V = 1.65 \quad (5.56)$$

where

$$V = \sqrt{\frac{c\, m_{j,i}\, L}{sz}} \sqrt{\frac{1 - p_i}{p_i}} - \frac{\sqrt{\frac{m_{j,i}\, L}{sz}}}{\sqrt{c\, p_i (1 - p_i)}} \quad (5.57)$$

Similarly, given a confidence that the schedule should provide, we can obtain the corresponding upper limit v for $\frac{X_{j,i}-\mu}{\sigma}$ (1.65 in the above example). The desired value for c can then be computed by,

$$c = \frac{v^2 + 2G_{j,i} + v\sqrt{v^2 + 4\,G_{j,i}}}{2\,G_{j,i}(1 - p_i)} \tag{5.58}$$

where $G_{j,i} = \frac{m_{j,i}L}{sz\,p_i}$. Equation (5.58) is derived directly from (5.56) and is the positive-sign solution to a quadratic equation involving $\sqrt{c}$ as the unknown. The other solution is invalid as the maximum usable v is below 3.5, while $\frac{m_{j,i}L}{sz}$ can be in the order of tens of thousands for a long duration movie, which would result in a negative value for c.

It can also be shown that

$$\frac{\vartheta c}{\vartheta m_{j,i}} = -\frac{v\left(2\,L\,m_{j,i} + p_i\,sz\,v\left(v + \sqrt{v^2 + 4\,G_{j,i}}\right)\right)}{2\,L\,m_{j,i}^2(1 - p_i)\sqrt{v^2 + 4\,G_{j,i}}} \tag{5.59}$$

which means that c decreases as $m_{j,i}$ increases. As the number of packets increases, the probability of packet losses deviating from the mean p_i becomes smaller and smaller, thus allowing for a c that is closer to $1 + p_i$.

If we assume that each of the N servers uses a different route to the client, thus allowing us to consider the $X_{j,i}$s random variables as independent, then the formula describing the probability of an interrupt-free playback becomes equal to:

$$\prod_{j=0}^{M-1} \prod_{i=0}^{N-1} P\left(X_{j,i} \le \frac{(c-1)\,m_{j,i}\,L}{sz}\right) \tag{5.60}$$

Determining c by putting a lower bound CP on Eq. (5.60) requires a prior decision on the individual values of the cumulative probabilities:

$$P\left(X_{j,i} \le \frac{(c-1)\,m_{j,i}\,L}{sz}\right)$$

The simplest solution is to assume that they are all equal. This assumption allows us to compute c as:

$$c = max_{j,i}\left(\frac{v^2 + 2G_{j,i} + v\sqrt{v^2 + 4\,G_{j,i}}}{2\,G_{j,i}(1 - p_i)}\right) \tag{5.61}$$

where $j : 0, \ldots, M - 1$, $i : 0, \ldots, N - 1$ and v is the upper bound for a standard normal variable so that its cumulative probability equals $CP^{\left(\frac{1}{N\cdot M}\right)}$.

The particular choice for c guarantees that

$$\prod_{i=0}^{N-1} P\left(X_{j,i} \leq \frac{(c-1)\ m_{j,i}\ L}{sz}\right) \geq CP$$

If all packet-loss probabilities are identical, i.e., $p_i \equiv p\ \forall i$, c can be determined by the minimum $m_{j,i}$. Since p_is cannot be easily determined or are not even constant over time for each of the communication routes used, a constant p representing worst-case behavior could be used instead to simplify our calculations.

The procedure depicted above stumbles on the fact that $m_{j,i}$s and c are interdependent. This means that the latter needs the former to compute and vice-versa! Given a value for c, from (5.58) and by solving for $m_{j,i}$, we can compute the minimum portion of the document that can be scheduled as,

$$m4c = \frac{c(1 - p_i)p_i\ sz\ v^2}{L(1 - c(1 - p_i))^2} \tag{5.62}$$

Thus, determining an optimum value of c would require the solution of a $N \cdot M$ equations of the form:

$$m_{j,i} = m4c \tag{5.63}$$

for c and selecting the largest of the $N \cdot M$ outcomes.

Each of the Eq. (5.63), for $i = 0, \ldots, N - 1$ and $j = 0, \ldots, M - 1$ can have multiple solutions. The one we are interested in, is the smallest one which is also greater than 1.

If we were to plot the curves $c = f(m, p)$ as given by Eq. (5.58) and the ones for parts $m_{j,i}$, then the intersections between the c family of curves (for each of the p_i) and the corresponding $m_{j,i}$ curves would provide the candidates for choosing the appropriate c, i.e. the minimum for a single $m_{j,i}$ curve and the maximum over all $m_{j,i}$s.

An example of this procedure is shown in Figure 5.4, where the delivery of a 100min MPEG-4 [1] MP@ML video stream by five servers using a single installment, is simulated. It is assumed that $R = 9.31sec/MB$ and $L = 645MB$ (see Section 5.8 for the reasoning behind these choices).

The server bandwidths were chosen as 10 times the corresponding Fibonacci number ($bw_0 = 10$, $bw_1 = 10$, $bw_2 = 20sec/MB$, etc.) for each server. o_is and δ were considered to be equal to 1sec, while the payload sz was

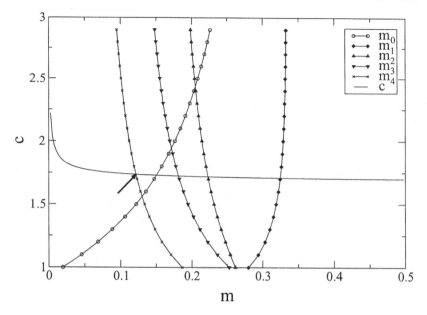

Figure 5.4. A plot showing how the individual parts m_i depend on the value of c. Also shown is a curve for c as computed from Eq. 5.58. The arrow points to the crossing which represents the optimum value for c in this particular setup.

assumed to be close to the maximum allowed by TCP/IP, i.e. 65000 bytes. The confidence on the resulting delivery schedule was set to 95% and packet loss probability was assumed to be 40%.

If packet loss probability is consistent across all channels ($p_i \equiv p$), then we only need to seek where the c curve intersects the minimum of all the parts, as indicated by the arrow in Fig.5.4.

Seeking the coordinates of this intersection can be accomplished by an iterative approach where successive $m_{j,i} \ \forall \ i, j$ and c values are computed in series. The details are presented in the form of a flowchart in Fig. 5.5. The algorithm shown is based on the assumption that the set of servers to be used has been already fixed.

In the algorithm of Figure 5.5, an initial guess for c is used to compute the minimum m_{min}s. This guess, which is generated from Eq. (5.58) by maximizing the number of data packets (i.e. by using $m4c = 1$), is the smallest possible for the given problem settings. The steps that follow are then used to reach our target by updating our c estimate through continuously halving the gap between m_{min} and $m4c$. It should be noted that although the algorithm

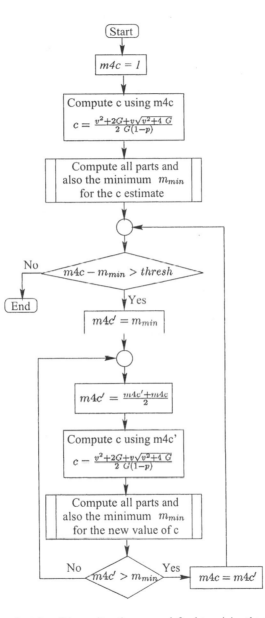

Figure 5.5. Flowchart describing an iterative approach for determining the optimum parameter *c*.

seems to go to unnecessary lengths for what is essentially a form of binary search, what is really attempted is a restriction on how the intersection is approximated. This restriction ensures that the algorithm converges, which is not the case if $m4c$ is allowed to oscillate back and forth the m-coordinate of the intersection (as has been actually observed under certain conditions, like very small document parts). Also, the right to left approach attempts (but cannot guarantee) to find the crossing with the smallest m-coordinate in the -unlikely- event that the instance of the partitioning problem exhibits the property of multiple crossings.

The probability p used in Figure 5.5 is the highest one among the servers employed. A simple modification to the algorithm of Fig. 5.5 can accommodate different packet loss probabilities.

5.7.   Coupling the Relaxation Parameter c and the Number of Installments M

The problem with a multi-installment strategy is that as the number of installments increases, the magnitude of $m_{j,i}$s gets smaller and smaller, resulting in increased c values and schedule overheads. The above hints to the fact that the *number of installments has to be carefully selected and should not be arbitrarily large*. Another important conjecture from the above discussion is that the c and M parameters have to be evaluated in tandem unless the number of installments is a fixed system parameter. The example displayed in Figure 5.6 illustrates vividly this problem.

In order to compute c and M we resort to an iterative procedure that is depicted in Fig. 5.7.

The algorithm in Fig. 5.7 can be broken down to two nested searches : an outer one where increasing values for M are evaluated and an inner one used to obtain an optimum value for c, given the number of installments and schedule confidence required. For the inner loop, a binary search procedure is used to find the value of c that produces a close match to the required CP (within a threshold $CONF\_ERR$). The initial search range is delimited by the c values for the largest ($= 1$) and smallest ($= \frac{sz}{L}$) possible parts correspondingly (i.e., $c_r = \frac{v^2 + 2p_i^{-1} + v\sqrt{v^2 + 4p_i^{-1}}}{2\,p_i^{-1}(1-p_i)}$ and $c_l = \frac{v^2 + \frac{2L}{sz\,p_i} + v\sqrt{v^2 + \frac{4L}{sz\,p_i}}}{\frac{2L}{sz\,p_i}(1-p_i)}$). The outer loop terminates when, either AT is no longer decreased, or the parts $m_{j,i}$ become so small (e.g. $< sz$) that no c in $[c_l\ c_r]$ can yield a match for CP.

Another issue with our treatment of packet loss, is that although c is calcu-

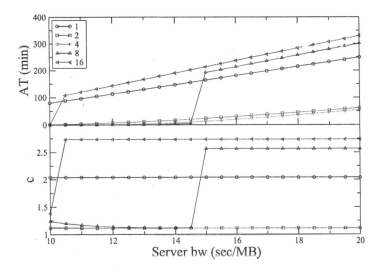

Figure 5.6. (a) AT offered by two identical servers, with bw ranging from 10 to 20 sec/MB and $o = 1sec$, for a 1 GB movie with $R = 8sec/MB$ to a client with an available bandwidth of $bw_C = 5sec/MB$. The number of installments is one of $M \in \{1, 2, 4, 8, 16\}$. (b) The optimum value of c is determined via the algorithm in Fig. 5.5, by assuming that $sz = 1500$, the confidence interval is 95% and the packet loss probability is 10%.

lated on the assumption of a linear retransmission cost (i.e. 10% loss requires an extra time cost of 10% for the retransmission of dropped data), TCP error control does not adhere to this assumption. TCP detects losses based on timeout and/or feedback. Successive losses could also cause a doubling of the time-out threshold (exponential backoff) with an upper limit of 64 sec, until an eventual connection reset after roughly 9 minutes [101]. Although precise modeling of TCP behavior is not incorporated in our model, the δ parameter can be used to provide an extra time delay "cushion". Calculating the appropriate δ for this purpose could be the target of future research.

5.8. Simulation Study

In order to evaluate the effectiveness of the multi-installment strategy, a number of simulations were conducted. The results reported here are based on the assumption that the transmitted documents are coded in MPEG-4 [1] format (MP@ML). MPEG4 can offer exceptional quality at low data rates. Although, MPEG-4 features a non-constant bit-rate, the following constant rate is assumed $R = 9.31sec/MB$, conforming to figures reported by DVD video transcoding experiments (880kbits/sec), where MPEG-4 codecs like the popular DivX codec (http://www.divx.com) were tested [45].

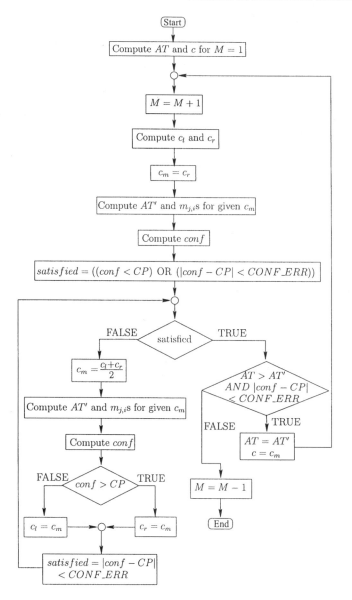

Figure 5.7. Algorithm for estimating the optimum c and M parameters given the confidence level CP that the delivery schedule should provide. $conf$ denotes the confidence provided by $c = c_m$.

All the tests reported in this section are based on the assumption of a single overhead per server and the optimum M and c are computed for a confidence of 95% and a packet size $sz = 1500$ bytes. Also the following values are used:

- $bw_C = 5.592sec/MB$ (1500 kbps ADSL line)
- $o = 1sec$
- $\delta = 1sec$ which is longer than a typical GOP.

The first set of tests aimed at quantifying the improvement our scheme can offer even under unfavorable circumstances when a 'slower' server joins a 'faster' one, speed in this case referring to their corresponding bw. By letting the slower server have 10 times the bw of the faster one, we get the results shown in Fig. 5.8. The remaining parameters used in this simulation were:

- $L : 774MB$, equivalent to a 120 minute feature-length movie.
- bw ranged from 10 to $20sec/MB$ in steps of $0.5sec/MB$. This is equivalent to the range $[51.2, 102.4]KB/sec$

As can be clearly observed in Fig. 5.8(b), the improvement in AT offered by our scheme, even with only a slight (10%) improvement in the consumed bandwidth, can be quite significant. This is even more so when the AT that can be achieved is smaller or at least close to the duration $R L$ of the movie. This effect is more evident for small values of p that lend to better access times. Also Fig. 5.8(c) and 5.8(d) show that as would be expected, more installments call for higher values of c, effectively limiting the maximum number of installment that would be beneficial to the streamlining of the delivery schedule.

A closer look into Fig. 5.8(b),(d) reveals that there is a coupling between the number of installments and the improvement in AT. As long as more than one installment can be used, the improvement in AT is superlinear as both servers are utilized for a longer period of time. The above simulation clearly shows that a multi-server multi-installment approach can greatly benefit situations when a single server cannot adequately service a request.

Actually, a very exciting feature of the multi-server approach is that a *superlinear access time speedup* is observed. If we denote as $AT(N, bw)$ the access time offered by N servers, each devoting bandwidth bw, then we can define the speedup as:

$$speedup(N, bw) = \frac{AT(1, bw)}{AT(N, bw)} \quad (5.64)$$

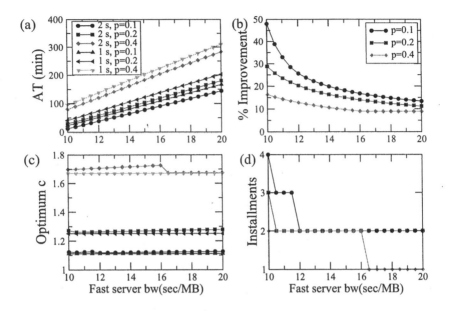

Figure 5.8. Simulation results for a pair of servers, one having one tenth the speed of the other one. Graph (a) shows the access-times for using the pair or just the faster of the two. (b) displays the improvement achieved by utilizing both servers VS only the fast one. Graphs (c) and (d) show the corresponding c and M values as computed from the algorithm in Fig.5.7. The horizontal lines in (c) correspond to the single fast server scenario.

In Fig. 5.9, the AT speedup curves show extraordinary improvements over the single server approach. The decline to the left of Fig.5.9(a) and (b) is due to the fact that AT cannot go any lower than $\delta + o_0 = 2sec$. Although the numbers shown in Fig. 5.9 seem unrealistically high, the fact is that they are a little bit lower than what could be achieved if the same client bandwidth was consumed by a single server (see also Fig. 5.11, explained below). For example, for $R = 9.31sec/MB$, $L = 774MB$ and $p = 10\%$ a single server with $bw = 22sec/MB$ offers an AT of 11729sec, while 2 such servers achieve 2372sec and a single server with $bw = 11sec/MB$ exhibits an AT of 2262sec.

As has been shown in [10], the use of fewer, faster servers provides a better utilization of a client's bandwidth, *at least when the number of installments is 1 or 2*. Increasing the number of installments has the effect of making many slow servers as efficient as fewer faster ones as far as the client's bandwidth is concerned. However, the results reported in [10] did not account

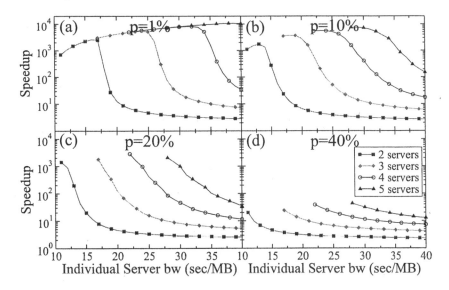

Figure 5.9. *AT* "speedup" for different packet loss probabilities p and number of servers N. The x axes display the individual server bw, which means that the consumed client bandwidth is $\frac{bw}{N}$.

for any schedule confidence or take into consideration the derivation of optimum M and c values. By computing the AT versus the consumed client bandwidth for a varying number of identical servers, Fig. 5.10 is derived. The strange behavior shown in the left side of Fig. 5.10(a) is due to the fact that AT levels off at around 2secs. The main point revealed in Fig. 5.10 is that more servers have to consume more client bandwidth in order to achieve the same level of service as fewer faster ones, although, the difference is not that significant.

The second set of simulations aimed at investigating the complex connection between the number of servers, packet loss probability and optimum installments, especially when guarantees are imposed on the delivery schedule. For this purpose, we estimated the bw that a varying number of identical servers would have to dedicate for delivering movies of different duration, given a modest target access time of 1 minute. The results were visualized with the aid of IBM's OpenDX[1] software and are shown in Fig. 5.11.

---

[1] OpenDX is freely available from IBM at www.opendx.org

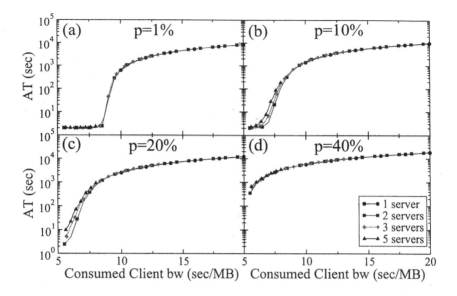

Figure 5.10. AT versus consumed client bandwidth for different packet loss probabilities p and number of servers.

A number of interesting observations can be made on Figure 5.11:

– Longer duration movies require more resources for achieving an access time on par with shorter ones. The difference can be quite substantial (a $1000MB$ movie could require as much as 15-23% faster servers than a $50MB$ one) and it is quite significant if we also consider that an optimum c for small movies was found to be 1-8% bigger than for longer ones. This can be attributed to several factors:

* Servers are released much earlier than the end of the delivery for long duration movies, inhibiting good server utilization.

* Also, a sufficient increase in M is not possible to counter-act the above effect, as it would lead to an increase in c.

* The most dominant influence though, is the selection of AT used in the simulation (60sec), relative to the total duration of a movie. While for $L = 50MB$, AT represents 13% of the duration, for $L = 1000MB$ it represents a mere 0.65%. Running the simulation with $AT = 5\%R\,L$, i.e. 5% of the movie duration, shows a totally different picture, with short movies requiring from 4%-21% faster servers than long ones.

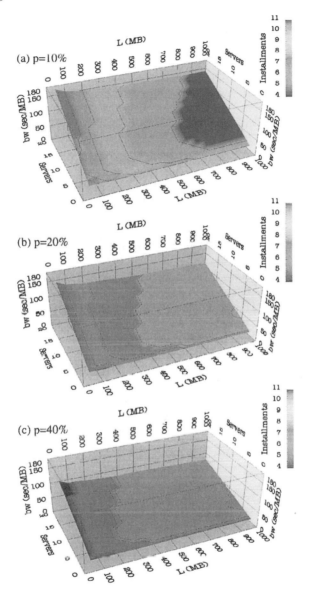

Figure 5.11. Bandwidth that has to be devoted by each of a number of identical servers for achieving an access time of 1 minute. The surfaces are pseudo-colored to reflect the corresponding number of required installments.

– Packet-loss probability has the greatest influence on M, greater than N or L do. Probability p is effectively dictating the region of optimum values for M.

Finally, Figure 5.12 shows how ATs relate to buffer requirements for different sets of identical servers. The buffer requirements are expressed as a percentage of L. As can be observed in both $L = 33MB$ and $L = 774MB$ cases, using more servers translates to higher buffer requirements for a given AT as long as packet loss stays low. This trend is reversed in the last row of graphs for $p = 40\%$, and partly in the middle row too (for very high AT). The reason is that when c and/or AT are high, the use of more servers translates to a higher ratio of server utilization, i.e. servers are active for a larger percentage of the total download time.

Figure 5.12 reports the buffer requirements for $M = 1$. Multiple installments are not examined in conjunction with the buffering requirements in this chapter because of the intricate timing assumptions that need to be established. A treatment of this aspect of the problem is presented in Chapter 6.

5.9.   Concluding Remarks

In this chapter we extend the idea of employing an MSR strategy three-fold: (a) by using a more realistic system model to describe the server-client transactions and movie playback, (b) by catering for network losses that plague user-experience and (c) by providing algorithms for optimizing the delivery schedule parameters, including the number of installments.

The introduction of the c parameter in our model, allows addressing both the minimization of the access time, and the elimination of playback artifacts, by giving enough time for all movie material to download *correctly*.

The simulations presented clearly show the potential of a real system based on the proposed approach in bringing a step closer the commercial exploitation of the Internet medium for movie distribution. The key to all these, is that the expectations and demands from the delivery mechanisms (both server and communications-wise) are relaxed. It should be stressed that even two combined servers can slash in less than half the access time a single one of them can offer. This superlinear access time speedup is on its own a tremendous advantage of the proposed method. Even if a single server is able to deliver the document in real time, i.e. $c\ bw < R$, using the proposed multi-server approach poses substantial benefits as it allows for:

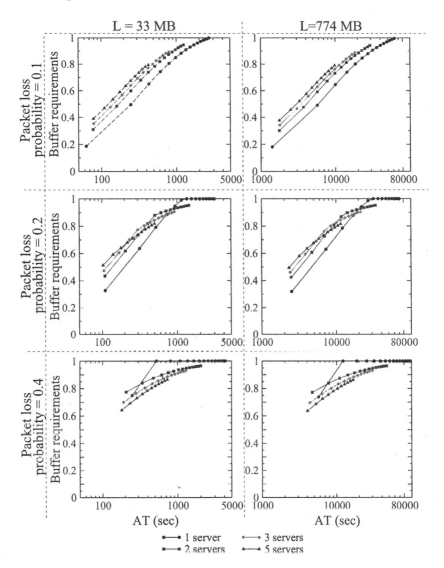

Figure 5.12. *AT* versus normalized buffer requirements for varying N and packet loss probability. The case of $L = 33MB$ (roughly 5min for $R = 9.31s/MB$) is indicative of movie clips. M is fixed at 1.

- The development and deployment of fine-grained server "load" balancing algorithms

- The introduction of fault-tolerance characteristics to the delivery schedule.

- A multi-vendor service provided under a unified umbrella. Multiple ISPs could jointly offer VoD services, adapting their policies according to client location and speed.

The main shortcomings towards the application of the presented framework in real-life are:

- How to determine the packet loss probabilities that are typically not constant over the duration of a download.

- How to adjust the delivery schedule in anticipation of the dynamic network characteristics.

These issues are addressed in Chapter 6.

Bibliographic Notes

The distributed multi-server approach presented in this chapter, can offer a universal solution for deploying VoD services that adapt to the client location and the available resources of each server. The result is that the best possible service can be offered to each client while at the same time maximizing both the server and the client bandwidth utilization. Thus, scalability and fault tolerance can be offered at the network connection level, similarly to how parallel video servers offer both at the storage level [66]. It should be noted that the framework presented in this chapter does not conflict with the parallel server or server array paradigm [36], as it is not concerned with server storage management. Various aspects of the multi-server approach have been studied in [11, 8, 9]

The main assumption on which our framework is based is that the document can be arbitrarily divisible, i.e. broken-up in independent parts as seen fit. Current state-of-the-art formats like the latest MPEG-4 standard [1], support this simplification to a large extent. Even if the delivery schedule computed by the proposed approach calls for intra-frame or intra-macroblock break-ups, during playback all necessary information for the decoding process will be present at the client side.

Multicasting [31] is the major network technology currently being used to maximize network utilization and alleviate server bottlenecks. A technique called patching -in various forms- has been also explored in order to accommodate clients having different playback starting times, with minimum communication overhead [23]. In [48], Horn et al. summarize a number of the techniques that have been proposed for addressing AT control, scalability and reliability issues in a multicasting environment. However, multicasting does not come free: it requires infrastructure changes like special routers, etc.. An alternative has been suggested in the form of the Simulcast protocol, which uses the clients as repeaters [35]. Requests directed to the server are used to build a binary transmission tree which does not require any network modification, as the extra functionality is embedded in the client software. A more advanced attempt at building a multicast tree using a P2P architecture, is reported in [103]. Tran et al. suggest a solution called Zigzag for live media streaming, that addresses the problems associated with the dynamic nature of the multicast trees, catering for fast, bounded tree updates. However, both simulcasting and Zigzag cannot fully utilize asymmetrical connections like ADSL, thus being suitable mainly for low bit-rate content.

In [70] the term simulcast is used to reflect the use of multiple streams with different rates targeting clients with different capabilities. A similar approach to Simulcast is being used by the BitTorrent[2] project and the Kontiki Delivery Management System[3] . BitTorrent uses the clients as content publishers, striving at the same time to satisfy fairness constraints. Files are split into $\frac{1}{4}MB$ pieces that are transferred between the peers. Other P2P file sharing approaches include the ever-popular KaZaa[4], eDonkey[5] and WinMX[6] systems.

The major difference of these systems with the presented approach is the scheduling of operations. Our framework allows a *robust, non-heuristic* calculation of the parts that are going to be uploaded by each server so that the playback can commence with a minimum amount of delay.

The idea of combining multiple geographically distributed servers for MM document delivery has been coined in [105]. Subsequently, client buffer space requirement has been studied by Dong, et al. [28]. An immediate extension to this work presented in [105], appears in [28] which attempted to use multiple server technique to service more than one client in the system. Also, in this study certain bounds on client buffer requirements are derived and rigorous simulation is presented. However, the system did not consider servicing the clients under real-life network conditions, especially

---

[2]http://bitconjurer .org/BitTorrent
[3]http://www.kontiki.com
[4]http://www.kazaa.com
[5]http://www.edonkey.com
[6]http://www.winmx.com

under unreliable communication media. In [28] the retrieval strategy derives the recommended bandwidth using a channel partition algorithm which essentially schedules each client data to be retrieved from each server. The challenge lies in deriving the schedule by taking into account the availability of the bandwidth so as to minimize the access times. The paper also considers a movie placement procedure to simulate a geographically distributed network.

Currently, possible communication errors like packet loss [20] or bit errors have to be dealt with concealment methods or by adopting error localization (e.g. video packets) or error correction methods, both of which increase the communication cost (e.g. in [44, 61], MPEG-4 [1] specific resilience methods, increase the data stream by 4%-11%). A side-effect of pursuing correct delivery of the data-stream is that the above mentioned overhead can be eliminated while at the same time maximizing the client bandwidth [56].

Jung et al. in [56] proposed a data partitioning scheme among servers that resembles data-interleaving in disk arrays. The video stream is broken in Groups Of Pictures (GOPs) and distributed in a round-robin fashion. This approach cannot in any way be considered a load balancing, network-characteristics-aware approach as the one presented in this paper. The idea of using multiple connections to geographically distributed mirror sites has been also suggested by Rodriguez et al. for minimizing large document transfer times [92]. Subsequently, in [34] Funasaka et al. suggest and evaluate a method for parallel downloads that computes the download assignments according to the servers' bandwidth.

Also, in an attempt to dynamically modify the quality of service according to network congestion, Rejaie et al. [90] proposed a layered video format and associated mechanism for tuning data volume to network capacity. A similar technique adapted to existing standards, was proposed by Pejhan et al. in [83], where it is shown that storing a single video along with the motion vectors needed for encoding it at smaller fps rates can be efficiently used for quality adaptation. A number of techniques have been suggested for offering video of varying quality and/or size [69]. Scalable video provides this capability by encoding the video in two or more layers using Hierarchical Layer Encoding Video (HLEV) or Multiple Description Coding (MDC) [115]. The base layer provides the elementary video stream in its most basic quality. Each additional layer, adds spatial and/or temporal details to the base layer, enhancing its quality and adding to the overall stream size. In [46] scalable video is discussed in association with multicasting by multiple replicated servers to multiple clients. Still, these methods cannot promise artifact-free playback while at the same time compromise quality.

Chapter 6

ADAPTING TO NETWORK VARIABILITY

6.1. Relaxing the constraints is not enough

In Chapter 5 we introduced a refined system model incorporating a "relaxation" parameter c that allows the computation of a delivery schedule that anticipates packet losses and provides room for their treatment.

The main problem associated with this approach is that it depends on fixed, a-priori known packet-loss probabilities and server connections speeds, both of which are typically constantly under change. Using just mean values for these parameters has the potential to create the following problems:

− If packet losses decrease and/or connection speeds increase over time, the computed AT would be overestimated, forcing the client to wait unnecessarily. Additionally, it would prevent a recalculation of the schedule that would "shift" responsibilities to faster servers yielding a smaller AT.

− If packet losses increase and/or connection speeds decrease due to congestion, interrupts would be introduced in the playback.

In this chapter we discuss methods for treating these deficiencies, by employing multiple installments. The notations and symbols used, adhere to the guidelines set in Chapter 5 (see Table 5.1).

6.2. Dynamic Schedule Adaptation

During the long time it takes to deliver a several-hundred-MB movie over slow links, many of the network parameters assumed constant in the previous chapters, change. In order to ensure the integrity of the playback, or in the worst case to minimize the number and duration of the interruptions, the delivery schedule has to be re-evaluated. The introduction of the multi-installment strategy in Chapter 5 is fertile ground for such techniques. Re-computing the delivery schedule can be done:

- Periodically. A multitude of approaches can be used to establish a periodic "calibration" of the delivery, including both time and data based ones. Examples:
  * Regular intervals (e.g. every 5 minutes)
  * At the end of an installment
  * At regular data intervals (e.g. after downloading each MB)
- Whenever such changes are detected (e.g. whenever a server connection stays inactive for more than 30 secs)

Of course, the problem of estimating the system parameters (in particular bw and p for each server connection) persists whatever the approach chosen. In this chapter we choose to deal with the network variability, whenever an installment is completed, thus any changes affect only the part of the re-quested movie that has not been scheduled yet.

This is not an optimum choice, especially if the movie part that has been already requested will not arrive in time (e.g. due to a server connection failure). The scenario of complete server connection failure is examined in Chapter 7.

After we use the algorithm in Fig. 5.7 to derive the optimum c and M parameters, we can start the delivery. At the beginning of each of the subsequent $M - 1$ installments that are to be performed, we can use the algorithm shown in Fig. 5.5 to adjust to any detected changes. The details are shown in Fig. 6.1.

Using the algorithm of Fig. 5.5 instead of the one in Fig. 5.7 is dictated by purely cost considerations (it is just too expensive to be performed for each and every installment). Hybrid techniques that change M every so often, could be also considered in future work.

Central to our capability to adjust the schedule 6.1, is the use of the o parameter for encoding the -expected- release time of a server, effectively shifting responsibilities to servers that can fulfill the duties faster. However, this prevents the use of the multi-overhead (MO) model presented in Section 5.3.2.2.

We will refer to the technique outlined in this section as **M**ultiple **I**nstallments **S**ingle **P**art (**MISP**).

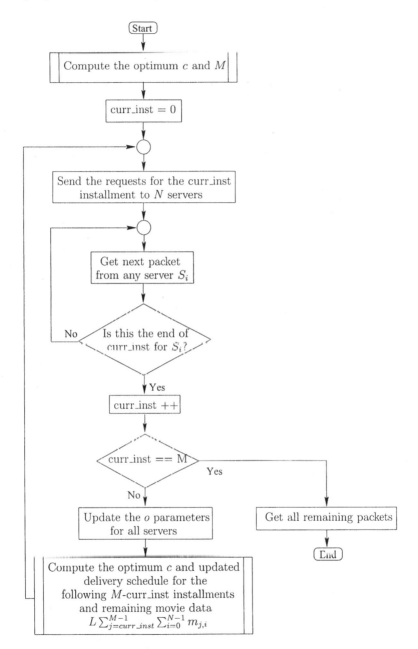

Figure 6.1. A pull-based scheme that a client can use to adjust the delivery schedule to system changes.

6.3. Single Installment Revisited

Similarly to a multi-installment strategy, we can use the single installment as a building block to an adaptive scheme.

The principle is to divide the delivery of the movie into M equal disjoint parts, thus having each server make M deliveries. This is conceptually equivalent to a *multi-installment* strategy [105] with the difference that *no constraints tie together the delivery of successive installments*. Each installment delivers $\frac{L}{M}$ data to the client. $m_{i,j}$ will be used in the following paragraphs to denote the i-th part delivered by the j-th server. The difference with the multi-installment notation is that $m_{i,j}$ is expressed as a percentage of $\frac{L}{M}$, hence $\sum_{i=0}^{M-1} \sum_{j=0}^{N-1} m_{i,j} = M$.

In the following sections, we will refer to the alternative technique as **S**ingle **I**nstallment **M**ultiple **P**arts (**SIMP**).

The benefits of the single-installment based approach over the pure multi-installment one of Section 6.2 are:

–   The closed-form solutions of Section 5.3.1 significantly reduce the cost of schedule calculations. This is important if M is large.

–   A multiple-overhead model can be easily incorporated (see Section 5.3.2.2). Actually, the overheads can even vary from one installment to the next.

The flowchart in Fig. 6.2 presents the sequence of operations for estimating the AT at the very beginning of the downloading process. If we denote the access time needed for installment k, $k : 0, \ldots, M - 1$, as AT_k, then the overall AT should be set so that the following condition is satisfied $\forall\, k$:

$$AT \geq AT_k - k\,R\,\frac{L}{M} \tag{6.1}$$

The computation of each AT_k is accomplished via Eq. (5.9), (5.7) and (5.10) for $\frac{L}{M}$ data and by setting the overheads o_i to reflect the delivery cost of all the previous installments up to k. Thus, when calculating how the j-th L/M part is going to be partitioned among the servers, we set:

$$o_i = \begin{cases} o_i^{(init)} + c\,bw_i\frac{L}{M}\sum_{k=0}^{j-1} m_{k,i} & \text{for single overhead} \\ (j+1)\,o_i^{(init)} + c\,bw_i\frac{L}{M}\sum_{k=0}^{j-1} m_{k,i} & \text{for multiple overheads} \end{cases} \tag{6.2}$$

where $o_i^{(init)}$ is the actual overhead associated with S_i.

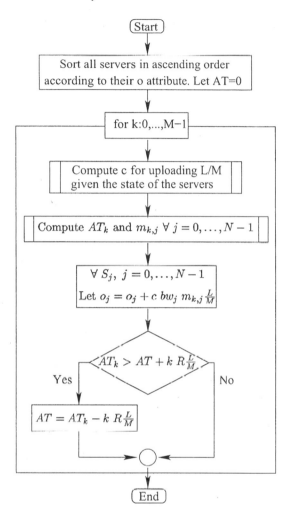

Figure 6.2. Algorithm for determining the AT and parts $m_{k,j}$ for M successive deliveries of L/M movie parts (a single overhead is assumed).

The process in Fig. 6.2 can yield parts $m_{0,j}$, but in order to accommodate changes in the network, we should recompute the delivery schedule at the beginning of each subsequent installment $k : 1, \ldots, M - 1$. For example, when S_0 completes (or is close to completing) sending its $k - 1$ part, the measured bw_i and p_i figures can be used to update: (i) the expected completion of installment $k - 1$ for each server S_j, $j \neq 0$, and (ii) the AT_k estimate and the parts $m_{k,j}$ to be used for installment k. Thus the client has

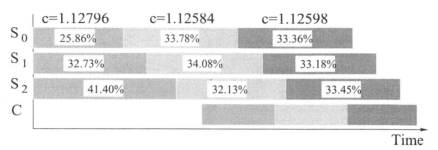

Figure 6.3. A 3-installment schedule for delivering the "Matrix Revolutions" trailer via 3 identical servers $S(10sec/MB, 0sec)$. It is assumed that $p = 10\%$ and $sz = 1500$ bytes. The corresponding c value is shown above each installment. Also displayed are the $m_{i,j}$ values.

to execute the loop body of Fig. 6.2, $\frac{M(M+1)}{2}$ times in total.

If condition (6.1) is no longer valid, an interruption equal to $AT_k - k\,R\,\frac{L}{M} - AT$ will have to be introduced into the playback. Alternatively, more servers could be employed for avoiding this.

An example of a 3-installment schedule as produced by the algorithm in Fig. 6.2, for the "Matrix Revolutions" movie trailer mentioned in Section 5.4, is shown in Figure 6.3.

Although the issue of a server failure is not explicitly treated above, it is possible that one or more new servers are introduced in the delivery schedule at the beginning of each installment.

One might suggest that an alternative to the above method might be to send requests for small, fixed portions to the available servers in a round-robin fashion, or whenever they become available. This approach can be considered a special case of the suggested method for very large M. However, Section 6.5 shows that this can yield inferior results, even without any regard to the additional network overhead.

A key point in the algorithm of Fig. 6.2 is that the value for c is computed for each installment and for every schedule update. Deciding on the optimum value of M for dividing up the movie L can be accomplished by using as a building block the algorithm of Fig. 6.2. However, the optimum M found this way may not necessarily be the best one under working conditions.

6.4. Simulation Study

In order to explore the potential of the proposed document delivery approaches and associated algorithms, two types of tests were conducted: analytical ones based on the models presented in the previous sections and discrete event simulations. In doing so, we tried to answer the following questions:

- Which is the best performing technique access-time-wise and by what margin?
- What is the best M for movie delivery?
- What are the buffer requirements of the suggested schemes?
- Given the unpredictable nature of the communication media, what can be expected in real-life in terms of playback interrupts?

For the analytical tests and in order to satisfy both simplicity and diversity, we focused on identical servers delivering a 100min duration CBR movie coded in MPEG-4 format (MP@ML), through identical communication links. MPEG-4 [1] is an emerging standard offering high quality at low data rates. MPEG-4 aims to solve the "global media" problem covering the coding, delivery, communication and synchronization of multiple media including among others natural video and audio, 2D and 3D mesh representations [14]. Given an MPEG-4 data rate of 880kbits/sec (reported as a mean data rate value in DVD transcoding applications [45]), we have $R = 9.31sec/MB$ and a document size of roughly $L = 645MB$ accordingly. For our tests, we also used a 5 min duration movie clip, representing short media, which for the same R noted above, translates to $L = 33MB$.

The number of servers ranged from 1 to 5 and the consumed client bandwidth ranged from 100% to 50%, evenly split among the servers. All servers were assumed of having $o = 1sec$. The client was assumed of having an ADSL-class connection at 1.5Mbit/sec, or $bw_C = 5.592sec/MB$. It should be noted that throughout this section a confidence of 95% is used for c estimation. In the case of the SIMP strategy, M parts translate to a confidence of $0.95^{\frac{1}{M}}$ for each part delivery, as per the discussion in Section 5.6.

Initially, we focus on SIMP and later in this section we provide figures comparing SIMP and MISP.

As can be seen in Fig. 6.4, the more servers we use, the less efficiently the client bandwidth is used. Also, the optimum number of installments as determined in conjunction with c can be quite large in order to achieve a small AT. For $p = 0.01$ the very high number of installments essentially

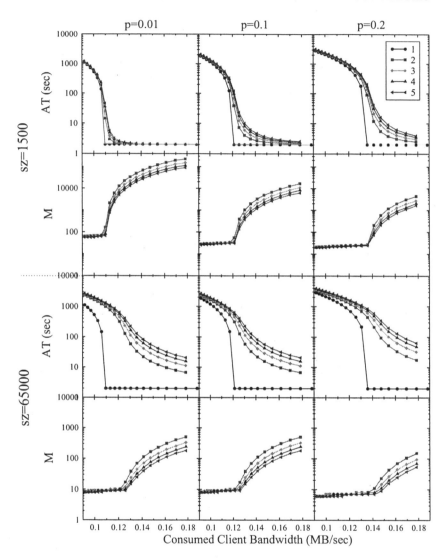

Figure 6.4. SIMP optimum access times and number of installments M for delivering a **645MB** movie using different portions of the available client bandwidth and a different number of servers sharing that resource. Plots depict different combinations of packet size sz and loss probability p. In order to make the graph easier to interpret, we use the normal and not the inverse of the client's consumed bandwidth in the x-axis.

translates to a round-robin assignment of packets to servers. Very high Ms equate to high upstream communication traffic (i.e. sending commands to servers) and a high cost for computing the delivery schedule. The former is not taken into account in this study and it is a parameter that deserves additional research. In practice though, gains in AT are insignificant after a few hundred (at the most) installments.

Similar results for the 33MB case movie are reported in Fig. 6.5. Similar to the case of the 100min movie, a smaller packet size allows for better utilization of the available bandwidth and can achieve smaller AT. Another significant trend that is visible in both Figures 6.4 and 6.5 is that increasing packet loss probability reduces the optimum M. The reason is the increase in c that comes with increased p and M.

Despite a less efficient use of the client bandwidth, multiple servers can offer a substantially better service that a single one. The following example is illustrative:

- Given the task of delivering a $645MB$ document with $sz = 1500$, a single server with $bw - 15sec/MB$ and p=0% offers an $AT = 3671sec$. If this server is assisted with another one consuming one tenth of its bw, i.e. 150sec/MB, we can achieve an $AT - 2841sec$ for $M=10$. This is a 22.6% improvement for 10% more bandwidth. Still a single server using the same bandwidth would produce an $AT = 2791sec$ but that may not be possible in every situation.

As can be seen from both Figures 6.4 and 6.5 a smaller packet payload sz improves the behavior of the system. For this reason, in the remaining results that are reported we use only $sz = 1500B$.

The maximum buffer requirements (in the spirit of Section 5.3) are reported in Fig. 6.6 and as can be seen, for offering the same AT SIMP requires almost the same amount of client space as a single server approach. The trend is for the multi-server scheme to require a bit more space, although this is reversed for small L and higher access times.

Just how SIMP stacks up against MISP is shown in Fig. 6.7. As can be observed, there is no consistent advantage of one approach over the other. What is clear is that the differences are minute both AT- and buffer-requirements-wise. When a large portion of the client bandwidth is used, MISP is dominant, while for a lower percentage of the available bandwidth, smaller access times and buffer requirements are exhibited by SIMP. Also the much larger number of installments utilized by SIMP (3-4 orders of magnitude bigger) allow for a much more aggressive adaptation of the de-

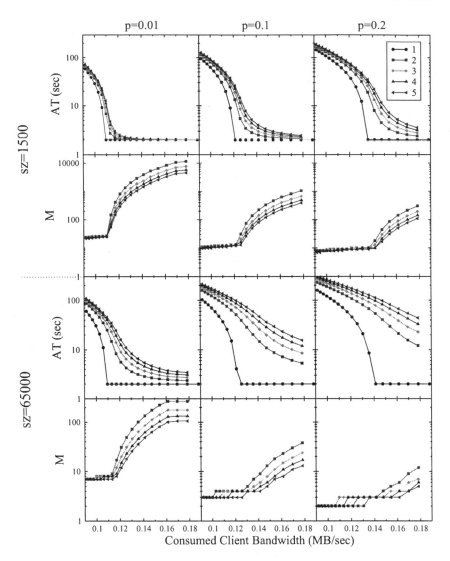

Figure 6.5. SIMP optimum access times and number of installments M for delivering a **33MB** movie using different portions of the available client bandwidth and a different number of servers sharing that resource. Plots depict different combinations of packet size sz and loss probability p.

livery schedule in response to system changes. In contrast, a MISP strategy would have to rely on an auxiliary mechanism to track potential problems

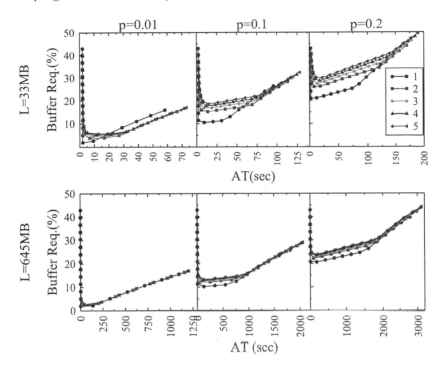

Figure 6.6. SIMP maximum buffer requirements versus AT for different number of servers and movie size L. The buffer requirements are normalized i.e. expressed as a percentage of L.

as the end of an installment would not come soon enough to allow for this. Complications in server and client implementations would be a certain result of this.

The only major problem that one might face in the application of SIMP, is the excessive computational effort required to produce the optimum M, especially under the light that in certain circumstances M can be in the order of one hundred thousand. This also translates to increased computational requirements for updating the delivery schedule. An alternative could be to use as many installments as would be necessary to render any further reductions in AT insignificant.

As can be seen in Fig. 6.8, where M is calculated as the point where further improvements in AT fall below 0.1% of the current estimate, such a policy can be a good compromise: AT are only marginally increased over the best that can be achieved, while M remains high enough for quick schedule

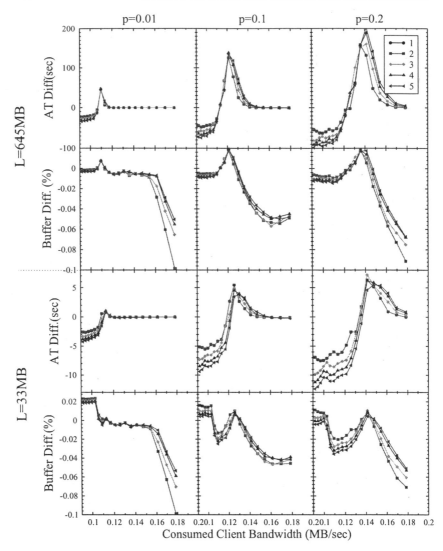

Figure 6.7. SIMP VS MISP. The plots display differences between SIMP and MISP corresponding figures, e.g. $AT_{SIMP} - AT_{MISP}$.

adaptations and low enough for computational efficiency.

As is the case for the MISP approach explored in Chapter 5, a super-linear speedup (see Eq. (5.64)) is also observed for SIMP. The curves shown in

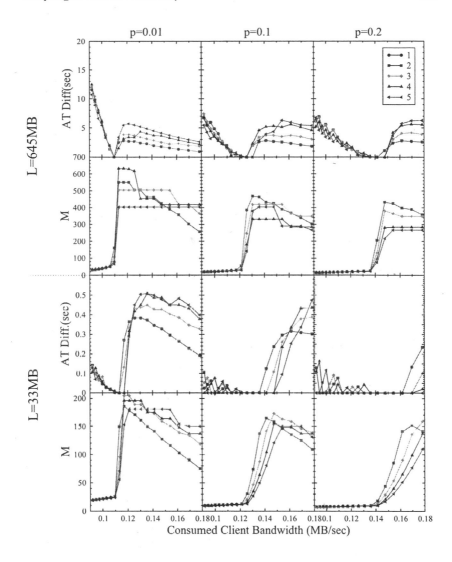

Figure 6.8. AT difference from an optimum SIMP strategy and associated M, when the number of installments is calculated as the threshold that makes any subsequent AT improvements over current estimates, fall below 0.1%. For both document sizes, $sz = 1500B$.

Fig. 6.9 are very similar to the ones in Fig. 5.9. In all the cases shown in Fig. 6.9 $speedup(N, bw) > N$. This is due to the fact that playback can start much sooner than in the single server case, without risking an interrup-

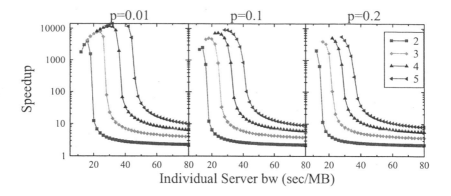

Figure 6.9. Speedup over a single server for $N = 2, \ldots, 5$ servers ($L = 645MB$ and $sz = 1500B$).

tion. The shape of the speedup curves is dictated by the total transmission time. Any access time improvements are marginalized if the duration of the document delivery is very long. Naturally, the total transmission time features a sub-linear decrease with the number of servers. The downturn of the curves for small p in Fig. 6.9 is produced because AT approaches the overhead o.

The above paragraphs show that SIMP is a strategy that can provide a service on par with MISP while at the same time allow for rapid adaptation to system changes. The level of SIMP's success in blocking playback interrupts is explored in the next section.

6.5.   Discrete Event Simulation Study

In order to probe the real-life behavior of a system based on SIMP, we performed a discrete event simulation of the delivery of a feature-length **CBR** movie stream. In order to get a realistic data feed from the servers to the client to drive the simulator, we used a modified version of the Open Source *ffmpeg* library by Fabrice Bellard (available at the SourceForge.Net site), to extract the header information from a MPEG2, stream. The movie used had a resolution of 528x224, $R = 17.6567s/MB$ (or roughly 463kbps), $L = 368.3MB$, n=155906 frames and $fps = 23.976$. The extracted header information was also used to get the best posteriori-calculated AT and compare it against the predicted AT. The best posteriori-calculated AT is found

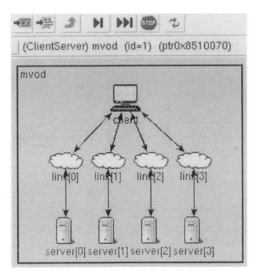

Figure 6.10. An instance of the OMNeT++ based discrete event simulator showing a 4 server setup.

in a similar fashion to Eq. (5.42) and is obviously of theoretical value:

$$AT_{post} = max_{\forall\, i} \left(deliver(i) - \frac{i}{fps} \right) \qquad (6.3)$$

The discrete event simulation software was based on the OMNeT++ Discrete Event Simulation System V.2.3 by Andras Varga [104]. The architecture of the simulation software is shown in Figure 6.10.

A separate module was used to model the packet loss characteristics of each individual link, based on the sine model suggested by Arai et al. [6]. According to the sine model, the loss probability p_k, $\forall\, k : 0 \ldots N - 1$ is time dependent and oscillates between a minimum min_k and a maximum value max_k as follows:

$$p_k = min_k + \frac{(max_k - min_k)\,(1 + sin\,(2\pi t/T + \varphi))}{2} \qquad (6.4)$$

where t represents time and T is the oscillation period ($T = 24$hours). φ represents a starting phase and it is used in our simulation to produce different loss behaviors. For each of the N links, $min_k = 0$ and max_k was generated from a uniform distribution in the $[0.1, 0.4]$ range. Figure 6.11 shows an example for $min_k = 0$ and $max_k = 0.2$.

The bw of each server was generated from a uniform distribution in the

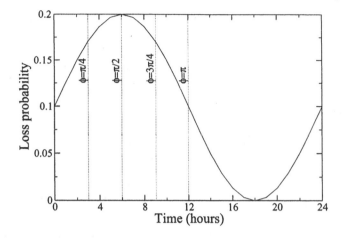

Figure 6.11. An illustration of the packet loss probability model of Arai et al. [6] for $min_k = 0$ and $max_k = 0.2$. The vertical lines indicate the different phases φ that are used in the discrete event simulation.

[20, 40]sec/MB range while a uniform distribution in the [1, 3]sec range was used for the client-server RTT. These ranges were chosen so that a multi-server delivery would be mandatory under the problem specifics. The o attribute of each server reflects the corresponding RTT overhead and thus we have $o = RTT$. bws and RTTs are assumed constant throughout the simulation. This is justifiable under the scope that bws represent resources that are dedicated by each server for a particular client. In a real-life scenario, a client could use the server-allocated and (most probably) fixed bws to derive a delivery schedule. RTTs can be easily computed by pinging the servers and are irrelevant after the initial requests are sent, since subsequent requests can be piped to the servers, i.e. a server will have the next request already delivered before the previous one is complete.

In order to assess whether the proposed scheme could cope in the absence of a detailed model of how the communication media behave, we set the links to begin "operating" in different phases of the cycle described by Eq. (6.4) (see also Fig. 6.11). At the same time, the client which calculates the delivery schedule, uses only the overall average loss behavior over the course of the delivery operation for the purpose of schedule derivation. The client calculates the initial schedule after collecting the bw, o and $\frac{max_k - min_k}{2}$, parameters for each server (the latter being the average loss probability for the particular link). Subsequently, the schedule is recomputed before the end of each installment for the remaining of the document, possibly shifting -not already assigned- content from one server to another, as depicted in the

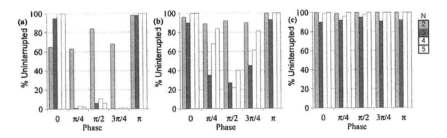

Figure 6.12. Percentage of cases where playback was not interrupted for (a) $M = 10$, (b) $M = 100$ and (c) $M = 1000$ for different starting phases φ.

algorithm of Fig. 6.1.

Because there is a possibility that the AT is set before the end of the first part delivery, we perform the update of the schedule also just before playback commences. Thus a delay can be introduced without risking an interrupt.

Figure 6.12 displays the results that were obtained by running the simulation 100 times for each combination of M, N and φ. For computing the optimum c values, a confidence of 95% was used. The packet size sz was set to 1500 bytes (as per the conclusions of Section 6.4), yielding an accurate representation of the network-level events. Finally, $\delta = 1sec$. Although an optimum value for M could be obtained for each instance, we chose to set M to three distinct values, in order to control this degree of freedom of our experiments.

As can be observed in Figure 6.12, large deviations from the estimated packet-loss percentages lead to interrupts even with our scheme. At first glance, it seems that increasing the number of servers can have a negative effect on the number of interrupts. The reason for this behavior, though, is that having only 2 servers produces a large AT that allows the client to get a better estimate of the packet-loss characteristics. As N grows, smaller ATs are produced, that can invariably lead to interruptions even for small loss fluctuations. However, as M grows, interrupts are minimized as any unpredictable behavior can be dealt with by shifting "duties" from one server to another in a rapid fashion. A second reason for this behavior is that as has been discussed in the previous section, c is inversely analogous to the parts m_k, i.e. more installments translate to an increase in c, in order to make each individual installment packet-loss-proof. This reflects negatively on the AT which on one hand prohibits interrupts, but on the other hand delays the beginning of the playback significantly. This effect is clearly visible in

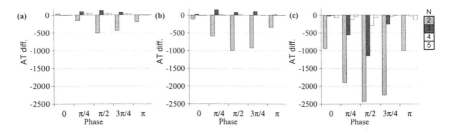

Figure 6.13. $\overline{AT_{post} - AT}$ difference expressed in seconds for different starting phases φ and for (a) $M = 10$, (b) $M = 100$ and (c) $M = 1000$.

Fig. 6.13. where the difference $AT_{post} - AT$ is displayed. In addition to minimizing interrupts, Fig. 6.13 also shows that the computed AT is only marginally higher than AT_{post}. These results re-enforce the conclusion of Section 6.4 that MSR strategies have the potential to aggressively monitor the status of the system and adapt to changes without compromising the client's experience.

6.6.   Concluding Remarks

This chapter describes a first attempt at deriving an adaptive multiple-server movie distribution scheme that can offer interrupt-free playback even in the absence of robust network error modeling and VBR streams. By using the single installment framework of Section 5.3.1 and by dividing the movie into M equal parts, we can cater for: (a) AT minimization and, (b) regular schedule updates which result in server load-balancing.

The experiments presented firmly establish SIMP as a great performer, capable of realizing VoD services over the public Internet with its current limitations and shortcomings. However, we are still a bit off the final target of a comprehensive multiple-server movie distribution scheme.

The set of policies that have to be specified in order to establish an adaptive scheme consists of:

– *Schedule Calculation Policy* : in this section we explore the properties of one such policy that (re)calculates the schedule at the end of each installment. Another -possibly better performing- policy would be to perform this calculation at regular time intervals. Of course, the problem of which interval is best is raised in this case.

– *Stream Partitioning Policy* : we compare SIMP and MISP policies. What about a MIMP scheme, i.e. one involving splitting the input in multiple parts and using multiple installments for each part?. This approach could potentially be superior to both SIMP and MISP. Many other possibilities that mix and match different policies for different stages of the distribution process are also possible.

- *Server Management Policy* : this part of the problem is not even implicitly mentioned in this section. We are currently assuming that all available servers are utilized for servicing each movie request. Clearly this is not an optimum solution and could also be the source of problems (what happens if a server fails without an available replacement). This is probably the least researched part of the problem.

- *Server Bandwidth Management Policy* : how much bandwidth should each server devote to a request?

- *Cost Management Policy* : it is possible that there is a different cost associated with using each individual server. The proposed approach can be extended to cover the monetary costs involved in providing VoD services by disjoint vendors. DLT has been already successfully applied in a similar problem by Robertazzi et al. [91].

Future work could also aim at further exploring/fine-tuning the parameters of the problem/model. For example, we could aim at using a different 'relaxation' constant c for each server. This would be desirable when each server connection exhibits widely different loss characteristics. Also, the study of a system comprising of many clients should provide more insight into the real-life benefits of SIMP/MISP and their variants.

Bibliographic Notes

The potential of SIMP has been explored for the first time for VBR media in [9]. Similar results for CBR media (MPEG2) are reported in [8].

Traditionally, the shortcomings of the public Internet and the associated heavy network loads that come with VoD services, have been addressed with network technologies such as multicast [101, 31]. Multicast achieves scalability by letting a video server/source send a packet only once to all the clients that should be receiving it, thus reducing the corresponding traffic substantially. The problem with multicast is that it requires infrastructure changes (e.g. like special routers) and it has been also reported that it suffers from configuration inconsistencies [87], leading to spatial and temporal routing instabilities.

Another major issue with the use of multicast is that the content must be delivered simultaneously to all clients, or at least within strict time limits. This effectively narrows the applications of interest to live news/sport feeds or collaborative/workgroup communication applications [33], unless special constraints are imposed as discussed below. The timing constraints also dictate the use of UDP instead of TCP as a transport mechanism. Since UDP is inherently unreliable, basic IP multicast is also unreliable. Hence, multicast requires special provisions by the video stream and/or decoder so that error correction/concealment is possible. SIMP/MISP on the other hand do not require such treatment, allowing a significant reduction of the video size (e.g. up to 11% for MPEG4 [44]).

To overcome multicast dependence on infrastructure changes, several researchers have proposed techniques that offer a form of multicasting by using peer-to-peer (P2P) unicast communications [35, 103, 17] also known as *overlay multicast* or *simulcast*. In [17, 16] Birrer and Bustamante compare a number of P2P multicast protocols against their P2P multicast protocol named Nemo. Nemo is based on a hierarchical organization of the peers into clusters.

In summary, all the techniques employing multicast in one form or the other, suffer from the need to have all the participating nodes receive data at a rate matching or exceeding the video rate. Hopefully, this chapter establishes SIMP and other multi-server unicast-based strategies, as valid alternatives to multicast and its variations.

Networking errors have been studied for a long time and under various domains as the effects of such occurrences are obviously dependent on the particular application. Packet-loss is usually being modeled by k-order Markov chain models [63]. The Bernoulli is the simplest of these models ($k = 0$), with more sophisticated ones (e.g. Gilbert for $k = 1$ and Extended Gilbert for $k > 1$) providing better prediction accuracy. An alternative approach called Markov-gap model is discussed by Lee and Varshney in [63], where gap refers to a loss-free run.

The sine model, a variation of the Bernoulli model, where the loss probability oscillates with a 24-hour long period between a minimum and maximum value, has been also described by Arai et al. to provide better accuracy than the Gilbert model [6]. The sine model also captures time variations that are typically observed in real-life situations. In our study we focus on the total number of lost packets during an installment and not on the duration or length of the loss bursts and that is why a Bernoulli distribution is sufficiently accurate for our purposes.

In [74] Maihofer and Rothermel study the effects of packet losses on the scalability of three multicast transport protocols, in view of lost/corrupted data retransmissions.

Chapter 7

FAULT-TOLERANCE ANALYSIS FOR MULTIPLE SERVERS MOVIE RETRIEVAL STRATEGY

7.1. What can go Wrong with an MSR strategy?

In the previous chapters we have seen a number of conspicuous advantages that MSR strategies can offer. In this chapter, we consider the fault-tolerance aspect, which is one of the crucial parameters in providing an attractive service. Since multiple servers are engaged in the retrieval process, failure of one or more servers, will allow the service to continue without any interruption as long as there is at least one server to provide the missing data. In fact, with a clever retrieval strategy design, the clients will continue to view the presentation, while certain number of servers may "die" and come back to "life" after some time. In contrast, with a conventional system, most probably the clients may need to be rescheduled or the presentation gets affected. Also, as shown in the rigorous simulation study from the literature[1], scalability of the physical system and heterogeneity of the system, can be easily accounted in the design, as the size of the portions retrieved from each of the servers depends on the available bandwidth and playback rate of the movie. Some of the key questions/issues to ponder are:

– When servers or links fail, how does the delivery & playback schedule get affected?

– A fault with a server may create a discontinuity in presentation owing to data loss. How can this "missing" data be provided to minimize any presentation hiccups?

– Faults could occur randomly. How should one react to these catastrophic events to prevent QoS degradation?

---

[1] See references [105, 66]

- What statistical data are required to safe-guard and quickly react to any failures?

- We demonstrated the effect of server sequencing on access times. Knowing server reliabilities, can the concept of sequencing be used to improve fault-tolerance or reliability of the entire server system?

We deal with the above issues in this chapter. We first consider the server and communication channel reliability in designing a multiple server re trieval strategy to provide a more reliable service. System reliability, or performance during playback, is one of the important factors in providing a high-quality reliable service to a client besides minimizing the access time of the movie. For instance, users may afford to tolerate a slight increase in delay in accessing a movie at a benefit of procuring a highly reliable system with a guaranteed QoS. Thus, we formulate the problem so as to incorporate these issues of reliability and analyze the performance in terms of *access time* and *reliability* considerations. Further, as with the practical systems, we assume that the server availability is determined based on the failure rate only and does not consider whether a server is busy or not. Without loss of generality, we assume that there exists an admission control module that takes into account the state of the server [2] to determine if it is busy or not.

Secondly, we identify an optimal sequence, the order in which data are to be retrieved from the respective servers, to achieve maximum system reliability.

Although the access time may not be influenced by sequencing[3], with this new formulation under fault-tolerance considerations, we will show that the retrieval sequence plays an important role in improving the system reliability. We attempt to identify an optimal sequence that maximizes the system reliability. Next, we consider analyzing the situation upon a server failure. Server failure amidst servicing the client results in data loss, and hence, a discontinuity in the presentation at the client site is expected. We first use a deterministic approach to analyze the single server failure scenario. We introduce two methods to recover the missing data, so that any severe performance degradation can be circumvented or minimized to the best possible extent. A parameter that quantifies the QoS is introduced to measure the extent of performance degradation. Further, this parameter recommends the client application to tune the playback rates in view of any delayed server recovery periods.

---

[2] Chapter 1 demonstrates an admission control algorithm for simple media servers.
[3] Refer to Chapters 2 & 5 for server sequencing.

Then, as an alternate means, we use a probabilistic approach to analyze the single server failure case. We analyze a single server failure scenario by assuming a constant failure rate of a certain participant server which is expected to fail between the time the server starts to send document to the time it completes its task. We derive an expression for the *Mean Time to Failure* (MTTF) of that server and an expected amount of document portion the server fails to deliver, referred to as *missing* data. Again, in this case, the above mentioned two methods will be used to recover the missing data, and the performance degradation will be quantified for both methods. By this analysis, server failures are very well estimated so that the Service Provider (SP) can plan in advance to allocate appropriate resources to ensure a reliable service.

We testify all the theoretical findings and highlight certain key features that are useful in designing such network based service rendering systems with rigorous simulation experiments. Finally, although MSR schemes are attractive in many aspects as discussed in the previous chapters, it is the reliability measure that remains to be explored to truly test the system performance, as the service provision is launched on a networked/distributed environment. In Chapter 8, a JINI-based implementation is used to conduct server crash tests and evaluate the reaction of the system in terms of providing a continuous presentation as well as load balancing. Further, the results from this research elicit several important aspects that a system and/or an algorithm designer must take into account while deploying a host of VoD servers. In fact, this study exposes interesting trade-off relationships between access time and the reliability (availability) performance measures.

7.1.1   Definitions, notations, terminology

As described earlier, the strategy is to utilize a pool of servers to retrieve the requested movie such that the access time is minimized and the system reliability is maximized. We shall now formally define some quantities and introduce the notations used in this chapter:

- N: Number of multimedia servers denoted as S_i, $i = 0, ..., N - 1$, in the system.
- m_i: Portion of the movie document retrieved from server S_i
- L: Total length of the movie expressed in Mbits or Gbits. Note that $\sum_{k=0}^{N-1} m_k = L$.
- bw_i: The inverse of the bandwidth of the channel between server S_i and the client. bw_i is defined as the time to download a unit amount of data over that channel, measured in *secs per unit load*. Without any loss of generality, we shall continue to refer to this quantity as bandwidth.

- R_{play}: Inverse of the normal playback rate of the movie at the client site. This is defined as the time to play a unit amount of movie data, measured in *secs per Mbits or secs per MBytes*.

- *Resource*: We refer to a resource as a single entity comprised of a server and the associated communication channel. Thus, a failure may correspond to either a server failure or a communication channel failure or both. A failure of one of the components or both will affect the presentation at the client site. Below, we attempt to quantify the *failure rate* and *reliability* pertaining to a resource, as opposed to failure rates and reliabilities for individual components. Thus, we avoid referring to a resource as *a resource pertaining to a MM server and its communication channel* explicitly every time.

- λ_i: This is the failure rate of the resource i and we assume it is constant. As mentioned above, this refers to the combined failure rate of server and link.

- r: This is the repair rate of the resource and we assume it is constant. We assume that all resources have the same repair rate because the SP practices the same recovery procedure for all the resources.

- $R_i = Pr_i(t > t_i)$: This is referred to as the reliability of a resource i, and it is defined as the probability that the resource will not fail before the data portion m_i has been completely transferred to the client.

- T_R: This is the time to recover a resource, i.e., the time interval between the instant at which a resource fails and the time instant at which the resource resumes its normal operation.

- τ: Time delay incurred in transferring the missing data in case of a resource failure.

- α: This is defined as a factor by which the playback rate is altered depending on data loss following a resource failure. Thus, $0 \leq \alpha \leq 1$ such that the playback rate at a given instant in time at the client, is given by R_{play}/α. Note that if the data loss is large, then we choose a small value of α, implying a slow playback rate and vice versa.

- t_c: The time instant at which a resource fails.

- t_r: The time instant by which the missing data has to be delivered to the client for continuous playback.

- $MTTR$: Mean Time To Repair a resource. We assume all resources have identical MTTR because a SP usually practices the same recovery procedure for all the resources.

- $MTTF_i$: is the Mean Time To Failure of resource i.

- A_i: This is referred to as the *availability* of resource i, and is defined as the probability that the resource is operating successfully over a period of time. It can be expressed as, $MTTF_i/(MTTF_i + MTTR)$ [29].

- $\sigma(0, ..., k, k + 1, ..., N - 1)$: The sequence in which the retrieval of media portions from the servers are sought, i.e., in the order of

$$S_0, S_1, S_2, \ldots, S_{k-1}, S_k, S_{k+1}, S_{k+2}, \ldots, S_{N-1}$$

respectively.

- $R_s(\sigma(0, ..., k, k + 1, ..., N - 1))$: The system reliability when the retrieval sequence is $\sigma(0, ..., k, k + 1, ..., N - 1)$.

7.1.2 Some remarks

As we know from the basic working style of the MSR strategies, when a request is placed by the client, the SP could return a schedule to the client and the respective N servers. Typically, the schedule consists of informing the servers on the starting time of downloading the data, the amount of data that each server has to render, and the order in which these portions are to be retrieved by the respective servers from their databases. For instance, for downloading a movie of length $300Mbits$, a typical schedule with a 3-server system may be as follows. The start time may be from say, $t = 0$, and $m_0 = 100Mbits$, $m_1 = 120Mbits$, and $m_2 = 80Mbits$, respectively. Further, the SP will also inform the first server that it has to download $100Mbits$ starting from the first byte of the movie, and the second server to download the next $120Mbits$ of data (giving the exact starting and ending locations) and the third server to download the next (the last, in this example) $80Mbits$ of data. From the basic recursive equations in Section 2.3 we can obtain the access times given by $AT = m_0 bw_0$, where bw_0 is the connection bandwidth from S_0 to the client and m_0 is obtained after solving Eq. 2.8.

Let us assume that the availability of the first server is $A_0 = 99.98\%$, second server is $A_1 = 90\%$ and third server is $A_2 = 99\%$. With these quantities, the SP may recommend a new schedule to the client is $m_0 = 120Mbits$, $m_1 = 95Mbits$, and $m_2 = 85Mbits$, respectively. Taking into account the availabilities of the servers, we allow the client to start the movie playback of the first data portion m_0 at time $AT = m_0 bw_0/A_0$, a longer time period than $m_0 bw_0$ (as in the above example) to guarantee that it receives the entire data portion m_0. Similarly, the client starts the playback of second data portion m_1 at time $m_1 bw_1/A_1$. Although there is an increase in access time in this new retrieval strategy, servers with high availability deliver relatively more data while servers with low availability deliver relatively less data, thus clearly accounting the failure possibilities of the resources. The system reliability can be improved by this retrieval strategy. This new retrieval strategy is formally introduced in the next section.

Thus, we will revisit the design of the MSR approach to seek minimum access times by taking into account the resource (server and/or communication channel) availabilities so that the overall system reliability is maximized.

7.2. Revisiting the Design and Analysis of MSR Strategy with Server Reliability

As mentioned above, we assume that the resource (by which we mean either a server and/or the communication channel between the server and the client) in this system has a constant failure rate λ_i and a constant repair rate r. Further, we shall assume that the reliability of each resource R_i, $i = 0, ..., N - 1$ follows an exponential probability distribution. That is, in general,

$$R_i = Pr_i(t > m_i bw_i) = e^{-\lambda_i m_i bw_i} \qquad (7.1)$$

The availability A, the probability that a resource is in normal operation, depends on both reliability and maintainability of the resource. Thus, in general, the availability can be expressed as $Availability = uptime/(uptime + downtime)$, where $uptime$ is the time duration in which the resource is in normal operation and $downtime$ is the time duration in which the resource is not available for service, respectively. The availability for a constant failure rate and constant repair rate resource is given as [29],

$$A_i(t) = \frac{r}{\lambda_i + r} + \frac{\lambda_i}{\lambda_i + r} e^{-(\lambda_i + r)t} \qquad (7.2)$$

The average availability over a period of time from t_1 to t_2 can be calculated as,

$$A_{i(t_2 - t_1)} =$$
$$\frac{1}{t_2 - t_1} \int_{t_1}^{t_2} A_i(t) dt = \frac{1}{t_2 - t_1} \int_{t_1}^{t_2} (\frac{r}{\lambda_i + r} + \frac{\lambda_i}{\lambda_i + r} e^{-(\lambda_i + r)t}) dt \qquad (7.3)$$

Then, the steady-state availability is given by,

$$A_i = \frac{r}{r + \lambda_i} = \frac{MTTF_i}{MTTF_i + MTTR} \qquad (7.4)$$

A resource can have an average availability ranging anywhere between 0 (low or no availability) to 1 (high availability). To ensure that the client receives the entire media portion, say m_i from S_i, the client starts its playback from time $m_i bw_i / A_i$ instead of $m_i bw_i$, thus allowing more downloading time, since $A_i < 1$, where A_i is the availability of resource pertaining to server S_i. If this resource fails during the communication time period, the SP will have more time to allocate any standby resources to recover the missing data or may wait for a failed resource to resume the communication.

Thus, to guarantee a continuous playback under a realistic (failure prone) scenario, the time constraint relationship is modified as,

$$\frac{m_{j+1} bw_j}{A_{j+1}} \leq \frac{m_j bw_j}{A_j} + m_j R_{play}, \quad j = 0, ..., N - 2 \quad (7.5)$$

We denote $(bw_j / A_j + R_{play}) / (bw_{j+1} / A_{j+1}) = \rho_j$, and (7.5) becomes,

$$m_{j+1} \leq m_j \rho_j, \quad j = 0, ..., N - 2 \quad (7.6)$$

We thus have a set of $(N - 1)$ recursive equations. Using equality relationship in (7.6) and $\sum_{k=1}^{N} m_k = L$, we obtain the portion m_0 as,

$$m_0 = \frac{L}{1 + \sum_{p=1}^{N-1} \Pi_{k=0}^{p-1} \rho_k} \quad (7.7)$$

Substituting (7.7) in (7.6), we obtain the respective portions that can be retrieved from each of the servers as,

$$m_j = \frac{L \Pi_{k=0}^{j-1} \rho_k}{1 + \sum_{p=1}^{N-1} \Pi_{k=0}^{p-1} \rho_k}, \quad j = 1, 2, ..., N - 1 \quad (7.8)$$

The access time is then given by,

$$AT = \frac{m_0 bw_0}{A_0} = \frac{L bw_0 / A_0}{1 + \sum_{p=1}^{N-1} \Pi_{k=0}^{p-1} \rho_k} \quad (7.9)$$

Note that the access time given by (7.9) is greater than $m_0 bw_0$ in the MSR scheme by a factor $1/A_0$ which is greater than 1.

The system reliability can be calculated using the reliability of each constituent resource. It may be noted that albeit the fact that all the N servers are involved in downloading the respective portions concurrently, this multi-server system with N servers basically functions as a set of resources connected in a sequential fashion from the client's perspective. That is, all resources must function for the entire presentation to be continuous, and if any one of the resources fails, the presentation will encounter a discontinuity. The system reliability for N independent resources in series is given as

[29],

$$R_s = \Pi_{i=0}^{N-1} R_i = \Pi_{i=0}^{N-1}(e^{-\lambda_i m_i bw_i}) = exp(-\sum_{i=0}^{N-1} \lambda_i m_i bw_i)$$

Using (7.8) for m_i, we obtain,

$$R_s - exp(-\sum_{i=0}^{N-1} \lambda_i(\frac{L\Pi_{k=0}^{i-1}\rho_k}{1 + \sum_{p=1}^{N-1} \Pi_{k=0}^{p-1}\rho_k})bw_i) \qquad (7.10)$$

Thus, the system reliability is not only dependent on the reliabilities of the individual resources, but also largely determined by the bandwidth of each constituent resource. Both factors will determine the size of each data portion to be retrieved. Example 1 below clarifies this aspect. Clearly, this is intuitively appealing and the model presented in this chapter elegantly captures this behavior of the strategy. Later, in the simulation study to be presented, we shall demonstrate the trade-off relationship between the access time and the system reliability.

7.2.1   Effect of sequencing

In this section, we shall investigate the effect of sequencing on the system reliability and access time. In Chapter 2, it has been shown that the access time remains unaffected when the order in which the movie portions are retrieved from the servers is varied. While this observation can be easily verified even with the mathematical model in this chapter as far as access time is concerned by following the same steps, it remains to be explored whether or not the system reliability is *sensitive* to sequencing. We investigate on this issue in this section and we attempt to derive an optimal sequencing of the servers to achieve the highest system reliability. We consider the following example which clearly shows that reliability is affected by sequencing.

Example 1. Consider a system with 10 servers that are required to deliver a 3-hour MPEG I [4] movie to a client. We assume that the bandwidth of all the channels to the client is $1 sec/Mbit$ and the availability of servers is $A_0 = ... = A_4 = 0.99$, and $A_5..A_9 = 0.67$, respectively. Let us assume that $\sigma(0, 1, 2, 3, 4, 5, 6, 7, 8, 9)$ be the retrieval sequence. Using 7.10, the system reliability is obtained as 0.14. However, if we adopt a sequence, say $\sigma(5, 6, 7, 8, 9, 0, 1, 2, 3, 4)$ the system reliability is obtained as 0.82. Clearly, we see an improvement in the overall system reliability.

---

[4]For MPEG I has a typical playback rate of 0.67 sec/Mbit.

If the bandwidth of all the channels to the client is $1.2sec/Mbit$, then for sequence $\sigma(0, 1, 2, 3, 4, 5, 6, 7, 8, 9)$, the system reliability is given by 0.1, whereas when the sequence of retrieval is $\sigma(5, 6, 7, 8, 9, 0, 1, 2, 3, 4)$, the system reliability is given by 0.74. We observe the effect of bandwidth in deciding the overall system reliability, as described by (7.10).

Thus, we observe that the overall system reliability is indeed affected by sequencing, which motivates us to investigate how to determine an optimal retrieval sequence. We state the following theorem, which is an important contribution.

Theorem 1. An optimum system reliability (in the sense of maximizing the system reliability) can be achieved when the order of retrieval from the servers is such that $\lambda_0 bw_0 > \lambda_1 bw_1 > ... > \lambda_{N-1} bw_{N-1}$, i.e., the retrieval of movie portions must follow an order in which the quantity $\lambda_i bw_i$ decreases.

Proof. Let $q = \sigma(0, 1, ..., k, k+1, ..., N-1)$ and $q' = \sigma(0, ..., k-1, k+1, k, k+2, ..., N-1)$ be two sequences of retrieval. Observe that in sequence q', servers k and $k+1$ are swapped. Let $\lambda_k bw_k = \beta \lambda_{k+1} bw_{k+1}$, where $\beta < 1$. Let the system reliabilities using these sequences be $R_s(q)$ and $R_s(q')$, respectively. The corresponding terms $\rho_{k-1}, \rho_k, \rho_{k+1}, \rho'_{k-1}, \rho'_k$ and ρ'_{k+1} for these respective sequences are given by,

$$\rho_{k-1} = \frac{bw_{k-1} + R_{play}}{bw_k}$$

$$\rho_k = \frac{bw_k + R_{play}}{bw_{k+1}}$$

$$\rho_{k+1} = \frac{bw_{k+1} + R_{play}}{bw_{k+2}} \qquad (7.11)$$

$$\rho'_{k-1} = \frac{bw_{k-1} + R_{play}}{bw_{k+1}}$$

$$\rho'_k = \frac{bw_{k+1} + R_{play}}{bw_k}$$

$$\rho'_{k+1} = \frac{bw_k + R_{play}}{bw_{k+2}} \qquad (7.12)$$

respectively. According to (7.10), we have,

$$\frac{R_s(q')}{R_s(q)} = \frac{exp(-T')}{exp(-T)} = exp(T - T') \qquad (7.13)$$

where, T' and T are the indices (expressions) appearing in (7.10) of $R_s(q')$ and $R_s(q)$, respectively. The denominator of T can be written as,

$$denom(T) = 1 + \rho_0 + \rho_0\rho_1 + \rho_0\rho_1\rho_2 + ... =$$
$$= 1 + \rho_0(1 + \rho_1(1 + \rho_2(...))) \quad (7.14)$$

Thus,

$$denom(T') - denom(T) =$$

$$\frac{R_{play} + \frac{bw_{k-1}}{A_{k-1}}}{\frac{bw_{k+1}}{A_{k+1}}}(1 + \frac{R_{play} + \frac{bw_{k+1}}{A_{k+1}}}{\frac{bw_k}{A_k}}(1 + \frac{R_{play} + \frac{bw_k}{A_k}}{\frac{bw_{k+2}}{A_{k+2}}}))$$

$$-\frac{R_{play} + \frac{bw_{k-1}}{A_{k-1}}}{\frac{bw_k}{A_k}}(1 + \frac{R_{play} + \frac{bw_k}{A_k}}{\frac{bw_{k+1}}{A_{k+1}}}(1 + \frac{R_{play} + \frac{bw_{k+1}}{A_{k+1}}}{\frac{bw_{k+2}}{A_{k+2}}})) \quad (7.15)$$

It may be verified that the above equation returns zero after some algebraic manipulations, thus yielding $denom(T') = denom(T)$. Also, it can be shown that $\rho_{k-1}\rho_k\rho_{k+1} = \rho'_{k-1}\rho'_k\rho'_{k+1}$ and hence, the expression for $(T - T')$ can be rewritten as,

$$T - T' = \frac{L}{denom(T)}(\rho_0\rho_1...\rho_{k-2})(\frac{bw_{k-1}}{A_{k-1}} + R_{play}) \quad (7.16)$$
$$\times \; A_k A_{k+1} R_{play} \left(\frac{(1 - \beta)\lambda_{k+1}bw_{k+1}}{bw_k bw_{k+1}} \right)$$

Thus, since $\beta < 1$, we have $(T - T') > 0$ or equivalently, $R_s(q') > R_s(q)$. This means that the system reliability can be improved by swapping the order of retrieval from servers S_k and S_{k+1} as $\lambda_{k+1}bw_{k+1} > \lambda_k bw_k$. Thus, any valid sequence of servers can be generated from a given single sequence by iteratively swapping the adjacent servers. The above proof establishes the fact that in each such iteration a definite improvement in the overall system reliability can be obtained. In another words, an optimum (maximum) system reliability can be achieved if we arrange the sequence of the servers such that $\lambda_0 bw_0 > \lambda_1 bw_1 > ... > \lambda_{N-1}bw_{N-1}$. Hence the proof. $\square$

The significance of this result is as follows. From the theorem, we can observe that resources with both high failure rate and small bandwidth are preferred to be used initially in the sequence of retrieval and also to deliver smaller portions of the document. Also, resources with both low failure rates and large bandwidths are preferred to be used later in the sequence of retrieval and to deliver a large portion of the document. Thus, by choosing such a retrieval order we will be able to utilize all the servers with low availability servers to transmit the first parts of the video.   .

7.3.   Failure-Recovery Analysis

We shall now propose strategies to recover the missing data upon a resource failure. We assume that at most only one failure can happen in the system during the playback time period, that is, we consider only the case of single resource fault in our analysis. In the current problem context, considering server failures is more crucial than considering channel failures, since a SP can attempt to provide the missing data via alternate routes in case of channel failures. Thus, hereafter in this chapter, we consider server failures and propose strategies to recover the missing data upon a server failure. Note that by a *server failure*, we mean that a server fails to deliver the intended movie data to the client. Whenever a server fails, a client's playback may be affected, thus deteriorating the quality of service.

We approach the problem from two different perspectives. Firstly, we use a deterministic approach, by which we mean that whenever a server fails, it is immediately relayed to the SP, or after a short time. Thus, knowing this failure time instant, we design and analyze certain policies for recovering the lost data that can be used by the SP. Secondly, we use a probabilistic approach, in which the server failure can happen at any random time instant. The purpose of this probabilistic analysis is to estimate the possible failure time and the resulting expected (average) amount of missing data. This *failure-aware* approach can be used by the SP to prevent any catastrophic failures in the system, by reserving additional resources, if any, required to ensure a continuous presentation at the client site. Also, in this approach, after estimating the failure times and the average data loss, we attempt to use the strategies designed for deterministic approach to recover the lost data. We also attempt to quantify the expected quality of service that the SP may guarantee a client.

7.3.1   Solution using a deterministic approach

While N servers are in the process of downloading a movie document to a client, consider a situation wherein one of the servers, S_j fails at a time t_c, as shown in Figure 7.1. At time $t = t_c$, S_j is amidst downloading the data portion m_j to the client. Let us denote the data portion which S_j fails to deliver as m'_j. To ensure a continuous playback, the missing data portion has to be delivered to the client site on time before it is needed. Two possible

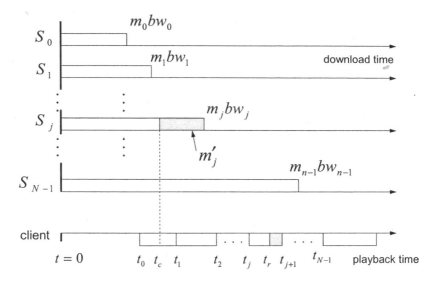

Figure 7.1. Single server(S_j) failure at time t_c. The shadowed area represents the missing data portion m'_j that S_j fails to deliver

approaches are proposed below to recover the lost data.

1. One or more idle servers (standby servers) replace a failed server and they can send the data m'_j to the client.

2. The client waits for a failed server S_j to recover and it will continue to download the data m'_j from S_j after it resumes to normal service.

The SP actively monitors the whole system to see if there is any server failure and as soon as a failure is sensed, recovery procedures will be carried out to recover the lost data as quickly as possible.

The choice between the above two approaches depends on *how busy the system is*. If the number of clients that are being serviced by the entire system is large and if the existing set of servers cannot admit anymore requests, there will be no idle servers available to perform the data recovery. In this case, approach 2 has to be selected. However, if there are idle servers available and the data portion m'_j is present in their databases, then approach 1 is preferred. Also, if the recovery time of server S_j is too long, the client may experience considerable delay, beyond the expected arrival time of m'_j. On the other hand, if idle servers are ready to be used immediately, data starvation can be avoided and the missing data can be supplied immediately.

If we choose approach 2, the time delay of the missing data is given as,

$$\tau = (T_R + m'_j bw_j) - (t_r - t_c) \tag{7.17}$$

where T_R is the time to recover a failed server, $m'_j bw_j$ is the communication time of the missing data portion, $t_r = t_j + (m_j - m'_j)R_{play}$, $(m_j - m'_j)R_{play}$ is the playback time of the part of m_j downloaded by the client before the failure. Thus if $\tau \leq 0$, the playback will not be affected. However, if $\tau > 0$, the SP informs the client to slow down the playback rate to account for the data delay as mentioned in [50]. As an alternative, SP could trigger stopping the playback and display the time to resume. Thus, the factor by which the playback at the client is altered is given by,

$$\alpha = \frac{t_r - t_c}{T_R + m'_j bw_j} \tag{7.18}$$

It may be noted that, if $\tau > 0$, i.e., if $T_R + m'_j bw_j > (t_r - t_c)$, then $\alpha < 1$, hence, the client will play the movie at a rate less than the normal playback rate R_{play}. However, if $T_R + m'_j bw_j < t_r - t_c$, or $\tau < 0$, the missing data portion m'_j will be delivered to the client before time t_r. Hence, there will be no delay in delivering the data and the client will continue to play the movie at its normal rate. In this case, there will be no discontinuity in the presentation at the client site. Since any discontinuity in presentation is affecting the quality of service, we refer to the parameter α as a QoS parameter.

Most of the time the client will play the movie at the normal rate R_{play} with $\alpha - 1$. However, during the time period from t_c to t_r, α may be less than 1 and the playback rate at the client site is less than the normal rate R_{play}, whenever $\tau > 0$, as mentioned above.

If we choose approach 1, we proceed as follows. Suppose we can select a standby server which satisfies the following condition to deliver the missing data on or before the required time. That is,

$$m'_j bw_s \leq t_r - t_c \tag{7.19}$$

where bw_s is the channel bandwidth of the standby server during this data recovery. However, if (7.19) cannot be satisfied using a single standby server the SP will attempt to utilize 2 standby-servers in such a way that $f_1 m'_j bw_{s1} = f_2 m'_j bw_{s2}$, where, $\sum_{j=1}^{2} f_j = 1$. We solve these two equations to obtain f_i, $i = 1, 2$ values, respectively. Of course, to deliver the missing data the following condition must be satisfied.

$$f_i m'_j bw_{si} \leq t_r - t_c, \; \forall i = 1, 2 \tag{7.20}$$

Thus, if the values f_i, $i = 1, 2$ obtained above do not satisfy (7.20), then SP will consider using 3 servers and repeat the above process. Thus, considering K standby servers to participate in the retrieval process, we derive the amount of portions to be retrieved from each of the standby servers as follows. Note that all the K servers will start to communicate the data to the client at the same time and then end the same time. In general, the following set of conditions must be satisfied to ensure that the missing data can be retrieved on or before the deadline.

$$f_i m'_j bw_{si} \le t_r - t_c, \ \forall i = 1, 2, ..., K \tag{7.21}$$

and we solve the following set of equations together with $\sum_{j=1}^{K} f_j = 1$

$$f_1 m'_j bw_{s1} = f_2 m'_j bw_{s2} = ... = f_K m'_j bw_{sK} \tag{7.22}$$

to obtain,

$$f_i = \frac{bw_{sK}}{bw_{si}} f_K, \ \forall i = 1, 2, ..., K - 1 \tag{7.23}$$

where,

$$f_K = \frac{1}{bw_{sK} \sum_{l=1}^{K-1} \frac{1}{bw_{sl}} + 1} \tag{7.24}$$

Thus, each of the K servers will deliver $f_1 m'_j, f_2 m'_j, ..., f_K m'_j$ respectively. Thus, the data portion m'_j will be delivered to the client site without any delay following the above distribution. Thus, if all the available servers are utilized and if (7.21) cannot be satisfied, then the SP will inform the client to slow down the playback rate, as specified in (7.18).

In the above discussion, we assume that all the servers in the system are identically configured, by which we mean that any one server in the system can replace a failed server so long as it has the required document in its database. A failed server after recovery is added back to the system. By this method, the server failures can be handled without any noticeable quality loss in service. Standby servers can be set aside as a regular measure to handle server failures. Some minimum numbers of standby servers are maintained to ensure normal performance when failure happens while serving the clients.

7.3.2 Solution using a probabilistic approach

As mentioned earlier, the purpose of this probabilistic approach is to estimate the failure time of a server so that additional resources (stand-by servers) can be reserved in advance, thereby guaranteeing a continuous presentation at the client site. Also, it may be noted that the reliabilities of the servers are actually estimates computed by the SP. Since the failure time estimation depends on the server reliabilities, their estimation accuracy plays a key role in this failure-aware approach. Hence, if the difference between the estimated time of failure and the time at which an actual failure happens is large, then the SP can tune the estimates of the reliabilities of the servers to improve the estimate of the failure time. This estimation process can be carried out continuously by the SP by accounting more past data on the server reliabilities.

Thus, instead of considering a server failure at a fixed time, we assume that one of the servers S_j can fail at any time between time 0 to t_j, where $0 \le t_j < m_j bw_j$. We also assume that this server has a constant failure rate λ_j. If server S_j fails before time t_j, it has the following conditional probability density function.

$$f(t|0 \le T_F \le t_j) = \begin{cases} \dfrac{f(t)}{\int_0^{t_j} f(t)\, dt} & \text{if } 0 \le t \le t_j; \\ 0 & \text{elsewhere .} \end{cases} \qquad (7.25)$$

and its expected failure time (conditional MTTF) can be derived as,

$$
\begin{aligned}
E\{T_F|0 \le T_F \le t_j\} &= \frac{\int_0^{t_j} t f(t)\, dt}{\int_0^{t_j} f(t)\, dt} = \frac{\int_0^{t_j} t \lambda_j e^{-\lambda_j t}\, dt}{1 - e^{-\lambda_j t_j}} \\
&= \frac{1}{(1 - e^{-\lambda_j t_j})\lambda_j} \int_0^{t_j \lambda_j} t e^{-t}\, dt \\
&= \frac{1 - (t_j \lambda_j + 1)e^{-t_j \lambda_j}}{(1 - e^{-\lambda_j t_j})\lambda_j} \qquad (7.26)
\end{aligned}
$$

Hence, the estimated amount of data that server S_j fails to deliver is given as,

$$m'_j = m_j - E\{T_F|0 \le T_F \le t_j\}/bw_j \qquad (7.27)$$

We can use both the approaches presented in the case of deterministic analysis here. When stand-by servers are not available, the client waits for a failed server to resume and supply the missing data. The expected time for a failed server to recover (T_R) is denoted as $MTTR$. The time delay incurred by the missing data to reach the client is then given by,

$$\tau = (MTTR + m'_j bw_j) - (t_j - E\{T_F|0 \le T_F \le t_j\} + (m_j - m'_j)R_{play}) \qquad (7.28)$$

However, if there are redundant servers (standby servers) available, the SP will first allocate redundant servers to replace a failed server. In this case, the following condition should be satisfied in order to facilitate the missing data to reach the client on or before the required time.

$$m'_j bw_s \leq t_j - E\{T_F | 0 \leq T_F \leq t_j\} + (m_j - m'_j) R_{play} \qquad (7.29)$$

where, bw_s is the channel bandwidth of the standby server for this recovery. As seen in deterministic analysis, the SP can allocate more than one server for data recovery in case one server is not sufficient. The following set of equations must be satisfied so that the missing data can be communicated to the client without delay.

$$(f_i m'_j) bw_{si} \leq t_j - E\{T_F | 0 \leq T_F \leq t_j\} + (m_j - m'_j) R_{play}, \forall i = 1, 2, ..., K \qquad (7.30)$$

Thus, the data portion m'_j will be delivered without any delay to the client site.

According to equations (7.26) and (7.27), the SP will have an estimate of the failure time of each server and the resulting missing data. Further, these equations serve as valuable guidelines for a SP to decide on whether or not stand-by servers are needed in case of a server failure. We will show later in the discussion section that the failure estimation can be useful to the SP for resource planning.

7.4. Performance Evaluation and Discussions

In this section, we shall test all the theoretical findings in a systematic fashion by rigorous simulation experiments. From a client's perspective, knowing the failure and repair rates of a resource, the availability of that resource can be calculated using (7.4). Based on the resource availability, the client starts the playback of each data portion from the time instant $m_i bw_i / A_i$ (assuming that the client makes a request at $t = 0$). The time window from 0 to $m_i bw_i / A_i$ is a longer time period than $m_i bw_i$, since $0 \leq A_i \leq 1$. This time period is an approximate estimation for the client to ensure that it receives the entire data portion within this time period. Note that, in reality, the entire data may be downloaded before time $m_i bw_i / A_i$, if the server and the communication channels are *highly available/reliable* during the data communication time period. Thus, in this model, by explicitly considering the availability of the server and its components, system *reliability* is considerably improved. Further, in this retrieval strategy, we observe that the servers with high availability will deliver more data while servers with low availability will deliver less data to the client, a feature that is naturally expected in a frequently failure prone system.

This feature can be observed in Figure 7.2 where we compare the single installment MSR scheme introduced in Section 2.3 with the failure-aware

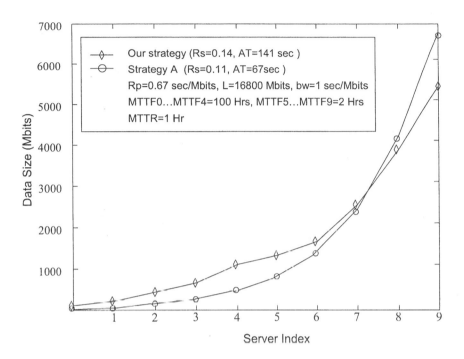

Figure 7.2. Data portions to be retrieved from the 10 servers for the refined MSR strategy and ideal MSR strategy (denoted as Strategy A in the figure)

MSR scheme of this chapter. We refer to the former as MSR or *ideal MSR* strategy and to the latter as modified/*refined MSR* strategy, hereafter. In this figure, we have shown the plots for a 3-hour MPEG-II video streams with $0.67 sec/Mbit$ playback rates for MSR and the refined MSR strategies presented in this chapter. The availability of servers can be calculated using their MTTF and MTTR values according to (7.4). The availability of server 0 to server 4 is 0.99 and the availability of server 5 to server 9 is 0.67. The data portions retrieved from each server are calculated using (7.8). As we employ the refined MSR strategy, we can observe that the size of the data portion retrieved from server 4 increases from $522Mbits$ to $1070Mbits$, the data portion retrieved from server 9 decreases from $6780Mbits$ to $5252Mbits$, respectively. Thus, the entire movie data are rescheduled in accordance with the availability of servers and hence, in this example, less data are downloaded from low availability servers (e.g. server 9) whereas, more data are downloaded from high availability servers (e.g. server 4). The system reliability is calculated using (7.10) based on each individual server reliability using (7.1). In this case, the system reliability increases from 0.11(given by MSR strategy) to 0.14 given by the modified MSR strategy in this chapter. Thus we have about 27% improvement! The access time, which is calculated using (7.9), increases from $67 secs$, given by MSR strategy, to $141 secs$, given by this refined MSR strategy, leading to 110% increase. Thus, a tradeoff exists between the system reliability and the access time. SP can use these relationships while pricing a customer. For instance, a service with highly available servers can be launched with higher pricing, guaranteeing a high quality reliable service than a service that uses a set of servers that are not highly available. In the later case, a more affordable pricing scheme could be in place.

We shall now investigate the influence of *sequencing*, the order in which the client retrieves data from the servers. It may be noted that the sequence of retrieval is actually planned by the SP. If a client retrieves a movie from N servers, there will be $N!$ retrieval sequences possible. The effect of sequencing on access time with our model, including availability factors, exhibits an identical behavior as the ideal MSR strategy of Chapter 2. That is, sequencing has no influence on access time. The proof of this claim is similar to the proof steps in Chapter 2, except we replace bw_i with bw_i/A_i. However, the sequencing of servers has an effect on the system reliability. As we vary the sequence in which the data portions are retrieved, the reliability of each individual server is affected, thus affecting the overall system reliability. In the above example, the original server sequence is $\sigma(0, 1, 2, 3, 4, 5, 6, 7, 8, 9)$ and if we adopt a sequence $\sigma(5, 6, 7, 8, 9, 0, 1, 2, 3, 4)$ the system reliability increases from 0.14 to 0.82. Thus, by utilizing low availability servers initially (and highly available servers latter) in the sequence of retrieval, the individual server reliability of the these low availability servers is significantly improved. However, this effect does influence negatively the dependability of highly available servers, as these are used latter in the sequence. Nevertheless, the overall system reliability is improved.

As we add more servers to serve a client, the access time given by the ideal MSR strategy (denoted as Strategy A) will decrease. Similarly, in the modified MSR strategy the access time will also be decreased when we add more servers to serve a client. Adding a server with low reliability will jeopardize the overall system reliability while adding a server with high reliability will improve the system reliability.

In the above example, if we add a new server 10 which is identical to server 5 (low availability), the access time decreases from $141 secs$ to $97 sec$ while the system reliability reduces from 0.82 to 0.42, as we have servers in sequence $\sigma(5, 6, 7, 8, 9, 0, 1, 2, 3, 4, 10)$.

On the contrary, if we add a server 10 which is identical to server 0 (high availability), the access time decreases from $141secs$ to $84secs$ while the system reliability increases from 0.82 to 0.87, as we have servers in sequence $\sigma(5, 6, 7, 8, 9, 0, 1, 2, 3, 4, 10)$.

We shall now show how the system could handle a single server failure in the above example. The client places the request for a movie of length $L = 16800Mbits$ at time $t = 0$. Each of the 10 servers has a connection to the client with a $bw = 1sec/Mbit$ bandwidth and the client's playback rate is $R_{play} = 0.67sec/Mbit$. The availability of the servers are $A_0 = ... = A_4 = 0.67$, $A_5 = ... = A_9 = 0.99$. The size of the data portion delivered by each server is calculated as $m_0 = 94Mbits$, $m_1 = 136Mbits$, $m_2 = 197Mbits$, $m_3 = 285Mbits$, $m_4 = 412Mbits$, $m_5 = 886Mbits$, $m_6 = 1474Mbits$, $m_7 = 2452Mbits$, $m_8 = 4078Mbits$ and $m_9 = 6784Mbits$ using (7.8). After the client receives the data portion m_0, it will start playback of m_0 at time $t_0 = m_0bw/A_0 = 141secs$.

We assume that server S_4 fails at time $t_c = 300secs$ when server S_4 has communicated $t_c/bw = 300/1 = 300Mbits$ to the client with $m_4' = m_4 - 300 = 112Mbits$ it fails to deliver. The missing data portion m_4' must be delivered to the client before it finishes the playback of data portion m_3 and the data portion S_4 has delivered before the failure at time $t_r = t_4 + (t_c/bw) * R_{play} = 614 + 201 = 815sec$ in order to avoid data starvation (due to time delay for supplying the missing data). The maximum time period allowable for this data recovery is calculated as $t_r - t_c = 815 - 300 = 515sec$. Assume a standby server with communication bandwidth $bw_s = 1sec/Mbit$ is available for this data recovery at this time (approach 1), the time required to deliver the missing data is given as $m_4'bw_s = 112 * 1 = 112sec$ which is smaller than the maximum time period allowable ($515sec$), and hence, there will be no presentation discontinuities in this case.

If there are no standby servers available at this instance, the client has to wait for a failed server S_4 to recover. Assuming that S_4 takes $T_R = 500secs$ to recover to normal operation and the server resumes data communications at this time, the time delay of the missing data τ is calculated to be $\tau = (T_R + m_4'bw_4) - (t_r - t_c) = (500 + 112 * 1) - 515 = 97secs$ using (7.17). Thus, in this case, the SP would recommend that the playback rate at the client is altered(decreased) right after the failure happens to prolong the playback time of the data portions before the missing data portion m_4' arrives, to avoid discontinuities in the playback. The factor by which the playback rate is altered can be readily computed using (7.18) and is given as, $\alpha = (515)/(500 + 112 * 1) = 0.84$. The playback rate from t_c to t_r

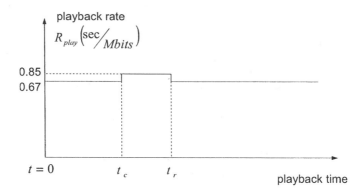

Figure 7.3. Playback rate variation at the client site in case of single server failure during movie retrieval

will be then $R_{play}/\alpha = 0.67/0.84 = 0.8sec/Mbit$ as shown in Figure 7.3. After the time instant t_r, the client will resume its normal playback rate R_{play}. To avoid the situation in which there are no standby servers available for a client, the SP estimates the failure probabilities of currently used servers to deliver the movie. In the above example, the estimated failure time $E\{T_F|0 \le T_F \le t_1\}$ of server S_4 is $315secs$ using (7.26). Hence, the SP would set aside one or more standby servers, in advance, for possible data recovery.

However, the actual time of failure for this resource is $300secs$. While the estimated failure rate $\lambda_1 = 1/MTTF_4 = 0.00014sec^{-1}$, the actual failure time can be substituted into (7.26) to calculate λ_1 as $0.00048sec^{-1}$ and it will be fed back to the SP to fine tune its estimation. The SP can gather a "history" of λ values for server S_4. If the sample size is large, λ follows a *Gaussian* distribution, the mean value of which can be a good estimator for λ.

Let us now analyze the behavior of AT as we add more servers into a group of servers downloading a movie to the client. To understand the relationship between the AT and number of servers N, we consider a case wherein all the servers have constant and identical availability A. We also assume that all the servers have identical communication bandwidth bw to the client. As expected, we observe that the AT decreases as the number of servers N increases as shown in Figure 7.4. This trend continues as more and more serves participate. Further, the system reliability remains unchanged as we add more servers to participate. This property can be readily realized using,

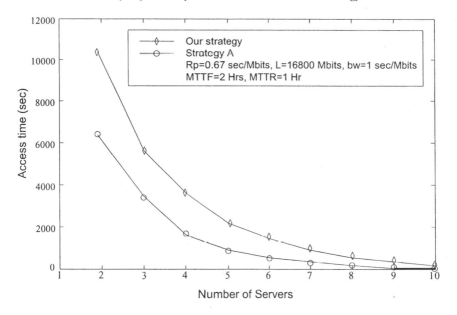

Figure 7.4. Access time vs. number of MM servers for the refined MSR strategy and ideal MSR(denoted as Strategy A in the figure)

(7.10). In this case, (7.10) can be reduced to ,

$$R_s = exp(-\sum_{i=0}^{N-1} \lambda m_i bw) = exp(-\lambda Lbw)$$

which is constant and independent of the number of servers. We shall now present some interesting experimental results where we have a set of 20 servers with different availabilities to deliver a 3-hour MPEG-II movie. All the servers are assumed to have a connection bandwidth of $1sec/Mbit$ to the client. We first generate a set of availabilities of the servers with the mean value of 0.9, following a uniform probability distribution. Based on the strategy described we determine the size of the data portion retrieved from each server. Further, the access times for a random sequence and an optimal sequence are given by, $1sec$ (as sequencing does not influence the access times) and the overall system reliabilities for the sequences are given by 0.61 and 0.85, respectively. Although there is a difference in the overall system reliability, the gain in performance is not significant, as the entire system of servers, in this case, are highly reliable. We can observe this from Figure 7.5.

However, when we change the mean value of the availability of the servers

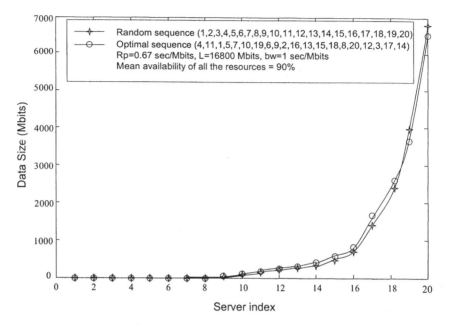

Figure 7.5. Comparison of a random sequence and an optimal sequence of servers in terms of data size. The mean availability of all the resources is 90%.

to 0.5, from Figure 7.6, we observe that the differences in the size of the data portions retrieved using a random sequence and an optimal sequence shows appreciable deviations. The overall system reliability is also improved from 0.01 to 0.02. This difference becomes prominent when the mean value of availability is 0.1. In this case, Figure 7.7 shows the size of the data portions retrieved from each server as before. Here, we can observe that the size of the data portions retrieved from each server, for the same randomly chosen sequence in the above experiment and an optimal sequence. We note that 18-th server in the chosen random sequence has been shifted to 14-th position in an optimal sequence; the data size to be retrieved from the same server decreases from $1520 Mbits$ (in random sequence) to $945 Mbits$ (in the optimal sequence). In this case, we clearly observe that there is a significant difference in the amount of data portions retrieved by servers in a random sequence when compared to the optimal sequence. In both cases, the idea of retrieving more data from highly reliable servers than from less available servers is followed. However, the main advantageous difference, comes from the fact that an optimal sequence indeed delivers an improved overall system reliability more than any random sequence. Thus, this experiment conclusively shows that the concept of sequencing has a significant effect

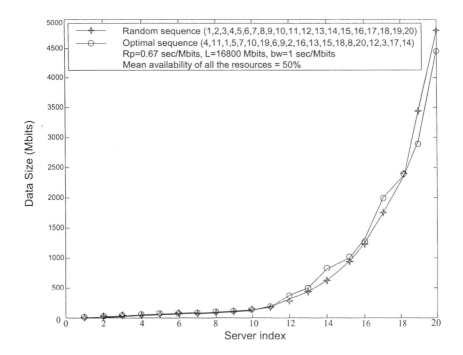

Figure 7.6. Comparison of a random sequence and an optimal sequence of servers in terms of data size. The mean availability of all the resources is 50%.

in improving the overall system reliability when the SP works with a group of low availability servers than with a group of high availability servers.

7.5. Concluding Remarks

In this chapter, we have discussed an important aspect in the design of MSR technology. We have fine-tuned the MSR strategy proposed in earlier chapters to incorporate fault-tolerance to provide more guaranteed and reliable VOD service. We have considered the reliability and/or availability factors of the multimedia servers and the communication channels which are contributing to the overall system reliability. This is one of the important contributions to this domain of research. With the mathematical model proposed, we have analyzed the effect on access times and identified an optimal sequence that maximizes the overall system reliability. We established a trade-off relationship between system reliability and the access time. We have shown that the access time of a multimedia document decreases as

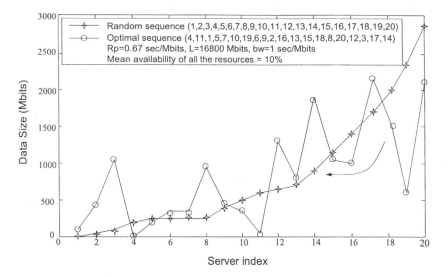

Figure 7.7. Comparison of a random sequence and an optimal sequence of servers in terms of data size. The 18th server in this random sequence is shifted to the 14th position in the optimal sequence. The mean availability of all the resources is 10%.

we include more servers to deliver the document to the client. Although access time remains unaltered when we change the retrieval sequence, an optimal sequence is shown to maximize the reliability/availability of the system (service).

We have rigorously analyzed the case wherein we have a single server failure during the retrieval of the document and presented two recovery methods to provide the missing data. The first recovery method employs standby resources to replace a failed server, while in the second method, we assume that there are no standby servers available and the client waits for a failed server to be repaired and to resume the data delivery. We have demonstrated the effect of these two methods and the impact of estimation on the server reliabilities by a SP via rigorous simulation tests. Further, to quantify the service quality, we have introduced a QoS parameter to measure the system performance in case of resource failure. We also analyzed all these issues from a probabilistic perspective in which we assume that a server may fail before it completes communicating its assigned data portion. However, the failure time of this server is not known in advance. We derived expressions for MTTF of this resource and the expected amount of missing data the resource failed to deliver. We have also demonstrated how a SP can make use of this estimate on the size of the missing data to plan for the deployment of standby resources.

The research contributions presented in this chapter are novel to the literature reported so far on movie retrieval strategies and can be used as a basis for future research to consider including reliability issues while employing a multi-installment retrieval strategy to minimize the access time of large size multimedia documents. It can also be used to analyze the reliability issues for a system which has a heterogeneous mix of resources with high and low availabilities. Following the treatment in Chapter 3, an immediate extension could be to analyze a multiple-server multiple-clients scenario using the strategies presented in this chapter. Further, with multiple servers rendering each portion of the media stream with certain availabilities, it would be natural to investigate the problem from the client's perspective. That is, given the fact that a client attempts to interact during presentation, one can study the performance in order to obtain a complete picture of a practically viable scheme.

Bibliographic Notes

Most of the contributions in this chapter appear in [106]. Apart from the recent attempts employing multiple servers in the literature, considerable research has been devoted in designing several retrieval scheduling strategies, e.g., retrieval scheduling for disk (single and arrays of disks) [80, 110, 100] and tape cartridge [62] for minimizing the access time of a requested document, while maximizing the number of continuous streams that can be supported and minimizing the buffer requirements at the client sites. These scheduling strategies are tightly related with the type of storage media. Besides, there are scheduling strategies not related to storage media. For example, the authors in [55] assign requests to servers with lighter load (load balancing ability) to maximize retrieval capacity. Some of the recent techniques attempt to study the optimization of buffer sharing by caching the data for successive requests [97]. The study in this work is exclusively on buffer sharing aspects and a simple yet powerful Markov model is also attempted to quantify the performance.

Also, there are scheduling methods devised exclusively for broadcasting. These include, the pyramid broadcasting [109], permutation-based pyramid broadcasting [3] and skyscraper broadcasting [51]. In these schemes, the basic idea is to partition each movie into several segments and broadcast them periodically, towards a goal of achieving a minimum access time. An excellent compilation and comparison of various VOD techniques proposed in the literature until 1997 appears in [41]. Finally, the study in [49] presents protocols for broadcasting for VoD environments.

The problem of data organization and storage is well studied in the literature [78, 88, 113]. Some studies also focus on the design of movie buffer caching strategies for effectively utilizing the memory and reducing disk I/O overheads [26] and dynamic network resource allocation for improving transmission rates with low jitter variation in media streams [32]. In [32], a dynamic bandwidth management policy that uses the concept of TDMA is proposed and its performance is evaluated. The authors also propose a scheme that allows a graceful degradation of the QoS, when the underlying LANs capacity is not sufficient to meet the total demand. These studies essentially deal with the data layout problems for easy and high speed access from a single disk or an array of disks (RAID technology). On the other hand, problems that deal with the provision of services are classified into three types, namely *data-centered*, *user-centered*, and *hybrid* [41]. Conventional broadcasting [41] and a recently proposed pyramid broadcasting [109, 3] are the examples of the data-centered approach. A very recent work in [85] considers employing multiple servers to retrieve MM objects, but from a different objective. In this work, the authors design a scheduling scheme, referred to as an *application layer broker*, at the client site. Typically, a client negotiates with a group of servers and identifies the best server to retrieve an object. This scheme attempts to minimize the buffer space requirements at the client site.

Chapter 8

AN AGENT DRIVEN PRACTICAL MSR SYSTEM: JINI TECHNOLOGY

8.1. Challenges in Realizing a Practical MSR System

Designing and implementing high fidelity Video-on-Demand (VoD) service systems for providing network based services is always a challenging problem. The design must carefully consider issues on optimizing various parameters, ranging from data storage level to customer satisfaction, in terms of providing high quality, reliable and interactive presentation. The main attraction of these network-based services is that viewing and presentation controls are completely handed over to the client, in contrast with the conventional broadcasting schemes. Such broadcasting schemes also have inherent disadvantages of making the client wait through the entire broadcast batch to get his/her choice and usually impose high expectations at the client-end. Further, VoD services are attractive from economic perspective in the sense that, depending on the popularity of the movie, the per user cost can be decreased when some effective *placement of movies*[1] on the network is carried out.

In the literature, the design of a VoD system employs several technologies, ranging from disk array technology to sophisticated scheduling policies during admission control , are in place to optimize several performance parameters of interest. Typically these parameters could maximize the number of clients that can be supported[2], minimize the access time of the users, provide efficient use of the available buffer space, etc., to quote a few.

---

[1]This also referred to as caching at vantage sites by researchers.
[2]This is the main concern of admission control algorithms. See [108]

When concerned about the design of such VoD systems from scratch, several issues come influential and probably they are highly inter-dependent. We list them now.

— Design of Service Architecture

Specifically this considers what should be the basic service infrastructure and how a client will be handled; This in a way reflects the "promises" from service provider's perspective. The service architecture must also consider if it is of *centralized* type or *decentralized* type. In either case, admission control algorithms must be in place, which assures quality to the clients. Pricing profile and policies are also some key issues to be considered here. For an attractive service, frequent offers in the form of packages, treating a long-standing customer different from a sporadic visitor, capturing an interactive profile of a long-standing user and catering to his/her needs in a customized way, proffering intangible benefits, etc. It may be noted that the system must allow a sporadic visitor to navigate through the system and be exposed to all service structures available. Finally, the size of the system in terms of amount of resources (servers, any intermediate repositories to be used, static placement of databases on the network at vantage locations, resources depending on certain service categories, etc) to be invested must be carefully weighed and an optimistic break-even must be pitched.

— Expectations at the client end

To the best possible extent, this should be kept very low. Of course, before availing service, if negotiation between client and service provider is allowed in the design, depending on the QoS demands of the client, expectations can be dynamically put forth. By and large, certain assumptions on the client-end can be made, such as the machine capabilities(one or two versions behind the current version floating in the market at present), a joy-stick (if relevant), and any other devices that are imperative for a requested service. To some extent, assumptions on the existence of software modules at the client end (say media players, etc) can be made. However, if the service infrastructure renders in any specialized formats, then the required components may be allowed to be downloaded by the client. Complete interactivity under VoD services must be exercised and for pay-per-view services, clients must be allowed to reserve in advance.

— Directory Services and Software Agents

A directory based service provision is almost a mandatory requirement as the number of clients availing this service is expected to grow exponentially. Thus, designing a directory based service infrastructure posses a challenge in the following ways - an appealing and flexible graphical user interface that allows users to be aware of the types of services and service packages with the service provider; Provision for a casual one-time visitor; Upon making a choice of a movie (in case of VoD services), a trailer video-clip and story particulars as narrated at the back side cover of a video cassette cover to stimulate interest, etc, must be provided; User must be able to navigate the site freely and for subscribed customers provision must be made to customize their settings.

Above these interface design details, on network based services spanning a large pool of customers, an agent driven service structure will be flexible in, scheduling resources, optimally using the available resources, searching the required documents, negotiating with adjacent cluster domains for seeking the requested media clip, etc. An agent can be servicing a local domain with authenticated services and can be treated as a messenger navigating beyond the domain boundaries to negotiate and to retrieve the requested documents. Thus, when a clip is not locally available, the agent-based service system will negotiate with adjacent domains and fetch the document. Depending on the current demand profile of this document, it may or may not suggest caching the document in its domain for future use. Beyond these, depending upon the service package, a user may be allowed to personalize agents themselves and such an agent can be made aware of the user profile and interests.

In this chapter, we attempt to describe a practically designed MSR system designed at the *Open Source Software* laboratory at the Department of Electrical and Computer Engineering at the National University of Singapore, Singapore. The system was designed using agent-driven pull-based policies for VoD service. Our VoD architecture employs the retrieval model proposed in Chapters 2 and 3 and implementation is done by using Jini technology. To the best possible extent, we have taken care of the above mentioned system design requirements for service infrastructure, clients, and directory and agent services. The object-oriented Jini technology provides a flexible infrastructure for delivering services in distributed systems. Concepts introduced by Jini technology such as leasing, discovery and the movement of objects over a network vastly simplify interactions on a network embedding a great degree of resiliency and scalability within a distributed system. For us, the simplicity inherent within the Jini architecture itself typically delivers gains in the design and development of our VoD system. Meanwhile, the retrieval model employed in our VoD system involves in retrieving the long duration movie (typically of 110 minutes duration) from multiple servers which host the entire data of the requested movie. Non-zero delays encountered due to the underlying network and the playback rate of the movie are considered while minimizing the access time and in providing a continuous presentation.

In fact, the retrieval model proposed in the literature by Bernhardt et al.[3] is very close to the model adopted in Chapters 2 and 3 and in this chapter. In the former model, a single video is distributed over multiple servers, whereas each server only stores a subset of the original video data. To retrieve a video, all servers storing pieces of the requested video must send their subset in a coordinated fashion to the client. Our model differs from this model in several ways. Firstly, in the former model, each server only stores a subset of the original video data. Hence, the client cannot watch a certain portion of the movie if any server storing this movie is off-line. In contrast, this scenario will not happen in our approach unless all movie servers storing this movie are off-line because the entire movie is available with all (or a subset of all) servers. Secondly, in the former model, the distribution of the subset of the video data must be re-organized once after adding the movie server to take advantage of the added bandwidth and capacity. The servers in our model can be simply added to the current working system, without re-configuring other servers, which means scalability is taken care easily. Finally, in the former model, all servers contribute an equal share to the overall effort of retrieving the video. This scheduling does not take into account the differences among movie servers, such as affordable bandwidth, current load, and so on. These factors have been explicitly taken into account in the design of our system.

8.1.1   Implementation challenges

While the retrieval model of a MSR strategy for long duration movies is fully studied in the previous chapters, no experimental evidence was presented to justify the feasibility of the ideas, their applicability and quantify the performance of the system. In this chapter, we study the design and implementation of a Jini technology based VoD system utilizing MSR strategy. We present a prototype which clearly justifies the applicability of MSR strategy to real-life network based service infrastructure. This prototype gives a hope of extending this technology to a WAN/MAN network to optimize several performance parameters further, which is the ultimate goal of this multiple servers system.

---

[3]See [15]

Following are some key issues that we will address in our design. Although few of them are addressed from a theoretical standpoint in earlier chapters, practical implementation demands a different treatment, as it will be exemplified in the design.

– How to design a service architecture with multiple servers coordinating with each other in retrieving the movie?

– How to sense server crashes and what are the adaptive measures to take upon a server failure?

– How does a client behave in this system, right from the start-up phase to the presentation phase?

– How to manage the available buffer space at the client site?

In this chapter, employing Jini technology, we present a software architecture that answers all the above questions. Several intricate aspects of Jini technology are thoroughly exploited to make this system less complicated to deal with the issues such as, service location, service upgrading and server failure, etc. For example, in the implementation, a Jini service and an agent are created to coordinate the activities between a pool of servers and a pool of clients. In addition, code migration from this agent to the clients, which is transparent to the clients, is carried out for instructing the client-end on certain events. In the design, the movie servers only send the specified data to the clients upon receiving the requests from the clients. We refer to this system as a Jini based Agent driven pull-based VoD system(JVoD) system. This design and implementation study will certainly benefit Internet service providers who wish to render an attractive VoD services on networks.

8.2. Service Description and Retrieval Strategy

In this section, we shall first describe the basic service infrastructure of the system which comprises components like, the Movie Server, the Agent, the JLS (Jini Lookup Service) and the client, respectively. We will also present the details regarding a typical client's interaction in the system. Then we will present the theory behind the design of a strategy to retrieve a long duration movie from a pool of servers. Finally, we shall demonstrate an illustrative example highlighting on the workings of the strategy.

8.2.1 Overview of the service architecture

In the existing implementation, the interconnection medium is a fast switching Ethernet network in which a set of processors will act as Movie Servers and a set of processors will act as clients. But it does not mean that this

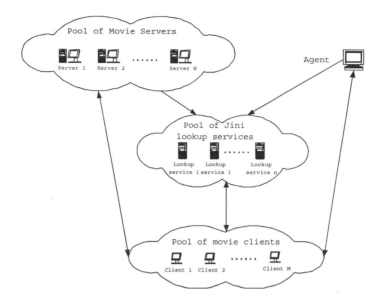

Figure 8.1. Overall view of the JVoD software architecture

VoD architecture is only valid on Ethernet network. The JLS also supports services over a WAN/MAN and the extension to WAN/MAN is clearly a study for the near future. The basic architecture of this JVoD system is shown in Figure 8.1 and comprises the following components.

A. Movie Server: The Movie Server is basically a host that stores the actual movie files that can be retrieved and viewed by the client. Besides movie files, each server also maintains a small database that is used to record the transaction history, which will be used to trace the server activities.

B. Agent: The Agent is the "brain" of the entire JVoD system. It is solely responsible on how the clients should behave in different situations. This is achieved by a downloadable part of the Agent, referred to as a *rule-base*, which enables the client to make a decision. The rule-base basically decides on *how*, *where* and *which* are the servers to contact and to retrieve different portions of the movies. In our design, the Agent not only aids the clients to carry out the required (streaming) transaction under normal conditions, but also instructs the clients (during the retrieval process) on how to handle the exceptions that might arise due to unpredictable server behavior, problem of some missing files, etc.

C. JLS: JLS holds the registration information of all services (the Agent and the Movie Servers in our case) available in the system. More precisely, a JLS maps interfaces indicating the functionality provided by a service to sets of objects that implement the service. The JLS acts as a conciliator to a client who is looking for a service. Any client who needs to make use of a Jini service will first contact the JLS. Then, the intended Service Object [54] is subsequently transferred from the JLS to the requesting client site where it will be used to set up the connection between the client and the Jini service. The Service Object contains the Java programming language interface for the service, including the methods that service consumers will invoke to execute the service along with any other descriptive attributes. Once the connection is established, the JLS is not involved in any of the subsequent interactions between that client and that service.

D. Client: The client is an application featuring a player. Further, through the preview screen, users can select and preview movies before they decide to view the entire movie. To fully utilize the multiple servers in the system, the client is allowed to receive concurrent (incoming) streams.

Thus, the above four essential components comprise the entire working system. Below, we shall explain on how a client typically interacts with the system, as an overview.

8.2.2   Interaction of a client with various components

The client in our system is "dumb" in the sense that it cannot make any decision regarding how the movie files are to be accessed from the Movie Servers registered with the JLS. After the client application is initiated, it downloads the rule-base from the Agent on-the-fly, then it can contact the respective Movie Servers, by using the strategies inside this rule-base. Exceptions that could arise are also handled by this rule-base. It would be meaningful to look on what exactly happens during a client transaction.

After the JLS and the Agent service are initiated first in the system, the components such as the clients and servers can become a part of the system anytime, since the Jini framework can self-recover as long as the JLS is available. Assuming that a new client application has been initiated, the client would first register itself with the JLS and obtain the necessary information regarding the Movie Servers from the JLS. However, the client will need to authenticate itself with the Agent before it can download the rule-base. Once the authentication requirements of the client are fulfilled (like entering the correct username and password), the client is said to be "logged on" to the current Agent, which will provide the algorithms(rule-base) that the client may use.

Once the user passes the authentication phase, he/she can then use the client application to open a comprehensive Movie-Selector that features a list of all the movies that are currently available (similar to a directory of available movies or yellow pages, with movie information) and a small preview screen. The generation of the list of movies is *dynamic*. This means that the elements in this list are subject to change, depending on the network environment. For example, when all the servers serving a particular movie are not currently available in the network for some reason, this movie will be immediately removed from the list. On the other hand, in the case where servers with new movies join the network, the information of new movies will immediately be available in the list. This dynamic mechanism is described in detail in Section 3.

With the Movie-Selector opened, the user can select any available movie and proceed to either view the trailer of the selected movie or to "buy" and view the entire movie immediately. When the user prefers to preview the trailer first, the client application is required to download the *Server Locating*(SL) strategy from the Agent. This SL strategy aids the client to locate a server from which the movie trailer can be retrieved. Our current SL strategy adopts a policy in which the client will select a server with a larger available transmission rate (depending on the current network and server loading conditions, the service provider can change the policy without involving the client), to retrieve the movie trailer. Once the trailer has been retrieved, it will be played in the preview screen. Further, once the SL strategy is transferred from the Agent to the client, the client need not download it from the Agent again until the client application is closed and restarted later. This means the client can reuse the strategy in its subsequent transactions (in a single session) till it quits the system.

After viewing some trailers, the user may then decide whether to buy the movies and view it. Once the user decides to view the entire movie, the client application needs to download more algorithms(strategies) from the Agent in order to fulfill this transaction. The strategies to be downloaded include, the *Streaming* strategy, *Buffer Management* strategy, *Scheduling and Retrieval* strategy, *Emergency Server Generating* strategy, etc. With these strategies, the client will proceed to start retrieving data streams from servers. Since this system supports multiple servers, the movie will most probably be streamed from more than one server. For example, if there are three servers hosting the requested movie, the algorithms from the Agent most likely will instruct the client application to stream the movie data from these three servers using separate connections. This implies that the movie data will be partitioned into three portions and streamed from each of these three servers. The algorithms also take care of assigning which portions should come from which of the servers. Once the connections between the client and servers are established, the movie data will be retrieved by the client and the buffering technique will handle these multiple incoming streams. After a *critical size*(as will be explained in Section 2.3.1) of the first portion data has been received, the client application will start the playback of the movie. The critical size guarantees that there is adequate data to play the movie *continuously* at the client site. This size is calculated by the algorithms provided by the Agent, taking into account the current network conditions.

As mentioned above, during the retrieval process, a number of critical situations may occur. Among these, there are two major critical situations including unpredictable failure of Movie Servers and failure of the Agent. The failure of Movie Servers definitely has a major impact on the performance of the system. Considering the case when there are three servers and one of them crashed during streaming movie data to the client, obviously, the client will not be able to stream the scheduled movie portion from that failed server. In this case, the Emergency Server Generating algorithm that was transferred from the Agent a-priori, will handle such a situation for the client. A *backup server* (one of the other two servers hosting the requested movie will act as a backup server) would be generated for the client to contact and resume streaming of the affected portion from the time instant where it stopped.

All these mechanisms are transparent to the user and the playback of the movie will not be affected, unless it is in a *race* with the data streaming (starvation of the movie data) at the client site. The possibility of this racing is extremely low, as the Agent algorithm had calculated the best possible critical size which ensures that the playback of the movie would circumvent this racing with the data streaming. However, it would be catastrophic if all the servers participating in the retrieval process were crashed before all portions were retrieved completely. If this worst scenario happens, the user would be notified that the playback of this movie would be affected. However, the user can continue viewing the available portions of this movie, or can go back to the Movie-Selector and select another available movie to view. On the other hand, the crashing of the Agent has no effect on the playback of the movie. This is because the Agent is not involved in the transmission of movie file after the connections between the client and the servers have been set up. However, in this case, the user would be notified that the Agent had exited the system and hence, it would not be possible to view other movies unless the client application is re-authenticated with the same or another Agent.

8.2.2.1   Strategy on a dedicated network environment: Equal Size Partitioning (ESP) strategy

The procedure described in Chapter 2 would be preferable, if the underlying network is a truly distributed one. However, in the existing implementation (and also when the underlying network is of small size), we have a fast switching Ethernet network comprising computers that are solely dedicated for this VoD system. Thus, the procedure described above has to be tuned for this environment. In contrast to the above strategies in which portions retrieved from different servers are of non-uniform in size, we propose an ESP strategy to obtain a better load balance among Movie Servers, as the communication speeds and server speeds are extremely fast and transfer delays are negligibly small in this dedicated infrastructure. In this strategy, the retrieval process from each of the servers is concurrent. In addition, in the earlier work a client is allowed to start the playback only after the client has received the entire first portion from the first server. However, in our retrieval strategy and implementation we relax this assumption and allow an *early start* of the playback which guarantees a presentation continuity. As soon as a *critical size* of first portion has been retrieved, the playback can be initiated on the client site. In other words, the client can start playing this portion while the remaining portion is being retrieved. This critical size indeed depends on the playback rate of the movie at the client site and the available transmission rates of the channels between the client and servers. For every portion that is to be retrieved from a server, our strategy recommends a critical size that should be retrieved in order to avoid data starvation.

As continuity is one of the major concerns during the presentation, the design of the ESP strategy must meet the following two important objectives. Firstly, the strategy must select the optimal set of Movie Servers that can be used to retrieve the requested movie. Secondly, it must derive the *critical size* of the portion to initiate the playback at the client site. The first requirement is used to minimize the access time of the movie and to guarantee a fault-free presentation while the second requirement is used to assure a continuous presentation at the client site. We let the size of portion retrieved from each Movie Server, measured in bits, as $m = \lceil L/N \rceil$. Note that we continue to use the same notations, i.e. $L, bw_i, R_p, cs_{i,j}$ for the length of the movie, the bandwidth of the channel, the playback rate and the critical size, respectively.

Now, we describe our retrieval strategy. Firstly, we show how the critical size is calculated with a given number of Movie Servers, which will be subsequently used to determine the optimal set of Movie Servers. Given that there is only one server, we will determine the critical size that has to be used to avoid racing. Similarly, when there are two servers available, we can have two concurrent streams. Thus, in order to utilize both the servers, we need to derive a critical size when two streams are to be retrieved from servers connected via different transmission rates. In the same way, if N servers are to be utilized, we need to derive a critical size when N streams are to be retrieved from servers connected via different transmission rates. Below, we will derive the critical size when there are, in general, k servers (k streams). To derive this critical size we proceed as follows. As a first step we consider only one stream and derive a critical size. Then in the second step, we consider including the second stream and determine a new critical size. Note that this critical size obtained guarantees a continuous presentation for the second stream alone, neglecting whether the first stream can be presented continuously. Similarly, in step k, we consider including the k-th stream and derive a new critical size, which guarantees that there will be a presentation continuity by considering the k-th stream alone. Finally, in order to obtain a ultimate critical size when there are k servers altogether, we consider choosing the maximum of the k values obtained from each of the above k iterations. Thus, this size is guaranteed to deliver a continuous presentation of the entire movie at the client site by employing k servers.

To clarify how this ultimate critical size is deduced, initially, let us consider a scenario when there is only one server in the system, i.e., $m = L$. In order to guarantee a continuous playback, the time to retrieve the remaining portion must be not greater than the entire playback duration of the portion when the playback is initiated. In other words, the following condition must be satisfied.

$$\frac{m}{R_p} \geq \frac{m - cs_{0,0}}{bw_0} \tag{8.1}$$

From the above condition, we can deduce $cs_{0,0}$ as,

$$cs_{0,0} \geq \frac{(R_p - bw_0)m}{R_p} \tag{8.2}$$

Thus, when there is only one server we have $cs = max\{cs_{0,0}\} = cs_{0,0}$. In this case, (8.2) gives the condition to choose the critical size that must be supplied initially so as to guarantee a continuous presentation.

Now, when there are 2 servers, we have $m = L/2$. Similar to (8.2), for the first portion, we have,

$$cs_{0,1} \geq \frac{(R_p - bw_0)m}{R_p} \tag{8.3}$$

Further, in order for the playback not to race with transferring of data in the second portion, we must have,

$$\frac{2m}{R_p} \geq \frac{m - cs_{1,1}\frac{bw_1}{bw_0}}{bw_1} \tag{8.4}$$

From (8.4), we derive,

$$cs_{1,1} \geq \frac{mbw_0(R_p - 2bw_1)}{R_p bw_1} \tag{8.5}$$

So, in order to meet the requirements in (8.3) and (8.5), the ultimate critical size is given by,

$$cs = max\{cs_{0,1}, cs_{1,1}\} \tag{8.6}$$

This rationale can be generalized for $(i + 1)$ streams originating from a system comprising of $(i + 1)$ servers as,

$$cs_{j,i} \geq \frac{mbw_0(R_p - (j + 1)bw_j)}{R_p bw_j}, \quad 0 \leq j \leq i, 0 \leq i \leq (N - 1) \tag{8.7}$$

Finally, from practical perspective, we have the ultimate critical size for $(i + 1)$ streams as,

$$cs = max\{cs_{0,i}, cs_{1,i}, ..., cs_{i-1,i}, cs_{i,i}, \delta\}, \delta \geq 0 \tag{8.8}$$

where parameter δ is the minimum size that a video player needs to initiate a playback and this value depends on different players. Note that when compared to the critical size obtained from (8.7), this parameter δ has a different interpretation. Critical size is used to guarantee a continuous presentation and is determined by our retrieval strategy, while δ is a codec and/or player-related parameter that reflects the minimum amount of data required to start the playback. Without loss of generality, we use $\delta = 0$ throughout this chapter. Thus, as soon as the critical size of the first portion has been retrieved, we can start playing the movie safely and the rest of the movie can be retrieved while the playback is underway. Thus, in our ESP strategy, (8.7) and (8.8) can be directly used to determine the size of the portion to be retrieved initially before playback commences. Further, in the following, we shall discuss how to determine an *optimal set of Movie Servers* that can be used to retrieve the entire movie, by using our ESP strategy.

8.2.2.2   Determining the optimal number of Movie Servers

The ESP strategy works on the fundamental assumption that the size of the movie portions to be retrieved from each of the servers is approximately equal. An immediate naive choice would be to use as many servers as possible to serve this request to minimize the access time of the client and to reduce the workload of every server. However, in some cases (the transmission rate(s) of one or more servers is(are) extremely slow), the access time does not always decrease when more servers are utilized. Hence, the problem now is to decide on an optimal number of servers to be used, satisfying the presentation continuity, using the transmission rate constraints and the playback rate constraints to minimize the access time.

To solve this problem, initially, all available servers (the servers holding the requested movie) should be located and sorted in a list according to their transmission rates, between each server and the client, in a non-decreasing order The first portion of the movie will be retrieved from the first server from the list (the "fastest" server). Similarly, the second portion will be retrieved from the second server from the list, and so on. After this list has been generated, an optimal set of servers and the ultimate critical size can be deduced by following the flowchart shown in Figure 8.2. Note that the complexity of determining an optimal set of servers is $O(N^2)$, where N is the number of available Movie Servers. To clarify how this ESP strategy works, without loss of generality, we now consider a scenario in which the requested movie is available at three Movie Servers, referred to as $JINI1$, $JINI2$ and $JINI3$. We assume that the transmission rates of channels from the above servers to the client are 1.2Mbps, 0.675Mbps and 0.45Mbps, respectively. The movie size L is assumed to be 900Mbits, and the playback rate at the client site R_p is 1.5Mbps.

First, we sort the Movie Servers according to their transmission rates. In our example, the order is "$JINI1 > JINI2 > JINI3$". Then, following the steps shown in Figure 8.2, the output (the optimal set of servers) is shown in Figure 8.3. As shown in the figure, there are altogether 3 loops. In the first loop, all the three servers are prospective candidates to participate in the retrieval process. Each of them is scheduled to cater a movie portion of 300Mbits. The critical size $cs_{0,2}$, $cs_{1,2}$ and $cs_{2,2}$ are calculated using (8.7) and the maximum of these three values, $cs_{2,2}$, is recorded. This recorded value represents the minimum amount of data that needs to be retrieved before the playback can begin in order to ensure a continuous presentation using all the servers. In the second loop, $JINI3$ (the last server in the current list of servers) had been excluded from the current list, which means that there are only 2 servers left to serve the entire movie, and hence, the size of the portion retrieved from each of the servers is increased to 450Mbits. Similarly, the critical size $cs_{0,1}$ and $cs_{1,1}$ are calculated and the maximum of these values is recorded. Then, in the third loop, $JINI2$ (the last server in the current list of servers) is purged. At this juncture, there is only $JINI1$

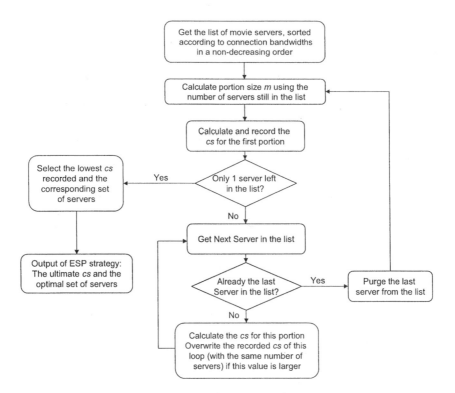

Figure 8.2. Flowchart of the ESP strategy

LOOP 1:

```
JINI1 serving 300Mb, critical size cs₀,₂ = 75Mb
JINI2 serving 300Mb, critical size cs₁,₂ = 54Mb
JINI3 serving 300Mb, critical size cs₂,₂ = 80Mb   ◀— Recorded
```

LOOP 2:

```
JINI1 serving 450Mb, critical size cs₀,₁ = 113Mb ◀— Recorded
JINI2 serving 450Mb, critical size cs₁,₁ = 80Mb
```

LOOP 3:

```
JINI1 serving 900Mb, critical size cs₀,₀ = 225Mb ◀— Recorded
```

Result :

```
Loop1 is selected, the final critical size  CS  is 80Mb

JINI1,JINI2 and JINI3 serving 300Mb, respectively
```

Figure 8.3. Typical output of the ESP strategy

left to calculate the critical size and this value, $cs_{0,0}$, is recorded.

Thus, after the last loop, we have 3 recorded critical sizes, $cs_{2,2}$, $cs_{0,1}$ and $cs_{0,0}$. Each one represents the minimum size of the first movie portion that a client needs to retrieve before the playback of the movie, by utilizing the corresponding set of server(s) comprising $\{JINI1, JINI2, JINI3\}$, $\{JINI1, JINI2\}$ and $\{JINI1\}$. In order to minimize the access time, the lowest value of these 3 sizes is chosen as the optimal critical size and the corresponding set of servers from which this value comes is chosen to supply the requested movie. In this example, the lowest value for the critical size, $cs_{2,2}$, comes from the first loop, and hence, all three servers participate to serve the movie data. In case where there are two or more loops with identical minimum critical size values, the server set with a maximum number of servers is chosen, since more servers obviously imply smaller portions to be streamed from each server and hence, lead to minimization of the access/serving time. Further, more servers means that there are more backup servers to select in case of any unforeseen failures.

So far we have presented the working style of the ESP strategy which employs multiple servers to provide a network based multimedia service. Following this strategy, we shall present the entire design of our JVoD software architecture.

8.3. Design of the JVoD Software Architecture

In this section, we shall present the design of our software architecture by considering the retrieval strategy which is addressed in the previous section. We shall describe the three components in our JVoD system:

- Movie Server
- Jini Agent
- Client

The functionality and implementation of the main modules of every component will be described. Further, we shall also describe the working style of each component.

8.3.1 Movie server : design and architecture

The Movie Server in our system is both a Jini service and a Jini client of the Jini federation, because it supplies service to JVoD clients, while it utilizes the service provided by JLS. When a Movie Server starts up, upon successfully registering with the JLS, the server is immediately ready for requests

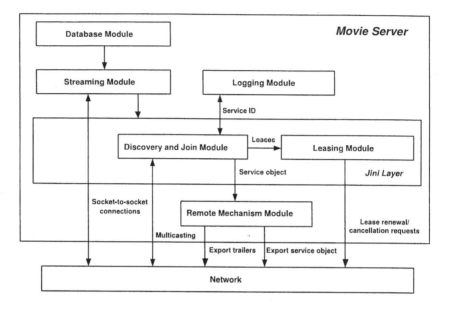

Figure 8.4. Movie Server structure design showing various modules

by activating its file streaming capabilities, utilizing socket-to-socket connection. One noticeable aspect of a server's file streaming capability is that it does not pose any constraint on the formats of the streaming file. As long as the client is able to play the formats of movie, any format can be used within the JVoD system. However, due to the constraints imposed by current technology of Java Media Framework (JMF) employed within the client component, the actual implementation concentrates currently only on MPEG media.

The Movie Server consists of several modules that interact with each other in a particular order, as shown in Figure 8.4. We shall now describe the functionalities of each of the modules.

8.3.1.1   Discovery and Join module

From Figure 8.4, we observe that there is an embedded Jini layer which has two modules: *Discovery and Join* module and *Leasing* module. These two modules are critical for the Movie Server to become a part of the Jini federation. When a Jini service is brought on-line, locations of the JLSs

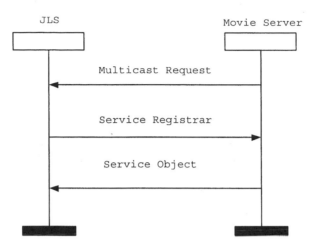

Figure 8.5. Discovery and Join Message Sequence Chart

are most likely unknown to the service, and hence, the service should find one JLS to register by using *Discovery protocol*. Jini defines two ways in which a Jini client can locate the JLS, using *Multicast Discovery* and *Unicast Discovery* [54]. In our design of the JVoD system, the former is adopted.

When the Movie Server starts, it will multicast a "special packet" to the entire network (this multicast will become a broadcast if the initial multicast group of the Movie Server is empty). How far this packet will go, or its *multicast radius*, depends on the routers deployed on the network. As long as the JLSs reside within this radius, they will respond to this special packet and this is how the initial set of JLSs is discovered. However, it does not mean that the JLSs have to be launched before the server in order to make this discovery possible. In fact, the administrator is absolutely free to start another JLS any time as desired. When this occurs, the new JLS will multicast a special packet to announce its availability to the interested servers within the multicast radius and this is the mechanism by which Jini clients locate new JLSs that have been added to the Jini federation. The significant implication of this approach is that the multicast discovery facility makes the startup sequence no longer important and the Movie Server or the JLS can be started in any order. This is also the reason why we employ the Multicast Discovery protocol. Then, the JLS that received the multicast will pass a *service registrar*, a *proxy* to the JLS, to the server. This service registrar enables a Jini client to interact with the JLS. After that, the service can register itself with this JLS by using the *Join* protocol. Then, a Service Object of the Movie Server is loaded into the JLS. The information about the Movie Server, such as server address, server port and titles of movies hosted on the server, can be obtained by invoking the methods inside the Service Object at the client site. Figure 8.5 shows the sequence of events occurring during a normal course of discovery and join process.

8.3.1.2   Leasing module

In a real-life distributed system, Jini components may fail at any time instant and the so far consumed resources by these failed components are locked. Further, there may be long delays encountered in waiting for a client to respond when the client had already timed out. This can potentially happen when service/response from a server takes a long time.To avoid these problems, some kind of relationship must be maintained between the server and the JLS and this is achieved by means of the *Leasing* module. When a service registers with the JLS, it receives a "lease" from the JLS. This lease represents the period of time after which the registration is considered void. The service must renew it before it expires, otherwise the JLS will assume that this service has expired and any resources associated with the lease will be freed at JLS. Basically, this is one of the ways in which a Jini federation achieves its self-healing robustness. Further, there is a trade-off between the duration of the lease and traffic generated due to the lease renewal process. For instance, if the lease duration is too long, then the registered list of services that the JLS is holding is potentially far from being updated. But, at the other extreme, where the service is expected to renew the lease very frequently, the lease renewal procedure will manifest itself very much like a constant polling, which could in turn affect the network efficiency. Apparently, depending on different conditions of traffic on the network and requirements of the service, the service provider may vary the value of the lease time to strike an optimal performance. In our system, a lease duration of 5 minutes (which is also the default period) is considered appropriate.

8.3.1.3   Remote mechanism module

The remote mechanism module is actually a HTTP server included in the Jini Starter Kit (JSK). This module is used to transfer the Service Object between clients and Movie Servers, which passes through one Java Virtual Machine (JVM) in passive form and is finally activated (brought to life) in the client's JVM. The additional functionality that the HTTP server provides is the movie trailer streaming capability. In this JVoD system, every movie that is hosted on the Movie Server comes with a trailer as well, and this file is usually about 5MByte in capacity. It is impractical to send it by means of the multi-threaded streaming protocol that entails some pre-calculations which is more suited for large-sized files. On a dedicated LAN environment, this streaming of the trailer normally takes only a few seconds time (typically, 5-6 seconds in our experiments, but it may not hold true in a large system) and thereby justifies this strategy.

8.3.1.4 Streaming module

The streaming module is built on top of the Jini layer to stream the movie data to clients. For each steaming thread created in this module mechanisms such as, handshaking, exception handling, garbage collection, etc, are carried out transparently. Further, this module is independent of any Jini specification. In other words, there is simply no communication between the Jini layer and this module anymore. This behavior appears to be slightly contradictory to the concept of robust Jini network, where automatic adaptation to the environment is expected. However, it is more appropriate to look at it in the following manner. As far as the streaming capability is concerned, the Movie Server is just a passive entity, as it never initiates any streaming by itself. Therefore it does not require holding any external information about the network like, *how many clients are there in the JVoD system?, is the client's request for a new movie or to resume a previous request?*, etc. In the case of any abnormal shutdown or streaming interruption (e.g. when the Movie Server crashes), the socket facility at the client site will "throw" certain *exceptions* in response to such situations, and as long as the client is able to react accordingly, there are no potential problems. Notice that all these exceptions are not tied to Jini in any sense, since they are just some standard classes defined in the Java Development Kit.

8.3.1.5 Logging module

For any commercial server, the logging facility is always one of the standard tools provided and it could be extremely useful in the event of debugging service failures. In our design, a fairly generic logging module has been created which allows the Movie Server to take a snapshot of a set of data related to the service state and then periodically update it.

This logging module does not merely capture the service state. In fact, the most significant function of this logging module is that it enables the service to recover the state of the data saved and recover its last saved state upon restart. This is similar to a *roll-back* service facility in the case of distributed transaction mechanisms [99]. In this way, the impact brought to the other entities of the network in the event of temporary service disruption is considerably minimized. In the actual implementation of this system, the only information captured is the *service ID*. A service ID is a 128-bit long number generated in a pseudo-random manner that uniquely identifies a service from the other services. When a service first registers with a JLS, it requests a service ID from the JLS. In the future, whenever the service restarts or new JLSs are found, it reuses this service ID for every registration. Further, this ID is an important piece of data to the client to discern service differentiation. If a client is searching services of the same type from different JLSs, the client can determine whether the objects represent the same instance of the service by comparing the service IDs. In addition, the service ID provides a way for the client to ensure that it can resume the same service again when the service is resurrected. Finally, we emphasize that this module is generic enough to handle most of the situations and certainly does not confine itself to storing service ID solely.

8.3.1.6   Database module

This module is developed to record all the transactions in a persistent storage space for future tracing purposes. This is a module residing on top of the Jini layer and is therefore well insulated from the Jini environment. For every transaction, the client's name, IP address, transaction type, date, etc, are all saved in the database. At a first glance, it looks as if it is rather similar to the logging module described above. In a sense, both are saving some information about the Movie Server. However, the key difference is that they are located in different layers. The logging module is meant for storing Jini specific parameters and retrieval of the last saved state of the Movie Server, whereas this database module purely manages the history of every streaming transaction, through the use of SQL.

Thus, we have described how a JVoD Movie Server in our system is designed and on the workings of various modules.

8.3.2   Agent : design and architecture

In the following, we shall consider the JVoD Agent design and describe various modules with respect to their functionalities. In the JVoD system, the Agent acts as a rule-base repository for the entire system, deciding on how the clients should behave in different situations. The rule-base is essentially a set of Java class files containing the necessary algorithms for the client. All these class files will be *serialized* to the client "on-demand", which is to say that a client will get these implementation classes whenever it makes a movie request. In other words, the rule-base logically resides on the Agent, but is executed on the client site. Depending on the network conditions and some other factors, these algorithms decide on *how* and *which* of the servers to contact in order to retrieve the different portions of the requested movie.

The Agent plays a crucial role in announcing a server failure. With the help from the Agent, the clients that are not actively contacting the server could be notified of the server failure even before the JLS notices this failure (due to lease mechanism). Other than performing the tasks above, the Agent plays the role of acting as a simple *Authentication, Authorization, Accounting* server. The JVoD system is intended to be a paid-service in the first place and therefore, some sort of identity confirmation is mandatory. The Agent authenticates any client who wants to join the JVoD system, then authorizes the eligible clients to negotiate with Movie Servers. After the transaction finished, the Agent updates the corresponding bill. This facility would help the service provider to manage the information of users.

As far as the Jini framework is concerned, the Agent is yet another Jini component providing services to the Jini clients. As a result, the structural design of the Agent resembles that of a Movie Server to some extent, especially the design related to Jini environment, as reflected in Figure 8.6. From the figure, we observe that there are mainly two groups of modules within the Agent component, the serializable module and other modules. The serializable Agent module is the rule-base while other modules provide functionality to the Agent application.

8.3.2.1   Discovery and Join module

Fundamentally, compared to the one belonging to the Movie Server, the Jini layer at the Agent works in the similar way.

8.3.2.2   Leasing module

As expected, the Agent needs to renew the lease regularly, otherwise the JLS will simply remove it from its managed set of services. Other than receiving leases passively from the JLSs, the Agent is also responsible for allotting a lease to clients. The Agent makes use of leasing to keep track of whether the clients are still alive as it is important for the Agent to duly release the resource that have been allocated for those "unresponsive" clients. For this reason, a lease (10 minutes) has been considered in our system (one can set this timing depending on the current performance). The client must renew it before it expires, otherwise the Agent service will assume that this client is "lost". If this happens, the Agent will drop this failed client and stop tracking this client.

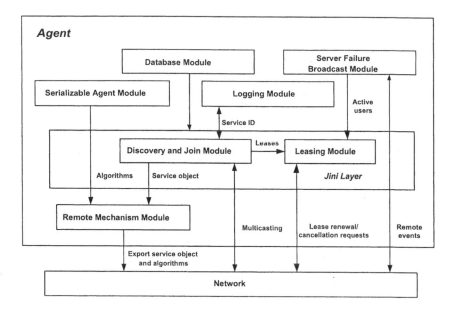

Figure 8.6. Agent structure design showing various modules

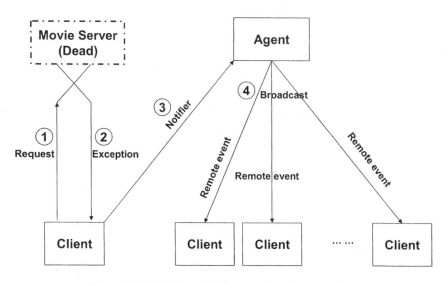

Figure 8.7. Movie Server failure event: broadcast mechanism

8.3.2.3   Remote mechanism module and Logging module

The Agent has also a standard HTTP server employed, as the protocol to export the Service Objects works in the same manner as the Movie Server does.

Also, the logging module works similarly to the logging module of the JVoD Movie Server. By storing the service ID of the Agent, this logging module enables the Agent to recover in the case of crashes. It must be realized that this module is generic enough to handle most of the adverse situations (Agent crash, link failure, etc) and certainly does not confine itself to storing service ID solely.

8.3.2.4   Fault Tolerance: Server failure broadcast module

Though it is a common belief that every component in a Jini infrastructure should be proactive in detecting failure conditions [54], it certainly does not have to be so at any time. In our design of the JVoD system, the Agent takes the responsibility of announcing failures of servers. The Agent uses the *remote events* mechanism to achieve this goal. Remote event is one of the Jini's APIs, which is referred to as the ability of one object to notify another object when some "event" has happened. The Agent does not create a remote event in any case, however, it stores and forwards such an event only when a client informs it to do so. The reason why the client can make sure that certain server is already down is because of the type of *Exception* thrown while it tried to contact this server. The following example should illustrate how powerful this mechanism can be.

Initially, let us suppose that there are m Movie Servers and n clients in our JVoD system. Suppose that one of the servers is abnormally terminated and there is no undergoing transaction between the clients and this server. When only the leasing mechanism is used, the JLS will not be able to know about this failure until the lease expires. As a result, the clients will not be aware of it too. The clients simply assume that all m servers are still alive. During this period of time, all requests of clients to this crashed server will fail. The scenario is totally different when the remote event mechanism is used together with the leasing. In this case, if one of the clients attempts to contact this failed server (obviously the client will not be served by this server), then this client will inform the Agent about the server failure by using the remote event. The Agent will broadcast the event of the server failure to the rest of the clients, who will then remove this server from their managed sets of servers. The sequence of events is shown in Figure 8.7. Effectively, the number of victims suffering from unnecessary connection has now been trimmed down to one. This is clearly a vast improvement, compared to the performance of the model using the leasing mechanism alone.

8.3.2.5   Database module

The user database held by the Agent is meant for restricting system access to only registered clients and keeping the bills of all clients. Besides these, the interface presented by the Agent also defines some methods for the client to change his/her password, update his/her profile, etc. Corresponding SQL commands will be generated when these methods are invoked, and since Java Database Connectivity (JDBC) was employed as an interface for executing SQL statements, the need for a low-level abstraction layer which does the actual connecting/transactions with the data sources is completely eliminated.

8.3.2.6   Serializable Agent module

This module is the rule-base of the entire system. This rule-base will be transferred to the client when the client needs it. The rule-base consists of the following strategies:

[A] Streaming strategy and Transmission Rate Testing strategy

The Streaming strategy allows clients within the JVoD system to initiate socket-to-socket connections with the servers. By defining the arrangement of streaming fragmented multimedia data from the servers, the strategy instructs the client to open connections with all the selected servers and start retrieving movie portions. Mechanisms such as, handshaking, exception handling, garbage collection, etc, are carried out transparently.

As the name suggests, Transmission Rate Testing strategy is used to approximate the transmission rate of each server-client channel before the actual streaming of the movie to the client. The reason to introduce this strategy is that even though the server can inform the client the upper bound of the transmission rate that it can afford, the actually offered transmission rate often differs from the upper bound and this difference will certainly affect the retrieval strategy. This strategy can be treated as a lightweight Streaming strategy as it has a similar algorithm to the Streaming strategy but the exception handling is somewhat simpler. In this prototypical implementation, we follow a simple testing procedure which basically averages out the transmission times after echoing several packets, using individual channel. Our strategy spawns daemon threads to set up socket-to-socket connections with the Movie Servers at the same time and start the transfer of dummy data, simulating the effect of streaming data from multiple servers. In order to get a more accurate result, this process may be repeated several times as the service provider desires and the average time taken to receive these packets is measured.

[B] Scheduling and Retrieval strategy

In our current implementation, the ESP strategy is adopted to retrieve the requested movie and minimize the access time.

[C] Emergency Server Generating strategy

The Emergency Server Generating strategy is a supporting strategy for the Streaming strategy. The main design objective of this strategy is to decide which Movie Server a client should contact in order to resume the streaming of an uncompleted movie portion that had been interrupted by errors. However, in the current implementation, the servers that the strategy can choose from are only limited to the servers provide by the ESP strategy, which means only servers selected by the ESP strategy can be allowed to participate in resuming operations. The logic for doing this is because that any server outside the server list generated by the ESP strategy would most probably slow down the performance of the streaming, since the ESP strategy had already evaluate all the available servers within the JVoD system before the streaming. Usually, when this strategy is invoked, the playback of the movie would still be executing without any effect.

[D] Buffer Management strategy

The multiple media data streams coming from the Movie Servers will be stored in the buffers (including RAM and hard disk) at the client site. Meanwhile, the client's system requirement has always been considered as one of the most important concerns during the design and implementation of the system. The main reason for the concern lies in the fact that any successful commercial application should always assume minimum requirements at the client site for the service to be attractive. In order for this system to meet this requirement, the approach of *memory releasing* is employed in the Buffer Management strategy to reuse the resource. In this approach, the buffer occupied is either flushed as soon as it had been consumed or been retained for sometime after it had been consumed. The former case is typical of an application such as *pay-per-view* kind of movie service and the latter is essential to achieve a simple *interactive* movie viewing service.

Having the rule-base stored in the Agent is actually very convenient, when it comes to upgrading. Depending on the current network and server loading conditions the service provider may vary the strategies inside this rule-base and this variation is transparent to clients. For example, the service provider may vary the Buffer Management strategy for clients, thus exercising different levels of interactivity with the service systems. This may also be a measure of QoS and hence, the pricing of the users may be varied for different interactive requirements. Otherwise, suppose if the rule-base is to be located at the client side and some improvements are to be made to the strategies, then essentially every client will have to go through some kind of upgrading process. This could be really cumbersome when a large number of clients are making use of this service infrastructure. However now, the existence of the Agent simplifies the process remarkably. If any change is to be made to the strategies, the serializable Agent module is the only part that has to be modified. The client will still remain as what it has always been and is yet equipped with the new capability transparently.

8.3.3   Client : design and architecture

In the following, we shall consider the design of the JVoD client and describe various modules with respect to their functionalities. In our JVoD system, it is noticeable that the JVoD client is a pure consumer which does not provide services in the Jini system. It is just a Jini application that consumes services available in the Jini system (the JLS, the Agent and Movie Servers, in this case). Further, all the intelligent parts of the client that are employed to fulfill the retrieval transaction will be transferred from the Agent (or in other words, they will be supplied by the Agent). This design requirement was intentional as, in general, resource expectations at a user side cannot be assumed by the Movie Servers. This in a way allows the scheme to be more attractive as any client satisfying the minimum requirements expected from the service provider, can also be a potential customer. As a result, the structural design of the client turns out to be quite straightforward, as shown in Figure 8.8. We shall now describe the functionalities of each of the modules.

8.3.3.1   Discovery and lookup module

The concept of multicasting discussed before also applies here. So long as the JLSs are within the multicast radius of the network, the client will be able to discover them. Unlike the Movie Server or the Agent, the client does not participate in the Join protocol, since it is a pure consumer and has no service to register with the JLS.

Right after the *discovery* stage, the client finds the appropriate services by looking in the JLSs and organizes all the Service Objects into a map. The map consists of entries involving pairs of objects. Each entry has a

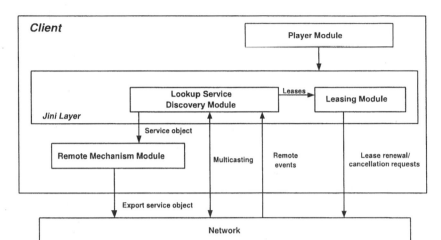

Figure 8.8. Client structure design showing various modules

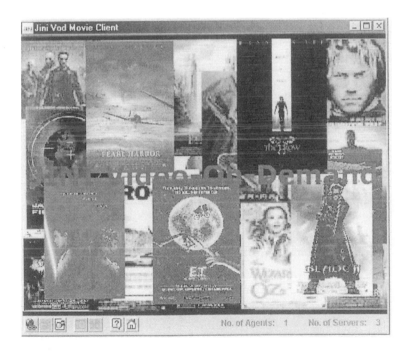

Figure 8.9. Accessing JVoD service through the client application - screen shot of the client

Service Object and an associated key object (service ID). In order to keep the most updated information about the services available inside this map, the Discovery protocol used so far is not enough. For instance, if a service that a client needs was started after the client, although the JLS is able to capture its existence, the client will not know about it (and hence could not show it in the map) because it only looks into the JLS only once. Apparently, a mechanism for the JLS to notify the client that a new service is now available is therefore required. This is where the remote event plays a crucial role in the design. The remote events that will be delivered to the clients relate to the changes in the registered services. Clients can then be informed if a new service has been added to the JLS or a service is being removed from the JLS. This is extremely significant, as the "bootstrapping" problem of a fixed starting sequence is completely eliminated.

8.3.3.2   Leasing module and Remote mechanism module

When a client registers for receiving remote events, either from the JLS or the Agent, it should renew the lease consistently. If the lease is cancelled or expired, the client will stop receiving events and release the resources associated with this lease. Then the serializable Agent module transferred from the Agent will become void to avoid further unnecessary traffic. Also, in order to ship the Service Objects, the standard HTTP server that is a part of JSK is employed in the Remote mechanism module.

8.3.3.3   Player module

Basically, the functionality of this module is to decompress the movie data so as to present the input streams in a viewable form. It does not decide where the input streams are fed in, nor does it have any control over when to start playing a movie, as all these commands are Agent driven. In our implementation we have used a JMF player capable of decoding MPEG streams, which is an expected application that a client must posses in order to avail this JVoD service facility.

8.4.   Implementation Test-bed and Discussions

In this section, we describe the experiments we have conducted to justify the applicability of our JVoD architecture. Below we describe our experience with our first prototype of the JVoD architecture in terms of measuring the exact access times, fault-tolerant ability, and impact of OS. The experiments are run with Pentium series dedicated PCs with Windows 98 Operating System (OS) or Windows 2000 OS, on a fast switching Ethernet network platform. Three computers are configured exclusively to participate as Movie Servers. One of the computers is configured to participate as a JVoD Agent. Finally, three computers in our system are configured to participate as clients. Each Movie Server, Agent and client has a 128MB RAM and a hard-disk of capacity 20GB. Each client is also a Pentium machine equipped with a JMF player (a built in player within the JVoD client). Each Movie Server is capable of storing 15 movies (typically of 110 minutes duration) together with the respective trailers for previewing. With all the description of our JVoD system in the earlier sections, it must be clear that the number of Movie Servers and clients can be arbitrary, however, only one Agent is allowed to exist in the current implementation of the JVoD system.

In our JVoD system, once the JLS, the Movie Servers and the Agent are ready, the client application can be launched. After launching a similar interface as shown in Figure 8.9 is displayed at the client site. From the status bar at the bottom of client interface, we can see that there are 3 servers and 1 Agent in this running JVoD system. After the user logs on to the system, he/she can browse the information of the desired movie from the Movie-Chooser and preview the trailer of a movie, as shown in Figure 8.10. The retrieval process begins when the user decides to "buy" the desired movie. The following events are triggered when the user chooses to buy the movie. Initially, the *transmission rate test* is conducted between all available Movie Servers and this client. Based on this information, ESP strategy determines the respective movie portions to be retrieved from the servers. The status of the retrieval process can be monitored from the interface of all participating Movie Servers, as shown in Figure 8.11. After downloading a critical size, as per (8.8) in our current implementation, the presentation will begin at the client site as shown in Figure 8.12. During the retrieval process, even when one or two servers crash, the lost portions can be retrieved from the backup server(s) and the presentation will not be interrupted. This mechanism is captured in the following experiment. In this experiment, at first, the client is scheduled to retrieve 3 independent portions from 3 different Movie Servers concurrently. During the retrieval process, we intentionally shutdown (to simulate a server crash) a Movie Server which is in the process of streaming the movie portion to the client. After the client detected the crashing of the Movie Server, the Emergency Server Generating strategy transferred from the Agent, selects a backup Movie Server from the remaining 2 Movie Servers to resume the retrieval of the lost portion. Thus, there are 2 Movie Servers to supply the movie file. While one Movie Server continues to render its original portion, the backup Movie Server renders its original portion and the lost portion, as indicated on the backup Movie Server's screen in Figure 8.13. In this experiment, it is of natural interest to determine the time it takes for this recovery mechanism to be in place

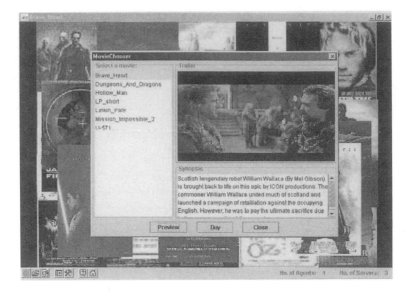

Figure 8.10.   Choosing and previewing the movie trailer - screen shot of the client

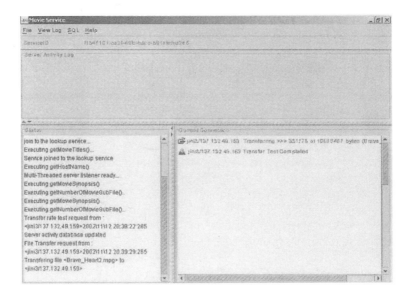

Figure 8.11.   Retrieving the movie portions - screen shot of the Movie Server

Figure 8.12. Presentation at the client site - screen shot of the client

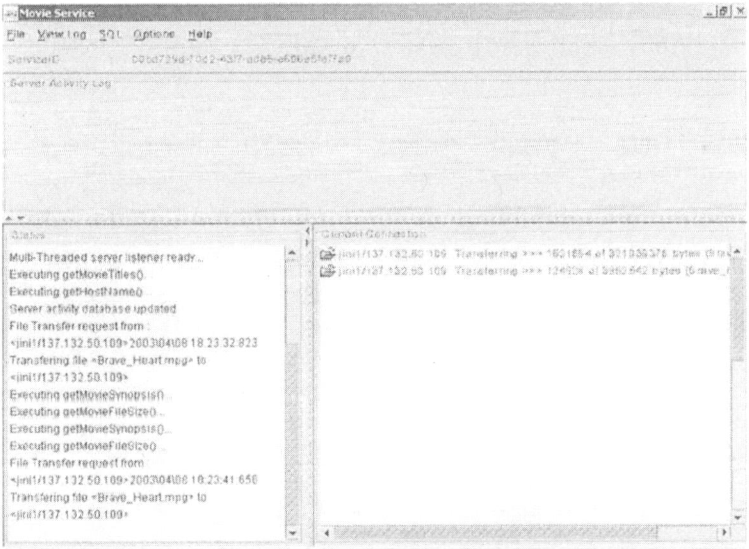

Figure 8.13. Retrieving the movie portions - screen shot of the backup Movie Server

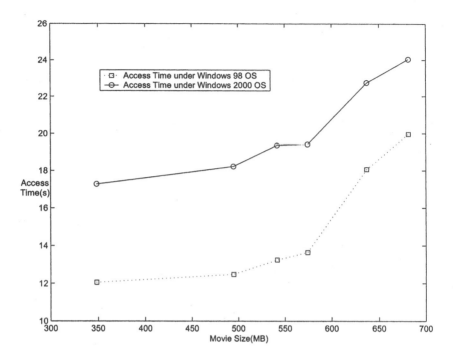

Figure 8.14. Access time with respect to movie size

in order to secure a continuous presentation. This experiment was repeated for 10 times and the average time it took the system to resume the trasfer of the lost portion was found to be 3.57 seconds. This clearly shows that the response time is significantly small to affect the presentation quality.

An important metric in quantifying the performance is the *access time*. It may be noted that the access time depends on several parameters, such as the size of the movie file, transmission rate of the channel, server capacity or the response time of the servers, etc. In our experiments, since the network infrastructure is somewhat dedicated, the access time will be mainly measured with respect to the size of the movies and the transmission rate of the channel. We conducted the experiments with 6 MPEG1 movies of different sizes and the upper bound of the transmission rate of the server-client channel was set to 1.5Mbps. To obtain an accurate result, we used the average access time over 15 trials for each movie. The results of the access time are shown in Figure 8.14. From the results obtained, the effects of movie size can be clearly observed. The access time increases when the movie size increases, as the computed critical sizes differ as per the lengths of the movies. We have also measured the average start-up delay of clients, defined as the average of the time from the time instant at which client application starts to the time instant at which it joins the JVoD system. This was measured to be 4.8 seconds, on average over the 15 trials in our experiments.

Finally, we have also observed that the underlying OS at the client site indeed has an influence on the performance of the system distinctly. Under Windows 2000 OS, the access times seem generally longer than that under Windows 98 OS (In our experience, the access time under Windows 2000 is about 5 seconds longer than that under Windows 98 OS, on an average over 20 trials). However, it should also be noted that under Windows 2000 OS, the CPU usage of the client application is relatively lighter. In our experiments, when the client application is retrieving the movie, its average CPU usage was 10.32% under Windows 2000 OS and 31.20% under Windows 98 OS, over 20 trails. This is because the JVoD system involves multitasking critical jobs and the two operating systems have different scheduling policies. Windows 2000 OS obviously behaves better than Windows 98 OS on multitasking in our experiments.

8.5. Concluding Remarks

In this chapter, we have carried out an extensive design and full-fledged implementation of the JVoD system, which is developed as a network based multimedia service employing the MSR technology introduced in Chapter 2. This infrastructure is built on the latest Java based Jini technology, which consists of the JLS, the Agent, Movie Servers and clients. To demonstrate the feasibility of this architecture, we have proposed a simple retrieval strategy that minimizes the access time and balances server load. Our prototype demonstrated that our architecture can achieve the goal to provide a highly fault-tolerant, distributed VoD service. Even amidst failure of servers, an uninterrupted service can be obtained through our fault-tolerant design. This clearly shows that our scheme is robust and has a load balancing capability.

The prototype presented in this chapter is a first attempt in the domain of distributed VoD services. The design and implementation reported here can be further improved in several dimensions as discussed below. As a first immediate improvement, interactivity could be introduced. While the interactions of Play/Stop, /Pause/Resume are provided in the current prototype, the modeling and implementation of other interactions, such as Fast Forward/Rewind, Fast Search/Reverse Search and Slow motion, are currently underway.Currently, as mentioned in the previous section, only one Agent is allowed to exist in our system. When the Agent is down, no transaction is possible even though all the Movie Servers are available. To eliminate this limitation, having multiple Agents in the system is one reasonable approach. However, several new issues arise from this method. For example, *should clients register with every Agent or with any single Agent?, How can Agents coordinate smoothly?, Should there be any coordination among the agents?, How can Agents update clients' information synchronously, if this is a requirement?* All these issues are challenging to address in a multi-Agent environment. Another important issue is introducing existing techniques to the current system in order to improve the performance. For example, the pre-calculated critical size which is used in our ESP retrieval strategy is computed by taking into account the current network conditions. This size may no longer be valid if the network conditions change, for example, the traffic in the network increases dramatically. Thus, either the future designs should be more adaptive to the changes of the network in order to support a continuous presentation at the client site, or a system with RSVP or Diff-Serv supporting should be developed to guarantee the QoS of the VoD system. Moreover, by employing techniques, such as batching, patching, and caching, in the JVoD system, the server resource will be saved considerably. Finally, in our current design, the placement of movie files is maintained manually. In a very large scale network system, an additional issue is in designing an automatic and efficient approach to replicate the popular movie files among servers and possibly place the moves as per the demands of the users at vantage sites. Efficient movie placement on the network is shown to minimize the access time in the literature. Also, this approach enhances the fault-tolerance of the JVoD. The contributions in this chapter clearly highlight the benefits and advantages of employing MSR strategies and serves as a basis for future research.

Bibliographic Notes

Most of the contributions in this chapter appear in [107]. As a standard for distributed architectures, CORBA has been extensively exploited to supply distributed multimedia services [57, 93, 114]. While Jini's lookup service (JLS) is somewhat similar to the *naming server* [102] used in other distributed network paradigms and in systems such as CORBA [47], Jini technology provides an easier and more flexible way to build, manager, and use the services of networks. There are several studies in the literature focused on the design methodologies for different aspects of a VoD system. Techniques such as batching [2, 27], chaining [94, 95] patching [22, 50] and piggybacking [42, 43] have been investigated to provide a VoD service. Also, some of these techniques can be combined to improve the efficiency further [38, 64, 77]. The effects of different techniques to reduce the aggregate bandwidth requirements are evaluated in [76] while providing interactivity for VoD system. These techniques include server replication, program caching in intermediate nodes and user sharing of video streams and caches. Further, an excellent compilation and comparison of various multicast VoD techniques and implementations proposed in the literature until 2001 appears in [73].

In the design of parallel server architecture, the concepts of using a *concurrent push* [67] and *pull-based* [65] have been proposed. In a pull-based design shown in [65], the need for inter-server synchronization is completely eliminated and also by a careful design of admission control algorithm the loads across the serves are carefully balanced. There is also a third approach that incorporates proxy at the client site [66]. With this scheme, a proxy located at client machine is responsible for requesting and processing data, thus avoiding further network communications. For, striping techniques see [66]. The work in [85] considers employing multiple servers to retrieve multimedia objects, but for a different objective. In this work, the authors design a scheduling scheme, referred to as an *application layer broker*(ALB), at the client site. Typically, a client negotiates with a group of servers and identifies the best server to retrieve an object. This scheme attempts to minimize the buffer space requirements at the client site. This can also be a part of the JINI implementation presented in this chapter as resource management module.

Chapter 9

FUTURE RESEARCH DIRECTIONS

Network based multimedia service rendering has posed several challenges to network and application programmers. Our direct experience in implementation of MSR technology presented in Chapter 8 elicits several design challenges. For this technology to mature and become commonplace among service providers, several issues need immediate attention. In the following paragraphs we discuss them in the context of developing MSR solutions and beyond.

Our discussion on Chapter 5 and 6, particularly the results of Chapter 6 cautions implementation specialists on certain key issues. The results of this chapter in fact account for some networking issues too, to some extent. With the Internet becoming a mainstream entertainment venue, handling a large client population becomes more challenging. The dynamic adaptation schemes discussed and the associated simulations show potential for MSR solutions. The preference of single or multi-installment based scheduling could be based on parameters other that the client access time which has dominated our discussions, as schedule calculation costs favor significantly the latter approach. Such decisions could be delegated to an admission controller at the server side. The important thing is that despite lack of detailed knowledge for packet-losses our SIMP or MISP schedules allow for adaptation to unexpected events via the relaxation parameter c. These techniques coupled with the channel-based partitioning discussed in Chapter 3, pose to efficiently handle multiple client scenarios. The extent to which the client population can be allowed to grow can be captured using similar derivations as in Section 1.2.3 for an exact physical model of the system. Thus, a combined influence of parameters such as, client population/arrival rate, overheads at the admission controller, media disk access delays (captured as seek delays), channel or data partitioning schedule generation, estimates of the relaxation parameter or some model of the network behavior, can lead to an ultimate performance quantification. This sequence of systematic computations will give more exact estimates of the overall performance one can expect, although going at such lengths may seem extreme given that it is clearly the case (at least the moment of this writing) that the network is the limiting factor.

Another immediate point worth noting is the means by which media distribution is carried out. Although single and multi-installment policies were proposed and shown to have a severe impact in determining the ultimate access times, implementing such strategies would pose a considerable challenge. Our experience on the Jini platform shows that in a dedicated environment, certain computations become somewhat redundant. For instance, network adaptability becomes easier and obviously the ultimate load fractions after speed-tests will recommend equal partitioning scheme, as the bandwidth is somewhat even. The only factor that could perturb (that too only to a certain extent) is when interactivity starts and overheads soon take control and dominate the cost! While server failures are not uncommon in real networks, unexpected server crashes can be easily taken care of with software control as demonstrated in Chapter 8. However, more performance sensitive events may be triggered when links start to fail, as transmission interruption and data loss occur. This phenomenon, although it is profusely analyzed in Chapters 5 and 6, a practical set-up demands explicit control to be exercised to recover the losses, if possible, and to re-initiate the transmission. Remember this re-initiation of events must prevent the clients from data starving. This especially becomes crucial when a link loss happens during an interactive session of a user. Fault-tolerance is an extremely imperative issue to be considered at the first place while designing such MSR based technologies. Emphasis of Chapters 5, 6 and 7 center around this goal. Of course, these chapters do not consider failures for all possible scenarios. In Chapter 7, we present both the deterministic and probabilistic approaches for data recovery amidst losses, however, exact control and signaling overheads in realizing such policies were never accounted.

In order for VoD to become a viable alternative to DVD rentals or mail deliveries (cost per GB for these, is still way lower than anything current network technology can offer) it must offer a user experience at least on par with what these methods can offer. The key word here is *interactivity*, i.e. the capability of the user to non-linearly and at-will access any of the requested content. The problem with MSR is that interactivity is a much more challenging capability to offer, compared to single server approaches, as one has to possible reschedule and reassign multiple streams. Although buffering techniques have been proposed in the literature these techniques may not be directly applicable for a MSR setting. The problem is two-fold. Even before buffer estimation or reservation can be made for rewind &/fast-forward operations, media portions have to be identified with respect to each server. This is because media portions from each server are independent and "server-switching " must be carried out seamlessly to circumvent any "hiccups" during presentation. Thus special "look-ahead" policies may be built-in (implementation issue) to avoid data starvation as well as for quick re-fetching in case the same server needs to be contacted. Thus user interactivity does impose severe work pressure on the system as it either speeds-up or slows-down the rate of the entire retrieval & display process.

Server activity can be sped-up to a certain extend by using concurrency and/or parallelism. The problem with MSR architectures is the maintenance of accurate system state information at all participating servers. Optimum resource allocation and access control require the existence of globally available, accurate client information. The cost of maintaining such exact information usually outweighs the benefits given that clients may join and leave (Markovian birth-death process) at any time! There are multiple server architectures that are currently in place and these are almost exclusively on small-scale networks and their predominant purpose is to provide an increased throughput. These, by and large, fall under the name of "parallel-server architectures" in the literature. These architectures provide high-bandwidth for multimedia applications by cleverly partitioning and replicating the data across multiple servers in terms of storage. These kinds of architectures (e.g. SANs) have been discussed in Chapter 1. Thus data organization and fetching is what has been the primary focus on these parallel-server architectures, while there are several inter-dependent as well as independent issues (in the domain of networking and data storage) to be dealt with our MSR technology.

It will be certainly interesting to probe further into implementation issues to realize a full-fledged working prototype with complete user interactivity. MSR technology can encompass technologies that use agent-driven solutions. A multi-agent scenario would be a very good solution for tasks such as fault-tolerance, inter-server communications, monitoring client activities, monitoring the loading of the network, etc, to quote a few. Presence of software agents enables collaborative and co-operative strategies to be in place thus easing the whole implementation process. With agents, admission control can have several inputs such as, network traffic information, client's current status, client's request patterns, interactivity pattern of the clients, etc. These naturally serve as value-added inputs to the schedulers running at the servers and aids efficient decision making.

Although MSR technology has proven to have complete flexibility, adaptability, guaranteeing minimum access times, fault-tolerance, a distributed approach is currently not in place. The contents of Chapter 3 come close to a distributed approach in realizing MSR technology. The design of a TGS scheduler can be tuned to work in a distributed fashion with additional processing and communication (message passing among servers) overheads, however this approach demands frequent status information to be availed at the servers. With distributed policies, there needs not be any centralized controllers and fault-tolerance at scheduling and managing resources become somewhat easy with above frequent status information support. A distributed approach can have movie replication and movie migration policies (transparently to the users) to optimize the access time and to maximize movie availability across networks. Popularity profile based approaches which are well-studied in multimedia literature can be attempted on such applications. Our Jini implementation in Chapter 8 allows easy migration to a distributed scheduling approach.

While MSR is the answer to many of the problems stemming from an under-delivering (in view of demand and not of technology) networking environment, we believe that a successful MSR system should incorporate a number of key technologies that have been developed under the single server paradigm. Multicasting is certainly one of these key technologies especially for live content (e.g. sports, news, etc.). Scalable video is the other key technology that has to be considered. Multiple layers do not offer only a way for quality adaptation, but also open a slew of possibilities on how a MSR system can offer content. Thus, one can envision a *hybrid* system that while based on MSR backbone, brings to the table the best of what technology has to offer.

Finally, the advantages of MSR must be weighed against the cost that a customer is expected to spend in hiring such networked services. Presently, the main sources of expense are the consumed server bandwidth (fraction of the time server is kept engaged in serving a particular client[1]), channel usage[2], and cost of renting a movie[3] While interactivity is allowed, on networked systems, there exist a maximum duration for which a movie is made available to a user. This parameter can also be priced, depending on the popularity of the movie and frequency of the availing the service by a user.

---

[1] This can also be based on service providers infrastructure on server deployment.

[2] For broadband/modem-based line subscribers, usually this will not accounted per request

[3] An amortized cost is usually recommended to service providers to minimize per-user cost of a movie, as the demand profile can be tracked.

In all, MSR technology shows very promising trends in realizing a full-fledged and complete workable system for deploying entertainment multimedia services over networks. Key research issues and the influence of certain vital parameters has been thoroughly studied in this book. MSR technology is completely technology driven, in the sense that most of the available technologies in the domains of networking and storage have to be carefully considered for a seamless integration. MSR demands additional support from other domains such as agent based approaches and collaborative &/co-operative strategies as exemplified above. As such, current research endeavors are more towards realizing an integrated approach for delivering a working, functional system, while the algorithmic challenges in designing a truly distributed operational scheme are yet to be ventured.

References

[1] MPEG-4 ISO/IEC 14496: http://www.cselt.it/mpeg.

[2] C. C. Aggarwal, J. L. Wolf, and P. S. Yu. On optimal batching policies for video-on-demand storage servers. In *Proceedins of the International Conference on Multimedia Computing and Systems (ICMCS '96)*, pages 253–258, June 1996.

[3] C. C. Aggarwal, J. L. Wolf, and P. S. Yu. Design and analysis of permutation-based pyramid broadcasting. *Multimedia system*, 7:439–448, 1999.

[4] Charu C. Aggarwal, Joel L. Wolf, and Philip S. Yu. On optimal batching policies for video-on-demand storage servers. In *1996 International Conference on Multimedia Computing and Systems (ICMCS '96)*, pages 253–258, June 1996.

[5] Charu C. Aggarwal, Joel L. Wolf, and Philip S. Yu. The maximum factor queue length batching scheme for video-on-demand systems. *IEEE Transactions on Computers*, pages 97–110, February 2001.

[6] Masayuki Arai, Atsushi Chiba, and Kazuhiko Iwasaki. Measurement and modeling of burst packet losses in internet end-to-end communications. In *Proc. 1999 Pacific Rim International Symposium on Dependable Computing*, pages 260–267, Dec. 1999.

[7] Gerassimos D. Barlas. Collection-aware optimum sequencing of operations and closed-form solutions for the distribution of a divisible load on arbitrary processor trees. *IEEE Trans. on Parallel & Distributed Systems*, 9(5):429–441, May 1998.

[8] Gerassimos D. Barlas. Simulating the effects of packet loss on the delivery of continuous media by multiple distributed servers. In *Proceedings of ICMSAO*, February 2005.

[9] Gerassimos D. Barlas. Vod on steroids : Optimized content delivery using distributed video servers over best-effort internet. *Journal of Parallel and Distributed Computation*, 65(9):1057–1071, September 2005.

[10] Gerassimos D. Barlas and Bharadwaj Veeravalli. Optimized delivery of continuous-media documents using distributed servers. In *ISCA PDCS 2002*, pages 13–19, Louisville and Kentucky and USA, 2002. ISCA.

[11] Gerassimos D. Barlas and Bharadwaj Veeravalli. Optimized distributed delivery of continuous-media documents over unreliable communication links. *IEEE Trans. on Parallel & Distributed Systems*, 16(10), October 2005.

[12] P. Basu, R. Krishnan, and T. D .C. Little. Optimal stream clustering problems in video-on-demand. In *Proc. Parallel and Distributed Computing and Systems*, Las Vegas, NV, October 1998.

[13] P. Basu, A. Narayanan, R. Krishnan, and T. D. C. Little. An implementation of dynamic service aggregation for interactive video delivery. In *Proc. SPIE – Multimedia Computing and Networking*, San Jose, CA, January 1998.

[14] Stefano Battista, F. Casalino, and C. Lande. Mpeg-4:a multimedia standard for the third millennium and part 2. *IEEE Multimedia*, pages 76–84, Jan.-March 2000.

[15] C. Bernhardt and E. Biersack. A scalable video server: Architecture, design and implementation. In *Proceedings of the Realtime Systems Conference*, pages 63–72, Paris, France, January 1995.

[16] Stefan Birrer and Fabian E. Bustamante. Nemo : Resilient peer-to-peer multicast without the cost. Technical Report NWU-CS-04-36, Northwestern University, August 2004.

[17] Stefan Birrer and Fabian E. Bustamante. Resilient peer-to-peer multicast from the ground up. In *3rd IEEE International Symposium on Network Computing and Applications (NCA'04)*, pages 351–355, August 2004.

[18] C. C. Bisdikian and B. V. Patel. Issues on movie allocation in distributed video-on-demand systems. In *Proceeding on IEEE International Conference on Communications*, pages 250–255, New York, 1995. IEEE Communications Society.

[19] C. C. Bisdikian and B. V. Patel. Cost-based program allocation for distributed multimedia-on-demand systems. *IEEE Multimedia*, pages 62–72, Fall issue 1996.

[20] Jill M. Boyce and Robert Gaglianello. Packet loss effects on mpeg video sent over the public internet. In *ACM Intern. Conf. on Multimedia '98*, pages 181–190, Bristol, 1998.

[21] M. M. Buddhikot and G. Parulkar. Distributed data layout, scheduling, and playout control in a large scale multimedia storage server. Technical Report WUCS-94-33, January 1995.

[22] Y. Cai, K. Hua, and K. Vu. Optimizing patching performance. In *Proceeding of SPIE/ACM Conference on Multimedia Computing and Networking 1999*, pages 204–215, January 1999.

[23] Ying Cai and Kien A. Hua. An efficient bandwidth-sharing technique for true video on demand systems. In *ACM International Conference on Multimedia '99*, pages 211–214, Orlando, 1999.

[24] K. S. Candan, B. Prahakaran, and V. S. Subrahamanian. Retrieval schedules based on resource availability and flexible presentation specifications. *Multimedia System*, (6):232–250, 1998.

[25] E. Casilari, A. Reyes, A. Diaz-Estrella, and F. Sandoval. Heavy-tailed distribution of scene lengths in vbr video. *Electronic Letters*, 35(2):134–135, January 1999.

[26] A. Dan and D. Sitaram. Multimedia caching strategies for heterogeneous application and server environments. *Multimedia Tools and Applications*, 4(3), May 1997.

[27] A. Dan, D. Sitaram, and P. Shahabuddin. Dynamic batching policies for an on-demand video server. *Multimedia Systems*, 4, 1996.

[28] Li-Gang Dong, B. Veeravalli, and C.C. Ko. Efficient movie retrieval strategies for movie-on-demand multimedia services on distributed networks. *Multimedia Tools and Applications*, 20(2):99–134, June 2003.

[29] Charles E. Ebeling. *An Introduction to Reliability and Maintainability Engineering.* 1997.

[30] Hossam El-Gindy, Chi Nguyen, and Antonios Symvonis. Scheduled-multicast with application in multimedia networks. In *IEEE International Conference on Networks 2000 (ICON 2000)*. IEEE Computer Society Press, 2000.

[31] Hans Eriksson. Mbone: The multicast backbone. *Comm. of the ACM*, 37(8):54–60, August 1994.

[32] H. Fahmi, S. Baqai, A. Bashandy, and A. Ghafoor. Dynamic resource allocation for multimedia document retrieval over high speed lans. *Multimedia Tools and Applications*, 8(1):91–114, 1999.

[33] Hugh Fisher. Multicast issues for collaborative virtual environments. *IEEE Computer Graphics and Applications*, pages 68–75, September 2002.

[34] Junichi Funasaka, Nozomi Nakawaki, Kenji Ishida, and Kitsutaro Amano. A parallel downloading method of coping with variable bandwidth. In *23rd International Conference on Distributed Computing Systems Workshops (ICDCSW'03)*, Providence, Rhode Island, USA, May 19 - 22 2003.

[35] Borko Furht, R. Westwater, and J. Ice. Multimedia broadcasting over the internet: Part i. *IEEE Multimedia*, pages 78–82, October-December 1998.

[36] Jamel Gafsi, U. Walther, and E.W. Biersack. Design and implementation of a scalable and reliable and and distributed vod-server. In *5th joint IFIP and ICCC Conference on Computer Communications*, Tunis, 1998.

[37] H. Gajewska. Argo: A system for distributed collaboration. In *ACM Multimedia 1994*, pages 433–440, 1994.

[38] L. Gao, Z. L. Zhang, and D. Towsley. Catching and selective catching: Efficient latency reduction techniques for delivering continuous multimedia streams. In *Proceedings of the 7th ACM International Conference on Multimedia '99*, volume 1, pages 203–206, 1999.

[39] D.J. Gemmell, H.M. Vin, D.D. Kandlur, P.V. Rangan, and L.A. Rowe. Multimedia storage servers: A tutorial. *IEEE Computer*, 28:40–49, May 1995.

[40] Mohammed Ghanbari. *Video coding: an introduction to standard codecs.* Telecommunication Series. IEE, London, UK, 1999.

[41] D. Ghose and H-J. Kim. Scheduling video streams in video-on-demand systems: A survey. *Multimedia Tools and Applications*, 2000.

[42] L. Golubchik, J. C. S. Lui, and R. R. Muntz. Reducing i/o demand in video-on-demand storage servers. In *Proceedings of the 1995 ACM SIGMETRICS joint international conference on Measurement and modeling of computer systems*, volume 23, pages 25–36, 1995.

[43] L. Golubchik, J. C. S. Lui, and R. R. Muntz. Adaptive piggybacking: A novel technique for data sharing in video-on-demand storage servers. *ACM Multimedia Systems*, 4(3):140–155, 1996.

[44] S. Gringeri, R. Egorov, K.Shuaib, A. Lewis, and B. Basch. Robust compression and transmission of mpeg-4 video. In *ACM International Conference on Multimedia '99*, pages 113–120, Orlando, 1999.

[45] Tom's Hardware Guide. Mpeg-4 - copying a dvd video to a cd-rom, 2000.

[46] Akihito Hiromori, Hirozumi Yamaguchi, Keiichi Yasumoto, Teruo Higashino, and Kenichi Taniguchi. A selection technique for replicated multicast video servers. In *International Conference on Parallel Processing (ICPP '02)*, pages 556–563, August 2002.

[47] Sungjune Hong, Youngjae Kim, Minsoon Kweon, Dugki Min, and Sunyoung Han. Object-oriented real-time corba naming service on distributed environment. In *Proceedings of Twelfth International Conference on Information Networking*, pages 637–640, January 1998.

[48] G. B. Horn, P. Knudsgaard, S. B. Lassen, M. Luby, and J. E. Rasmussen. A scalable and reliable paradigm for media on demand. *IEEE Computer*, pages 40–45, September 2001.

[49] A. Hu. Video-on-demand broadcasting protocols: A comprehensive study. In *Proceedings of IEEE Infocom 2001*, pages 508–517, 2001.

[50] Kien A. Hua, Ying Cai, and Simon Sheu. Patching: A multicast technique for true video-on-demand services. In *Proceedings of ACM Multimedia 1998*, pages 191–200, September 1998.

[51] Kien A. Hua and Simon Sheu. Skyscraper broadcasting: a new broadcasting scheme for metropolitan video-on-demand systems. In *Proceedings of the ACM SIGCOMM '97 conference on Applications, technologies, architectures, and protocols for computer communication*, Cannes France, September 1997.

[52] Chung-Ming Huang and Hsu-Ying Kung. A multicast multiple-stream multimedia presentation system over internet. In *4th International Symposium on Autonomous Decentralized Systems*, pages 353–360, March 1999.

[53] E. Hwang, B. Prabhakaran, and V. S. Subrahmanian. Distributed video presentations. In *Proceedings of International Conference on Data Engineering (ICDE '98)*, Orlando, February 1998.

[54] Sun Microsystems Inc. Jini technology core platform specification.

[55] D. Jadav, A. N. Choudhary, and P. B. Berra. Techniques for increasing the stream capacity of a high-performance multimedia server. *IEEE transactions on knowledge and data engineering*, 11(2):284–302, March/April 1999.

[56] Gwang S. Jung, K.W. Kang, and Q. Malluhi. Multithreaded distributed mpeg-1 video delivery in the internet environment. In *2000 ACM symposium on Applied Computing 2000 (volume2)*, pages 592–597, Como, 2000.

[57] V. Kalogeraki, L. E. Moser, and P. M. Melliar-Smith. A corba framework for managing real-time distributed multimedia applications. In *Proceedings of the 33rd Hawaii International Conference on System Sciences*, volume 8, 2000.

[58] M. F. Khan, A. Ghafoor, and M. N. Ayyaz. Design and evaluation of disk scheduling policies for high-demand multimedia servers. In *ICDE 1999*, pages 592–599, 1999.

[59] C. W. Kong and Jack Y. B. Lee. Slice-and-patch - an algorithm to support vbr video streaming in a multicast-based video-on-demand system. In *9th International Conference on Parallel and Distributed Systems*, pages 391–397, December 2002.

[60] R. Krishnan, D. Venkatesh, and T. D. C. Little. A failure and overload tolerance mechanism for continuous media servers. In *Proc. ACM Multimedia*, Seattle, WA, 1997.

[61] G. Kuhne and C. Kuhmunch. Transmitting mpeg-4 video streams over the internet: Problems and solutions. In *ACM International Conference on Multimedia '99*, volume 2, pages 135–138, Orlando, 1999.

[62] S. Lau and J. C. S. Lui. Scheduling and data layout policies for a near-line multimedia storage architecture. *Multimedia System*, (5):310–323, 1997.

[63] H. Lee and P. K. Varshney. Gap-based modeling of packet losses over the internet. In *10th IEEE Intern. Symp. on Modeling and Analysis and and Simulation of Computer and Telecom. Systems (MASCOTS'02)*, pages 507–510, October 2002.

[64] J. Y. B. Lee. On a unified architecture for video-on-demand services. *IEEE Transaction on Multimedia*, 4:38–47, March 2002.

[65] J. Y. B. Lee and P.C. Wong. Performance analysis of a pull-based parallel video server. *IEEE Trans. on Parallel & Distributed Systems*, 11(12):1217–1231, December 2000.

[66] Jack Y.B. Lee. Parallel video servers: A tutorial. *IEEE Multimedia*, pages 20–28, April-June 1998.

[67] Jack Y.B. Lee. Concurrent push-a scheduling algorithm for push-based parallel video servers. *IEEE Trans. on Circuits and Systems for Video Technology*, 9(3), April 1999.

[68] A. Leff, J. Wolf, and P. S. Yu. Efficient lru-based buffering in a lan remote caching architecture. *IEEE Trans. Parallel and Distributed Systems*, 7(2):191–206, February 1996.

[69] Gary Lilienfield and John W. Woods. Scalable high-definition video coding. In *International Conference on Image Processing (Vol 2)*, pages 567–570, October 1995.

[70] Jiangchuan Liu and Bo Li. Adaptive video multicast over the internet. *IEEE Multimedia*, pages 22–33, January-March 2003.

[71] Chen Long and Bharadwaj Veeravalli. A play-while-retrieve strategy for distributed multimedia applications using multiple servers. Technical Report TR-04-02,, Open Source Software Lab, Dept of ECE, National University of Singapore, Singapore, 2004.

[72] Haibin Lu, Junqiang Lan, and Xinhua Zhuang. Advanced pyramid broadcasting for video-on-demand. In *IEEE 6th International Symposium on Multimedia Software Engineering (ISMSE'04)*, pages 28–34, December 2004.

[73] Huadong Ma and K. G. Shin. Multicast video-on-demand services. *ACM Computer Communication Review*, 32(1):31–43, 2002.

[74] Christian Maihofer and Kurt Rothermel. A delay analysis of generic multicast transport protocols. In *2001 IEEE International Conference on Multimedia and Expo*, pages 24–27, August 2001.

[75] J.S Milton and Jesse C. Arnold. *Introduction to Probability and Statistics*. McGraw-Hill, 1995.

[76] J. P. Nussbaumer, B. V. Patel, F. Schaffa, and J. P. G. Sterbenz. Networking requirements for interactive video on demand. *IEEE Journal on Selected Areas in Communications*, 13(5):779–787, 1995.

[77] J. H. Oh, K. A. Hua, and K. Vu. An adaptive hybrid technique for video multicast. In *Proceeding of the 7th International Conference on Computer Communications and Networks*, pages 227–234, 1998.

[78] B. Ozden, A. Biliris, R. Rastogi, and A. Silberschatz. A disk-based storage architecture for movie on demand servers. *Information Systems*, 20(6):465–482, 1995.

[79] B. Ozden, R. Rastogi, and A. Siberschatz. A framework for the storage and retrieval of continuous media data. In *Proceedings of IEEE International Conference on Multimedia Computing and Systems*, Washington D.C, May 1995.

[80] H. H. Pang, B. Jose, and M. S. Krishnan. Resource scheduling in a high-performance multimedia server. *IEEE transactions on knowledge and data engineering*, 11(2), March/April 1999.

[81] Jehan-Francois Paris, Steven W. Carter, and Darrell D.E. Long. Efficient broadcasting protocols for video on demand. In *6th International Symposium on Modeling, Analysis and Simulation of Computer and Telecommunication Systems*, pages 127–132, 1998.

[82] Jehan-Francois Paris, Steven W. Carter, and Darrell D.E. Long. A low bandwidth broadcasting protocol for video on demand. In *International Conference on Computer Communications and Networks*, pages 690–697, October 1998.

[83] S. Pejhan, T.H. Chiang, and Y.Q. Zhang. Dynamic frame rate control for video streams. In *ACM International Conference on Multimedia '99*, pages 141–144, Orlando, 1999.

[84] Fernando Pereira and Touradj Ebrahimi, editors. *The MPEG-4 Book*. Multimedia Series. IMSC Press, Prentice Hall PTR, Upper Saddle River, NJ 07458, 2002.

[85] B. Ping, B. Prabhakaran, and A. Srinivasan. Retrieval scheduling for collaborative multimedia presentations. *ACM/Springer-Verlag Multimedia Systems*, (8):146–155, 2000.

[86] Cai Qingsong, Li Zimu, and Hu Jianping. Suffix caching techniques of streaming media based on batch patching. In *11th IEEE International Conference and Workshop on the Engineering of Computer-Based Systems (ECBS'04)*, pages 94–101, May 2004.

[87] Prashant Rajvaidya and Kevin Almeroth. Multicast routing instabilities. *IEEE Internet Computing*, pages 42–49, Sept.Oct. 2004.

[88] P. V. Rangan and H. M. Vin. Efficient storage techniques for digital continuous media. *IEEE Trans. on knowledge and data engineering*, 5(4), August 1993.

[89] P. Venkat Rangan, M. H. Vin, and S. Ramanathan. Designing an on-demand multimedia service. *IEEE Communications Magazine*, pages 56–64, 1992.

[90] Reza Rejaie and Mark Handley. Quality adaptation for congestion controlled video playback over the internet. In *ACM SIGCOMM Conf. on Applications and Technologies and Architectures and Protocols for Computer Communication '99*, pages 189–200, Cambridge, 1999.

[91] T.G. Robertazzi, S. Luryi, and J. Sohn. Load sharing controller for optimizing monetary cost. United States Patent and No. 5,889,989, March 1999.

[92] Pablo Rodriguez, A. Kirpal, and E. W. Biersack. Parallel-access for mirror sites in the internet. In *Proc. of Infocom*, Tel-Aviv and Israel, March 2000.

[93] Douglas C. Schmidt, David L. Levine, and Sumedh Mungee. The design of the tao real-time object request broker. *Computer Communications*, 21(4):294–324, 1998.

[94] S. Sheu and K. A. Hua. Virtual batching: A new scheduling technique for video-on-demand servers. In *Proceedings of the 5th International Conference on Database*

Systems for Advanced Applications, pages 481–490, Melbourne, Australia, April 1997.

[95] S. Sheu, K. A. Hua, and W. Tavanapong. Chaining: A generalized batching technique for video-on-demand systems. In *Proceedings of the IEEE International Conference on Multimedia Computing and Systems*, pages 110–117, Ottawa, Ontario, Canada, June 1997.

[96] Simon Sheu, Kien A. Hua, and Wallapak Tavanapong. Chaining: A generalized batching technique for video-on-demand systems. In *International Conference on Multimedia Computing and Systems (ICMCS '97)*, pages 110–117, 1997.

[97] W. Shi and S. Ghandeharizadeh. Controlled buffer sharing in continuous media servers. *Multimedia Tools and Applications*, 23(2):131–159, June 2004.

[98] W. D. Sincoskie. System architecture for a large scale video on demand service. *Computer Networks and ISDN Systems*, 22:155–162, 1991. North-Holland.

[99] A. P. Sistla and J. L. Welch. Efficient distributed recovery using message logging. In *Proceedings of the 8th ACM Symposium on Principles of Distributed Computing*, pages 223–238, August 1989.

[100] A. Srivastava, A. Kumar, and A. Singru. Design and analysis of a vide-on-demand server, multimedia systems. *Multimedia Systems*, 5:238–254, 1997.

[101] W. Richard Stevens. *TCP/IP Illustrated and Vol1 and The Protocols*. Addison-Wesley, 1994. ISBN 0201633469.

[102] Andrew S. Tanenbaum and Robbert Van Renesse. Distributed operating systems. *ACM Computing Surveys (CSUR)*, 17(4):419–470, December 1985.

[103] D. A. Tran, K. Hua, and T. Do. A peer-to-peer architecture for media streaming. *IEEE Journal on Selected Areas in Communications*, January 2004. Special Issue on Service Overlay Networks.

[104] Andras Varga. The omnet++ discrete event simulation system. In *European Simulation Multiconference*, Prague, June 6-9 2001.

[105] Bharadwaj Veeravalli and Gerassimos D. Barlas. Access time minimization for distributed multimedia applications. *Multimedia Tools and Applications*, 12:235–256, November 2000.

[106] Bharadwaj Veeravalli, Chen Chaoyang, and Viktor K. Prasanna. Fault-tolerant analysis for multiple servers movie retrieval strategy for long duration movie retrieval. Technical Report TR-03-04, Open Source Software Lab, Dept. of ECE, National University of Singapore, Singapore, 2003.

[107] Bharadwaj Veeravalli, Long Chen, Hun Yen Kwoon, Goh Kar Whee, See Ying Lai, Lim Peng Hian, and Ho Chin Chow. An agent driven pull-based distributed video-on-demand system - multiple server retrieval technology. Technical Report TR-03-01, Open Source Software Lab, Dept. of ECE, National University of Singapore, Singapore, 2003.

[108] H. M. Vin, A. Goyal, and P. Goyal. Algorithms for designing large-scale multimedia servers. *Computer Communications*, 18(3):192–203, March 1995.

[109] S. Viswanathan and T. Imielinski. Metropolitan area video-on-demand service using pyramid broadcasting. *Multimedia Systems*, 4:197–208, 1996.

[110] Y. Wang, J. C. L. Liu, D. H. C. Du, and J. Hsieh. Efficient video file allocation schemes for video-on-demand services. *Multimedia System*, (5):283–296, 1997.

[111] Anna Watson and M.A. Sasse. Measuring perceived quality of speech and video in multimedia conferencing applications. In *ACM Intern. Conf. on Multimedia '98*, pages 55–60, Bristol, 1998.

[112] J. L. Wolf, P. S. Yu, and H. Shachnai. Dasd dancing. In *Proceedings of ACM Sigmetrics conference*, pages 157–166, May 1995.

[113] Y. Won and J. Srivastava. Smdp:minimizing buffer requirements for continuous media servers. *Multimedia Systems*, (8):105–117, 2000.

[114] S. Yucel and T. Saydam. An architecture for realizing corba audio/video stream specification over ip technologies. In *IEEE Globccom 2001*, volume 4, pages 25–29, San Antonio, Texas, November 2001.

[115] Michael Zink and Andreas Mauthe. P2p streaming using multiple description coded video. In *Proceedings of EUROMICRO*, pages 240–247, August 2004.

Index

GLOSSARY

Access Time The time between the instant a client is making a request and the beginning of the playback

B-frame Bidirectional predictive frame

Buffering A popular technique for streaming video data, whereas a certain portion of the data has to be stored at the client before a playback can be attempted. The buffer is used to smooth out the network speed irregularities.

CBR Constant-Bit-Rate

DCT Discrete Cosine Transform

FEC Forward Error Correction

Frame A digital image. Usually part of a sequence in a movie.

GOP Group of Pictures

I-frame Intra-coded frame

ISP Internet Service Provider

Initiation Latency See Access Time

JLS Jini Lookup Service

Jini A pseudo-acronym: Jini Is Not Initials. It refers to a Java technology for the construction of distributed systems.

MAN Metropolitan Area Network

MISP Multiple Installments Single Part

MSR Multiple Server Retrieval

MTBF Mean Time Between Failures

MTTF Mean Time To Failure

MTTR Mean Time To Recovery

MoD Movie on Demand

Multicasting A communication technique involving a single data stream, from a single source to multiple recipients.

NACK Negative ACK (acknowledgment)

P-frame Predicted frame

P2P Peer to Peer

PAR   Play-After-Retrieval

PWR   Play-While-Retrieve

QoS   Quality of Service

RAID   Redundant Array of Inexpensive Disks

RTT   Round-Trip-Time

SAN   Storage Area Network

SIMP   Single Installment Multiple Parts

SNR   Signal-to-Noise-Ratio

SP   Service Provider

SSRS   Single Server Retrieval Strategy

Scalable video   A technique that splits the video data into multiple streams.

Strand   An immutable, sequence of continuously recorded audio samples or video frames.

TGS   Task Generation & Scheduling

VBR   Variable-Bit-Rate

VoD   Video on Demand

WAN   Wide Area Network